The Victory of Mind

The Psychology of Humanist Art, Modernism, and Race

Thomas Martin

Ostara Publications

Dedicated to the memory of anthropologist
Claude Levi-Strauss,
who woke me from my dogmatic slumbers.

Contents

Reviews of *The Victory of Mind*

"This book makes a probing argument with the same clarity the ancient Greeks were known to present their philosophical insights: from the nineteenth century onwards the West has witnessed an inversion of values from noble to base values. The very same period as hailed as "progressive" by our current liberal elites is to Thomas Martin the era when Westerners abandoned their dedication to high cultural accomplishments in the name of cultural equality across all ethnic groups and classes. With the abandonment of the aristocratic elitism of the past, the worst side of our human nature has been given free reign, and, what is worse, this has happened right inside our universities through the promotion of political correctness and diversity." — Dr. Ricardo Duchesne, author of *The Uniqueness of Western Civilization.*

"In this revolutionary work, Martin shows that during the *ancien regime* the upper class controlled the lower classes, but during the nineteenth and twentieth centuries this became inverted, and so the low increasingly started to control the high, in both politics and culture. This process of inversion is so well documented it is clear the author has achieved what most scholars thought impossible: a unification of the apparent diversity of modern culture with a few basic principles from philosophy and evolutionary psychology. He also shows the origin and nature of the fear of biological determinism prevalent today. This book will cause a paradigm shift and allow us to get our emotions, values, culture and politics back under control. Highly recommended." — Prof. Richard Webster, received Ph.D. from Cambridge, author of several books.

"There is much to admire in this work." — Kevin MacDonald, Ph.D. Professor psychology, California State University.

"Martin has written a work of critical importance about American life that merits our attention. His thoughts are well phrased and reflect the author's detailed knowledge of the American cultural scene. Martin moves easily from highbrow to lowbrow culture and can write intelligently about both." — Prof. Paul Gottfried, Ph.D., author *of Leo Strauss and the Conservative Movement in America* (Cambridge University Press, 2012).

Wonders there are many, none more wonderful than Man.
— Sophocles
"Ode to Man"
Antigone

The king's grandeur and majesty derive from the fact that in his presence
his subjects are unequal....Without gradation, inequality, and difference,
order is impossible.
— Le Duc de Saint-Simon

"All men are brothers," said Schiller, but it won't happen in my lifetime...
and it probably won't happen for hundreds of years. The men of today
aren't brothers to me. They are beggars, slaves, clods. I soar above them
as my music soars above the music of my contemporaries. We exist on
different planes. For them, that other line of Schiller's would be more to
the point: "Against stupidity, even the gods fight in vain."
— Beethoven

At a certain level, humans have the same brain as sheep.
— Psychology Professor
Harvard University

Acknowledgements

Although the first edition of this book took only four years to research and write, in important ways it is the result of a lifetime of thought and writing.

My first college English professor, Peter Sharkey, made me feel that I had potential, and this was inspiring to me. I kept reading and thinking during the delirium of my twenties in part because of his encouragement.

I wrote to an Oxford philosophy professor that, "The universities are dead."

And he responded, "You're right, with a few exceptions." Some of those exceptions are the several wonderful professors who have made courses for the Great Courses. This company finds the best professors in the West and tapes them lecturing on their subjects.

While I had learned only a small amount during the course of obtaining my bachelors degree, I learned an immense amount from the Great Courses lectures, and this book would have been unthinkable without their wisdom.

I would like to thank my parents, without whose assistance this book may not have been possible. I would like to thank my friend Charles Thompson who has been very encouraging of my writing efforts, and who read this book several times in its many forms from infancy to completion.

I would like to thank Paul W., who edited my first book, and whose encouragement over fifteen years has been very helpful. And I would like to thank my publisher for being willing to go against the popular current in academia.

During the seventeenth century, while a small group of men were heroically creating the modern world, the universities were still in the dark ages. Today the universities are in a new, taboo driven Dark Age, are "dead", politicized, while a handful of writers and publishers are creating a new, enlightened, and more accu-rate understanding of human nature.

Introduction

A professor once said that the ancient Greeks saw things with a clarity that we have lost today. When I first heard this, I was not sure if he was right, but after years of research I have concluded that he was correct. For instance, Plato realized that without justice, there can be no peace in a political community. So the next question was, "How to create a power structure that represents justice?"

I shall try to show that the Greeks were hierarchical in their thinking, as the West is today, so they realized that, as parents rule their children, the better must rule the inferior to create social justice, a functional polity and a beautiful cultural life. Some people are smart and creative, and fit to rule, while most are average or worse in intelligence. James Madison makes this basic point in the *Federalist*. The founding fathers of the United States knew their Plato well, so they did not create a direct democracy, which had a bad history, but a republic, which at the founding was hierarchical, more so than today. To rise in power and even to vote, you had to be smart. In terms of obtaining political office today, things have not changed that much.

But underneath the political thinking of the founders was a Platonic psychology and culture. Plato believed that the mind or reason should use the will to rule the passions. As we can see in today's technological innovations, mind really is superior or really does rule, at least a good bit of the time, or when we are in our good senses. The passions mostly get us into trouble by creating crime and chaos, while reason allows us to rise above our animal nature and create form: form for our state, form for the arts, and a constructive social hierarchy. As parents rule their children, reflecting intrinsic or natural justice and hierarchy, reason should rule the passions to create a natural or just hierarchy in both the soul and the state. The founders were aware of this, and it is one reason that there is a minimum age to be president, and why at the time a citizen had to own property to be able to vote. Owning property meant that one could afford an education, which was viewed as essential for civic participation. It also meant that one was intelligent enough to maintain an estate and a staff of employees or slaves.

People also believed at the time that religion was essential for developing the sense of virtue and a rational demeanor. Virtue and reason were seen as connected. A citizen had to have both. If one lacks virtue, and is prone to anger like a child or wild animal, then one cannot be rational.

Virtue was also necessary to stop a republic from degenerating into mob rule. John Adams said that the Constitution was only for a moral population. Benjamin Franklin was aware of this. As he was leaving the constitutional convention a woman asked, "So Dr. Franklin, do we have a monarchy or a republic?" Franklin responded, "A republic, if you can keep it." He was alluding to the potential of a population endowed with natural rights to degenerate into a wild mob. We have seen this come to fruition to a degree since the 1960s.

The natural rights that Jefferson outlined in the Declaration of Independence are positive rights: the right to life, liberty, and happiness. By "happiness," he meant the right to live a life of virtue, not of debauchery. During the 1960s, the West embraced negative rights: the right to take drugs, rob, and even murder, or at least many try to argue this, as we shall see.

Excuses given today for such behavior would not have been countenanced during the nineteenth century. Franklin's dire prediction has come true. Much of society has abandoned the moral foundation of the Republic.

William J. Bennett and others have noted a coarsening of the culture. This is putting it mildly. Humans have lived 99.9% of our lives on earth as hunter-gatherers, so take a hunter-gatherer, put him in the streets, and you have a crude and swaggering "criminal." Put him on TV, and you have a popular entertainer. Such behavior and the desire to defend it are natural and do not really require explanation. But that some populations have developed virtue, self control, or inhibitions is what requires an explanation.

Who is the culprit here? The decline of the West is too vast and complex to blame any one group. The answer is most likely found in popular psychology and modes of reasoning. As will become clear, the blame lies with natural rights run amok or gone *Rabid* (the title of a movie discussed later). It did not happen overnight, but over a century and a half. By the "roaring 20s," the West was well on the way to its present position. Rome did not fall because of a conspiracy, but, at least in part because of bad values, which is similar to today. As we shall see repeatedly, bad values lead to incorrect notions of causality or, in general, bad thinking and decision making.

During the last two centuries, the vote was gradually expanded in the name of greater representation or natural rights. The increasing power of the lower classes produced, by association in the Platonic psychology, an empowering of the passions or appetites. Recall that the culture of the eighteenth century was Platonist and hierarchical. The lower orders and their passions were kept under control by their betters, but by the nineteenth century this started to reverse.

As the lower class became empowered and started to command the government, the passions, by association, started to tell the will and reason what to do in both politics and culture. The process happened gradually during the nineteenth century, but was accelerated in the twentieth, with bursts occurring during the '20s and '60s. To call someone today "wild and crazy" is to praise them. In the media and on the streets today, vulgarity and violence are intense, and crime has risen. But this makes the common people happy and the people rule, so critics are muted as we saw with Dr. Bennett's quote. Professional wrestling is now the cultural ideal, as it is in a state of nature.

In short, what we have seen during the past two centuries is an inversion of Platonism. The subject of this book is a description of that process in the areas of psychology, politics, and culture. We see this inversion in all areas of Western culture, from novels, music, film, and dance, to academic psychology and other theories of society.

The cultural transformation during the past two centuries would shock many of the Founders, but not all. Some, like Franklin, predicted some form of self-destruction, the primary subject of this book. There is a bright side. I show, at the beginning and at the end of the book, that the legitimacy of rationalism, and the gratification from Classical humanism are more profound and real than the vulgar and subhuman trash that passes for culture and values today.

I hope to show that a real victory of mind is possible. Today, it may be found only within the covers of this book, but under the right circumstances it can spread. If the human mind was victorious in the past, it can be again in the future.

Summary of the Model

During the *ancien regime*, it was commonly believed, following Plato, that it was just or legitimate for reason to use the will to rule the appetites; by analogy, to create social justice an educated, disciplined, and conscientious upper class should rule the less educated and more emotional lower classes. After the Bible, Plato's *Republic* is the most influential book in history. As Louis the 14th said of his own appetites, "I'm under control."

With the Enlightenment, this status hierarchy was inverted. The rise of the new God-endowed natural rights resulted in the legitimacy or justice of popular sovereignty. This new source of "low" power occurred in the context of the prevalent Platonic psychology and justice—so, by association, the popular will started to enforce a culture more of the emotions: at first, during the eighteenth century, more of the higher sentiments, and then eventually, by the late nineteenth century, of the lower appetites. And, in turn, by association with the emotions, we see a growing interest in dynamic and empirical nature. Victor Hugo said, "Be rabid," arguing that Romanticism is liberalism in art. And Jeremy Bentham captured the new era well when he said, regarding animals, that the issue is not whether they have reason, but if they suffer. This is perceived to represent justice, and so moral insight. This impulse is the norm today on both the left and most of the right.

The Left rose to power during the last three centuries with the cry, "We want social justice!" Hence the cultural ideal eventually became, "Sex, drugs, and rock and roll!" or a popular culture of bottom-up individualism, self-expression, catharsis, increasingly percussive music since the 1950s, obesity, narcissism, and increased crime; human intuition is commonly extolled today. People think that popular culture is legitimate, just, and good. As noted, at a certain level, humans have the same brain as sheep. It is a big part of popular culture to believe in "going with the flow" and "letting it all hang out," and, consistent with the inversion, to denigrate the mind, the new "low."

A recent pop song included the phrase, "Do you have street smarts, or are you just an intellect?" Woody Allen says, in his film *Annie Hall*, that "the mind is an overrated organ." And in his film *Midnight in Paris*, a character says, "Logic dictates…, but who cares about logic!" And I recently saw a huge billboard in Rome that read, "I'm with stupid, be stupid." A young female attorney I know, who was raised and educated in California, said that it's fashionable to be a fool today. This body over the mind perspective is what is perceived to represent justice, and so moral insight or righteousness.

A recent study has found a strong trend of anti-intellectualism among the young.[1] The inversion of Platonic justice is also shown in the rising status of cathartic popular culture and the lowering of the status of "illegitimate" high culture—the implication being that high culture has elaborate, oppressive modes of mental control. A recent study has found that fewer young people today attend performing arts events than did thirty years ago.[2]

Others have noticed the inversion. Sir Joshua Reynolds stated, in his *Discourses*, that the Romantics were inverting the academic hierarchy, that "scale of perfection" of rationalized or controlled human body, history, and nature.

---

[1] Mark Bauerlein. *The Dumbest Generation: How the Digital Age Stupefies Young Americans and Jeopardizes Our Future*, (New York: Penguin, 2008).
[2] Ibid.

And Arthur Lovejoy, in *The Great Chain of Being*, says that developments in science and theology by the early nineteenth century resulted from the inversion of Platonism. Prof. Joseph Kerman wrote: "All human experience, said Schopenhauer, consists either of emotions and drives—which he called 'the Will'—or of ideas, morals, and reason, which he downgraded by the term 'Appearance.' He insisted that the Will always dominates Appearance."[3] This is a clear inversion of Platonism, right down to the aesthetics of mere "Appearance." Again we have a perceived just relationship or accurate moral perception. So we see that political and cultural changes in the last three centuries pivoted on the firm idea of justice and power in the context of a retained Platonic dualism. This, apparently, is real.

The inversion of Platonism is reflected in opera plots. Because of their resistance to the new popular sovereignty, the upper classes and government are often portrayed as illegitimate and evil, as in the Count in Mozart's *The Marriage of Figaro*, the Nibelungen and Gods in Wagner's *Ring*, the Duke in Verdi's *Il Trovatore*, and the chief of police in Puccini's *Tosca*. The inversion also explains the increasing realism in opera, literature, and art during the nineteenth century. It also explains the extreme subjectivism of modernism and post-modernism that is perceived to be just, good and accurate.

I believe that this model supports Foucault's idea that culture is a pattern of control, but also corrects his portrayal of power as arbitrary. What is new in this research is the conclusion that human beings function in a hierarchical structure and are not, among other things, rational actors. Human psychology is profoundly social, and this is consistent with evolutionary psychology. It is commonly observed that if you put together a group of people that within a minute they start to form a dominance hierarchy.

During the nineteenth century, sex and the body were viewed as evil, but notions of race, class and gender were viewed as good and legitimate. With sexual liberation, evil was displaced to the public sphere, creating the evil images of race, class and

---

[3] Joseph Kerman & Gary Tomlinson. *Listen*. Sixth Edition. (Boston and New York: Bedford/St. Martin's, 2008), 286.

gender, which were to be "purged" in the name of justice. As we were in a state of denial over sex, now we are in a state of denial over race, class and gender. As talking about sex caused embarrassment and consternation, now talking about the biology of race, class, and gender causes embarrassment and consternation. As it was lamentable that our lives were pervaded by sinful desires, now it is lamentable that our lives are pervaded by sinful race, class and gender, our sinful social bodies as I will refer to it. The traditional notion of the "irrational" has become "society." As emotion was viewed as the negation of reason, now "society" is viewed as the negation of authentic emotion and reason. Race, class and gender are commonly viewed as unreasonable and dangerous passions. This perspective generates the social sciences. As it was a sure sign of virtue to deny the importance of sex, now it is a sure sign of virtue to deny the importance of race, class and gender. As expressing and enjoying sex was viewed as evil, now expressing and enjoying race, class and gender, at least for whites, is viewed as evil and unjust. As we were in a constant state of anger against the evil body, now we are in a constant state of anger against evil race, class and gender. Only whites are guilty of "racism." The nonwhites can hate all they like, and this is viewed as righteous as they are putting the evil whites in their place. This represents justice.

This is why the fear of biological determinism is common today; when one starts to mention biological factors in an area of culture, most people become nervous, because they fear the slippery slope to unjust race, class and gender or to the evil desires for these uppity impulses, perceptions and categories. Temptation! As we were in a state of fear of slipping back into the body, we now fear slipping back into race, class and gender—"society" or the nineteenth century. Harvard psychologist Steven Pinker makes this point in his recent study *The Better Angels of our Nature*, or that it is the fear of racism that causes the fear of biological determinism. I once praised *The Bell Curve* to a female college student and she gave me a shocked and disgusted look.

As a strategy to attack the evil, people have conveniently concluded that everyone is perfect and loveable. As we wanted to defeat the evil body with love, now we want to defeat evil race, class and gender with love. Any fact about people that implies less than universal love is automatically rejected. All negative facts about people have to spun so as to make people innocent victims, pitiable and lovable. It can't reflect negatively on their nature. This tyranny of love is what is perceived to be righteous, just and good. As we wanted to rise above the body, now we want to rise above race, gender and class.

This is what is perceived to be just and good. And it is indeed taboo to be judgmental today, and with it comes the risk of being accused of being biased or evil. Because it was whites who "succumbed" to race in the first place, their "original sin," they are viewed as evil and needing to be disciplined, socially controlled, attacked and enslaved or made subordinate to the good and righteous blacks, whites' natural, or more loving and erotic masters. As whites used to control the blacks for their own good, now blacks control whites for their own good. An elementary school recently offered tutoring, but not if the student was white, and this impulse is common today. The blacks' control of whites makes whites feel like their being well taken care of. This is "progressive," this assimilation of whites to blacks. Most whites are penitents: they're so sorry for the sins of race, class and gender. As glorifying God was a spiritual exercise, now glorifying the blacks etc is a spiritual exercise. St Ignatius of Loyola considered that if he didn't cry at least 3 times during Mass, that he didn't have sufficient solace. Similarly, if you don't cry at least 3 times during a sociology lecture, you clearly have a problem.

During the 1950s, whites were righteous, and blacks were submissive, while today, blacks are righteous, and whites are submissive. It is taboo for whites to get uppity. If someone succumbs and proposes that the different groups are unequal, he is automatically accused of being evil or a "witch". Hence the witch hunts against scholars like Jenson and Rushton, who promoted a biological understanding of race, and the taboos in mainstream publishing about race and gender.

Put more generally, all that has happened during the last century is that the evangelical culture of the nineteenth century has become reconfigured, and produced modern political and cultural taboos, on both the left and most of the right. As we will see in this study, the only difference between today and the past is that instead of moving from sin to salvation, now we believe in moving from salvation to sin. In other words instead of wanting to escape the conflicted world and move toward heaven, now we want to move away from stifling heaven and toward dynamic nature and hell. The stimulating, earthy blacks are now the vision of salvation. This is the new vision of exciting salvation, and so the blacks now appear to be inviting, to most.

Today the entire traditional Christian culture and all the biblical narratives are built on this new idea of escape or moral movement toward the dynamic world. Instead of seeing the primordial threatening predator, or evil, in sex and wild nature, now we see it in stifling heaven and civilization, and so have feelings of avoidance. This is why the left and right mostly agree on the recent social developments. They only disagree on details, not on fundamentals. Very few want to go back to the kind of high moral and cultural standards of the nineteenth century and their social, aesthetic and political implications.

So multi-racialism and the rest of the left does not result from a conspiracy, but from a historical accident. The Ancients had a very biological perspective, so they did not any illusions about people. We today have simply lost that subject centered perspective, and subtlety of perceptions, because of our new manias and blind rush toward the body and world. Instead of a blind rush toward the heaven of civilization, like during the nineteenth century, now we have a blind rush toward sex, nature and more natural people. This is the new vision of heaven and salvation. Musician Billy Joel said in his song *Only the Good Die Young*, "I'd rather laugh with the sinners, than cry with the saints." And a white woman got out of a car with a black man, and she said to herself, "Beam me up." This is the new heaven and so represents righteousness.

Chapter One: The Body in Mind, Art in Mind

The most difficult thing is to subordinate
your will to that of another.
—Roger Bacon,
Medieval Philosopher

I've seen much finer
Women, ripe and real,
Than all this nonsense of
Their stone ideal.
— Byron

She possessed both types of beauty—style and rhythm. Style is the
force of the ideal, rhythm is its movement… Proportion his song
to his nature, and you shall see!
— Victor Hugo
Les Miserables

When I read, it was I who gained knowledge through myself. Or
was it?
— St. Augustine

During the last two centuries, the West has undergone an important transformation in what it expects from body imagery presented in art and the media.

This is of fundamental importance for understanding the change during the same period in the West's perceptions of "race." At that earlier time, Western society presented to itself images that celebrated European descent and culture. In contrast, today's visual culture is designed to present and celebrate diversity.

What connects the two visual cultures is an emphasis on the human figure. While today the figure may be out of fashion in high art, overall the figure is with us more than ever because of the rapid development of the media during the last century. Before about 1800, images were expensive and rare, while today they cost pennies and are ubiquitous.

Prior to the nineteenth century, there was a clear emphasis on portraying the upper and middle classes while they engaged in gentle and even ascetic activities such as praying, adoring a religious figure or celebrating the humanist virtues of modesty and temperance; angels were the ideal. They celebrated a vision of individual self control, of mind in control of the body, and reviling bad, hubristic people; this vision was viewed as representing justice, peace and beauty.

During the nineteenth century, with the rise of naturalism, greater importance was placed on portraying the lower class doing menial activities, like farming or even breaking stones. This trend has gone further since the 1960s with increased portrayals of vulgarity in the media. For instance around 1975, the televised situation comedy *All in the Family* was the first in which the viewer could hear a toilet flush. This is mild by today's standards.

Advertisers and film producers today use indulgence, phantasmagoria, and vulgarity to get people's attention, enthusiasm and commitment. This represents the body over the mind, and our new notion of justice.

Celebration of diversity fits easily into this visual culture since both have a discontinuous nature. The visual culture of the mainstream is no longer self-centered, morally controlled and beautiful, or angel-oriented, but indulgent, vulgar, flamboyant and diverse.

The decline has found its way into scholarship. In a study on Beethoven, an author noted, "since part of the historian's task is to sift through the refuse of the past, what could be a better place to begin this tale than amid the same trash bins in the city that Beethoven called home for most of his life."[4]

These kinds of associations and putdowns in the context of high culture are common today. And this was written by a conductor, and not just a professor or journalist. This kind of "humility" or perceived justice, regarding high culture and the upper classes, as we will see, is common. When a titanic figure like Beethoven is treated in this fashion, you know there are self-destructive currents at work in the culture. Obviously, the modern world is fundamentally a product of the mind and not the body, but we are not morally aware of this as we were during the nineteenth century when we had a traditional Platonic sense of justice.

In order to understand the visual culture of today, we must start at the beginning of Western history to see the extent and psychological nature of the traditional portrayal of the figure. The importance of the figure to ancient and early modern art is due to its centrality in human psychology. This is apparent in that there is agreement or resonance between felt emotion in the body and imagined emotion emanating from dreamed body imagery. The same emotions are attributed to real and imagined bodies, and they refer to each other creating a bond.

The emotionally expressive images of the body in the mind or dreams refer to and bind to our own bodies by association with our felt emotion. Because of this connection, desires always want to push out or move out into culture through the medium of bodies and body images.

We want to contact others through similarity and resonance, and fashion ethical reasoning in our relation with others to fulfill our own ends and the group's social and political ends. This is a fancy way of saying we naturally want to have emotional reactions to others.

So the modern, inverted justice, as we will see, is indeed the natural one. This is clear in history and anthropology, as we shall see in the discussion of the state of nature.

---

[4] Harvey Sachs, *The Ninth: Beethoven and the World in 1824* (New York: Random House, 2010), 6.

Body imagery also binds to our bodies through similarity of physical parameters. Both of these similarities result in people feeling continuity between their own bodies and those that they see. In addition, psychologists have found that babies can recognize their mother's voice and odor. This results in part from the first nine months of life in the womb. It creates a special sensitivity and attachment to the human body, and the sense that the body is an extension of themselves. People project when they see a human figure; the viewed figure is experienced as being an extension of the viewer and of having a self-referential quality: this is how we experience our own existence. This is what we are naturally inclined to see and judge to be good or just.

As St. Augustine thought, we gain knowledge through ourselves. We are prone to explore and express ourselves through portrayals of the figure.

Depending on our values and character, we either respond positively or negatively to an expressive or vulgar and diverse emotional vocabulary among people and the visual culture. During Classical antiquity, most people adhered to the ideal of rationality and emotional self-control. This notion of justice had a profound impact on their portrayals of the figure.

One of the central questions that has vexed art historians and critics since the Classical world is the status of the human figure. From the extreme of the stick figures of Paleolithic cave art to the perfection of Michelangelo, the human form has experienced every possible permutation. But a common fact that is often overlooked by professionals is that it is a persistent and serious theme.

Artists gravitate towards it. While a few artistic schools have rejected it outright, like Islam and modern abstraction, most artistic schools throughout history have embraced the human form because of its intrinsic appeal. Even landscape artists, like Claude, included the human figure. People find emotional self-fulfillment in viewing the human figure and, by extension, in curved forms or ornamentation in the decorative arts.

The human body is curved and flexible, and so we resonate with similarly curved objects in the decorative arts or in our visual culture. In addition, it is common that when one sees an ambiguous picture that resembles the body, one jumps to the conclusion that it is, until one can see precisely what the picture is. So we ere on the side of seeing the human figure because of its status in the mind. Whether the figure is in action or in contemplation, people want to see other people. We can find the reason in human psychology.

Fundamentally, the individual unconscious is comprised in part of body images that are taken from the history of one's peer relations or from the perceptions of one's peer environment. In addition, studies have found that people have a body map in their brain and that it is very likely innate,[5] so this creates special sensitivity, and probably facilitates taking in historically specific and relevant information about bodies in our environment.

For example, a person will often dream of family members, acquaintances and anonymous people in modern dress. When dreaming, one feels the agreement or resonance between the desires expressed by the bodies in the dream and the desires of one's own body. Thus, when the people in the dream express fear, happiness, or sexual arousal, one will feel this in the body at the time of dreaming and immediately after awakening. This, very often is experienced as an exciting and positive thing.

Even while awake and calm, sudden sexual or frightening mental images can instantly evoke those emotions in one's body. Studies have found that humans are hard wired to imitate, and this influences our experience of dreamed body imagery. For instance, neonates can imitate facial expressions. If a person sticks out his tongue, a baby will often do the same thing. And studies have found that children will imitate acts of aggression that they see.[6] In addition, people tend to imitate higher ranking individuals.[7] If we are inclined to imitate the perceived images in our environment, it is reasonable that we feel and imitate dreamed body images.

---

[5] For a summary of this research on body image, see Ogas & Gaddam, p. 142-143; individual studies are: Aleong & Paus (2010), Arzy et al. (2006), Poliakoff (2010), Chan et al. (2004), David et al. (2007), Peelen & Downing (2007), Urgesi et al. (2004), Karremans et al. (2010).

[6] Stuart A Vyse, *Believing in Magic: The Psychology of Superstition* (New York: Oxford University, 1997).

[7] David Buss. *Evolutionary Psychology: The New Science of the Mind*, (New York: Allyn & Bacon, 2012).

Our felt connection with body imagery is so profound that we can mistakenly assume that our own emotions come from society or an external source. This misconception drives much popular and academic thought today about the nature of psychology and character formation.

People ask, "Do my emotions come from me or from out there or society?" To imagine that our emotions come from an external source is easy because of the power of dreamed images of the body. As we shall see, the power of dreamed body images can be so powerful that they are experienced as intrusive or confining.

The importance of body imagery and emotion can be seen in gender psychology. The agreement or resonance between male-specific emotions and male-specific body imagery creates a gender identity of masculinity. Similarly, resonance between female-specific emotions and female-specific body imagery creates a gender identity of femininity.

Men resonate with male imagery, and women resonate with female imagery. In the context of genetic similarity theory, evolutionary psychologist Burnstein uses the concept of phenotype matching.

He describes how "individuals compare another's trait (e.g., odor or voice) with a memory code representing the same trait in themselves or in a close relative. Besides pheromones, much of the work on adult human phenotype matching and detection of genetic relatedness involves the face."[8]

So of course this can be seen in gender and race leading to a kind of solipsism. So there is a circular relationship between native desire and imagined desire, and the physical body and imagined body image, and this leads to imitation. For instance, in the past, women were expected to be dainty, docile, and modest, and men were strong, dominant, or rugged.

These are simple projections of the natural, imagined state and were viewed as appropriate, good, just and proper. Heterosexuality and marriage are global norms, so a sexual charge

---

[8] Eugene Burnstein, "Altruism and Genetic Relatedness." David Buss, ed, *The Handbook of Evolutionary Psychology*, (Hoboken, N.J.: John Willey & Sons, 2005), 533.

exists in the mind between the dreamed images of the opposite sex and between felt emotion of an individual and the imagined emotion of the opposite sex.

For instance, people can achieve a certain degree of sexual satisfaction by fantasizing about a member of the opposite sex. There is a profound connection and resonance between felt and imagined emotion.

I recently had a dream that exemplifies this. I first saw a man who is a colleague, and my response was one of comradery and respect. In addition, I looked up to the image of his face. The dream then cut a woman who had a modest look on her face, and whom I looked down on.

My response to her was slight sexual arousal. So we see in these two examples how human relations are mirrored in dreams, and as I have a certain relationship or resonance with real people, I have the same relationship or resonance with my dreamed images of people. All of this starts with a native or deep social psychology which is projected onto other people in both real life and imagined or dream life. The basis for this is phenotypic matching.

Another example is that physical conditions felt while sleeping are automatically represented in dreams. For instance, if you are warm you dream about being warm; if you need to urinate you dream that you need to urinate. I once went to bed with a stomachache, had a dream that I had a stomachache, and when I awoke, still had the stomachache.

The mind can automatically represent the conditions of the body solely with feelings even without perceived images. Imitation is at work here. The mind has the ability to blend emotion with standard images of the body. For example, people can often describe their physical conditions with great accuracy.

I recently had a talk with an older man and he went into great detail about his failing health. I definitely felt how he felt about his health. So the mind and language have the ability to communicate with precision subjective states like those that are dreamed and real. Again we see imitation, and that cognition and values are inclined to be influenced by the innate sense of the rightness or justice of the emotions. We saw this in gender.

Another factor is what we observe. White Americans mostly dream of White people and African Americans' dreams are mostly populated by Blacks. This is consistent with genetic similarity theory. In many grade schools, Asians associate with Asians, Blacks with Blacks, Whites with Whites, and so on, even though there is every opportunity to associate with other groups. Neighborhoods spontaneously self-segregate and are as about as segregated today as in the 1950s. So spontaneous distancing results, in part, from an interruption of resonance or racial solipsism. But we will see later that this is a bigger problem for white men than white women. A neutral example of this solipsism is that it is common in many societies for men and women to socialize separately because of gender solipsism.

Resonance and projected desire from a person creates expectations or ideals for himself or herself and for others like in the areas of gender and race. And when people collectivize their desires they create norms or social ideals, which are then reflected in the media. So at this point we see that unless the group inculcates a mind centered sense of superiority or justice, that the mind will automatically project an emotion and body based sense of values and justice. We will see this body based value system in the discussion of the state of nature and recent trends in sexual selection.

The resonance between felt and imagined emotion is what allows us to detect gender deviance. The body image that enters our senses clashes with the imitative resonance between our own emotions and our own body imagery. (We saw this with race.) For instance, in the film *Little Women* (1949), one girl says to another, "You act boyish." The first girl is making a comparison in her mind between male and female norms. But she feels the emotional clash in her body, which results from an interruption of imitative resonance.

The alien behavior/body introduces a dissonant note. Female bodies should exhibit female emotions and behavior. She feels and seeks emotional self-fulfillment in the resonance, in the ideal, and in the harmonious image of another appropriate female. Similarly, when a woman sees an effeminate male, she feels disappointment, or the conflict between her desired image and the image of the man she sees. (Keep this in mind when we examine women's rape fantasies.) During the 1950s in San Francisco, city ordinances required women to wear a certain number of female articles of clothing. This resulted from the collectivization of desire. These laws are important because we will later see that women are indeed prone to imitate men. Men represent for women an attractive image of greater power, at least in certain contexts.

That memory plays a role is evident in that men and women can imitate each other, but usually rather badly, due to lack of resonance. And when individuals feel that their own specific constitutions or emotions do not allow for easy resonance with their official or representative mental images, as with homosexuals, they feel the discrepancy and discomfort. Homosexuals don't just feel like misfits when they see men and women together in public, but is something that they carry around in their memory and nervous system.

This is an example of the intrusiveness or confining quality of body imagery. Men and women do not really feel social pressure, but rather body image pressure in memory and body. This explains why homosexuals tend to reproduce heterosexual roles, styles and relationships. This is what is perceived to be good and is a good example of how the body can influence thought and values. This imitation results from a blending of native homosexuality with the power of heterosexual body imagery and emotions. Homosexuals feel an impulse to line themselves up with either one side or the other just as do heterosexuals. We saw this in race and from the girl's comment in *Little Women*. It is an example of the confining quality of body imagery.

After body imagery binds to felt emotion, imagery in the mind, in language, and in public then enforces desires and norms and its patterns or ideals. This explains why homosexuals adapt to a degree to the images of heterosexual norms, and is, again, an example of the confining pressure people feel from images. Cultural norms and linguistic expression result from observing, memorizing, and feeling attracted to patterns in attitude, emotion, and behavior. People do not experience social conditioning, but rather body image conditioning in the mind.

As people feel attached to their body image, through imitation, and that of the opposite sex, they feel attached to body images seen in public, and have an impulse to imitate them, especially if they are impressive. This is evident in the popularity of the human image in human-interest magazines. There is also greater resonance with a member of ones own race, and even with similarity of spoken language, body language and emotional tone. A cross-cultural comparison of developmental psychology makes clear the power of body imagery.

I once was speaking with two 12 year-old Swedish girls, and I was stunned by how poised they were in comparison to Americans of the same age, who tend to be giddy. This reflects that Swedish adults are less emotional and more focused than are American adults. There is a severity to most Scandinavians in comparison to Americans, who in turn are more relaxed. The children's behavior reflected body image vocabulary derived from perceiving adults.

Similarly, linguists know that children adopt the accent of their peers, not of their parents. So the general image that is imitated and that comes in from the populace is decisive. I once met a man whose parents were Italian, and he looked Italian, but he was raised in Germany, and he had a German personality. During the sixteenth century, the English had the same personalities as modern day Italians.

Sometimes you hear people say in the television shows from the 1950s, "How can you say that in front of the children?" At the time people believed that individuals had to constantly present the proper ideals of rationality or set a good example to others. We have the same practice today of social pressure but we just have different, inverted ideals of justice.

This practice of social pressure is evident in our taboos about expressing self-centered notions of race, gender and class, at least for whites. Recall here that these taboos resulted from the displacement of the old taboos about sexual expression and enjoyment. As it was wrong for whites to express and enjoy sex, now it is wrong for whites to express and enjoy race or any other of the old, self-centered identities. But notice that this taboo only applies to whites, and this is predictable given the origin of the taboo. In other words, it just moved to a different part of our personalities and social lives.

If unimpeded, body image resonance is attracted to the appropriate or idiomatic images seen in nature and social values. As people seek and ideally achieve imitative resonance with their own body image, they seek and achieve resonance with objects in nature. This creates the common impulse to anthropomorphize. And even today, men tend to earn more money than women because of their perceived greater physical power. More money is an idiomatic object that both men and women desire for men. As women want men to be impressive and powerful, so both men and women instituted social values and practices to empower men.

For instance, women are often compared to bunnies and men are big apes, or "rich and powerful." Mammals, such as mice and bears, are more easily anthropomorphized than reptiles and inanimate objects like rocks. This is so even though most people have more experience with rocks than with bears. In design, watches for men are usually larger than those marketed to women. As these non-human images, like bears and bunnies, fulfill, to a degree, desire and expectations or ideals for our gender differences, we are similarly attracted to the image of the human figure in general, in areas such as in the media, the public and in visual representation or art.

It is, obviously, the most fundamental and appealing "idiomatic" image. A mediating factor is that ideals from the group, like about good and evil, can create different kinds of associations with what is an appropriate body image to represent us: either a high one, like an angel, representing peace and mind, if that is perceived to be good, or a low one, like an ape, representing emotion and body if that is perceived to be good.

Recall here that Billy Joel would rather "laugh with the sinners than cry with the saints." This kind of cultural imagery influences people, and people made this point during the nineteenth century. At that time people experienced the world and others in the context of innate desire and its problematic moral status.

People seek emotional self-fulfillment in the figure in general, both in the image of their own sex and that of the opposite sex. The striving for ideal bodies compels many men and women to try to get a good figure. This pressure can also be experienced as confining.

So notice that fundamentally people judge others by an innate, internal standard, as regarding body type, for instance. We can all agree on who have the great bodies, for the most part. Desire and ideals move from the body into the public sphere, not the reverse. People sometimes think the reverse because of the confining pressure on the self from the body imagery in the mind and public. For instance, if you had a nightmare of being chased by a growling monster, you would experience it as intrusive and confining. Nightmares are more the exception than the rule, so for the most part there is resonance or a positive flow that moves back and forth between self and images in the mind and in public. Though it should be said that 70% of dreams are negative.

And some of these are universal, like being chased.[9] So as will become clear in our later discussion of the state of nature, and human conflict and ethics, these negative dreams help to explain why we are very prone to feel and cultivate conflict with other people, to view this as just, and to project it onto the order of nature. In addition we will examine later that there are more idealized or, in contrast, more average or realistic figure types in art and in the human population.

If the mind passively mirrored the body, then all groups would be similar, at least in the area of gender, and there would be no historical change. Obviously this is not the case, so we must examine the dynamics of change. Because of ideals from other sources than the body, such as from political forms, religion and philosophy, people can project different emotions, which are then collectivized and internalized.

We saw this with Billy Joel and his inversion. This results in change or at least pressure on the group and the vocabulary of body images in the mind. We saw this change in ideals with the inverted definition of justice. Recall that people are prone to imitate high status individuals, so what high status people believe and do can

---

[9] David Linden, *The Accidental Mind: How Brain Evolution has Given Us Love, Memory, Dreams, and God*, (Cambridge, Mass: Harvard University Press, 2007).

influence others. Again, there is resonance, and pressure can move in either direction, from images to body, or from body to images depending on, for instance, the kind of images and values in the media. We saw this with Billy Joel.

Before the twentieth century, aggression between peers was stigmatized as uncivilized or barbaric, and gender was conceived largely in terms of social status and qualities of mind. Starting during the early twentieth century, aggression became a larger source of gender values in the West, and this changed expectations and patterns of sexual selection. This will be explored in detail later, when we discuss the state of nature and early film history.

Humans are not endlessly changeable in a physical sense, but there is room for change in ideals. We have seen significant change in gender ideals during the past century. Women's natural modesty was seen for centuries to be the feminine ideal, as it was what men found sexually attractive.[10]

But this ideal was abandoned during the past century. Now strength is often a feminine ideal, at least in the area of self-reporting. Hence, we have heroic actresses today like Angelina Jolie. These values did not drop from the sky but were adopted from men.

Popular feminism is largely driven by imitation of men, and this is a modern development. Men are not expected to imitate women, but women are expected to imitate men. It is common for women to dress like men, but men almost never dress like women. It is common in popular and academic culture to romanticize women acting like men, but men acting like women is usually seen as humorous or pathological.

This relationship of women imitating men actually grows out of the relationship that existed between the sexes during the nineteenth century. At that time, women were socially male-dependent. They obtained social status from fathers and husbands. They obtained status by an act of imitation or submersion with bigger and stronger men.

It was easy for feminists to propose that women, in imitation of men, work themselves in the job market to obtain their social status. So as women dress like men, they now work like men, and

---

[10] Nancy Etcoff, *Survival of the Prettiest* (New York: Doubleday, 1999).

male-like attire is common among female professionals. Modern studies find that women are still concerned about the status of men, regardless of their own status.[11] Even high status women want high status men and are sensitive to questions of status for men. This shows that women are pre-wired to be status conscious in their selection of men. This makes evolutionary sense, so it will not go away, as we have seen when women obtain official existential independence from men.

Even when independent of men, women feel compelled to imitate men in obtaining their social status, because their deeper desire is to obtain their status from being a subset of men, which, as we have seen, is a form of imitation. Even high status women are concerned about the status of a potential mate. They feel that it reflects or rubs off on them, as it did during the nineteenth century. We can see that women's deeper concerns lie below superficial imitation of men in obtaining status in the job market.

As we can see in recent trends in sexual selection, women's financial independence from men allows them greater power in choosing men or influencing the kind of values that animate gender relations. As we will see in the discussion of the state of nature, women then and now promote and pursue more body based values in men in comparison to the nineteenth century. This of course is consistent with the inversion of values we have seen in the last century in all aspects of life.

So instead of the ideal of men being high minded, like during the nineteenth century, they now should be low minded, cool, bestial or "hip." I once heard two men in London talking, and one said to the other, "Girls like it when you act black." We will put these newly reemerging values, from both men and women, into their full evolutionary context during the discussion of the state of nature.

This study will show that status is a foundational structure in psychology. Almost every major and minor point will fit into a hierarchical structure. We will see that hierarchy is as important to humans as it is to any other group-living species from ants to apes.

---

[11] David Buss, *Evolutionary Psychology: The New Science of the Mind*, (New York: Allyn & Bacon, 2012).

As will become clear, our only option is how we animate it with different values, ideals or definitions of justice, what we aspire to, and who is in charge.

Feminism derives in part from the application of natural rights to gender roles and relations. If men may have political rights and be economic aggressors, then so should women.

This is a new development, and few thought this way during the eighteenth century, when the concept of natural rights emerged, as people were nativistic in their understanding of gender or sex. Politics and sex were viewed as separate domains, and in fact were viewed as incompatible.

Today, with a new, inverted value system in place, Westerners start to feel, project and collectivize different values and this influences ideals and behavior of self and others in part through resonance. Both men and women are more aggressive than they were a century ago as can be seen in the history of film, and with higher crime incidence today than in the 1950s. The mind is not a passive reflector of the body. Though, the mind does move more easily toward expressing the emotions than toward adapting to social pressure for rationalism and self control. This can be seen in the area of crime.

Crime skyrocketed all around the West during the 1960s. Today in the United States, the victim data shows about a 1000% increase since the 1950s, from about 1.5 million white crime victims, to 13 million,[12] and property crime in Europe has increased so much it is almost out of control, with a total of 23 million more crimes every year.[13]

World-wide the increases are 82 million every year. During the last 50 years over a billion people have been killed, injured and robbed, so the situation is serious. (For a full discussion of this problem see *Religion of Macho* by London and Smith.) I mention crime because the issue of how we conceive of the aggressive impulses, a sense of justice, and our bodies more generally, will

---

[12] Dane Archer & Rosemary Gartner, *Violence and Crime in Cross-National Perspective* (New Haven: Yale University Press, 1984); Bureau of Justice Statistics, 2012.

[13] Archer & Gartner; Interpol, 2004.

recur frequently in this study. In fact I can say it is the foundational issue as we saw in dreams.

As is evident with the increases in crime, the minds of self and others can adopt values other than the natural and positive, the truly just, and change mental imagery, emotion, behavior, and the ideals that are projected. It could be argued that some cultural ideals, specifically gender ideals, are more natural, desirable, and easier to adapt to than others. As it is easier to anthropomorphize a mammal than a rock, it is easier and more desirable for modesty to be a feminine ideal, at least from the male perspective. Yes, women can be more aggressive, but does this make women more or less attractive? It may appeal to our historically specific ideals for sex roles, or patterns of self-reporting, but does it appeal to our deepest and most universal currents of sexual desire?

For instance, marriages are less stable today, with men and women jockeying for power, than a century ago. Similarly, some ideals are more functional than others from a social cohesion or crime perspective. This will be explored further when we analyze the deep logic of modernism and Platonist psychology as they have developed during the last two centuries.

An interesting example of the desire for physical movement lies in the historical preference for marble in architecture and interior design. In comparison to other stones types, the texture of marble has more movement or apparent flexibility and softness. This contrasts with the appearance of harder stones like granite. Some types of marble appear to flow, and this gives it warmth similar to the living and flexible human body.

One motive for anthropomorphism is a desire for physical power, a desire to commune with another body and to share its power. This is common in animal behavior, called "dependent rank." A lower-ranking individual raises its status by aligning itself with a higher-ranking individual or, in the case of humans, with the power intrinsic to another body. It is easy to see why people imagine images like professional wrestlers, Vikings, or like Bacchus, who is stimulating, or Superman flying around the sky and capturing bad guys and knocking over buildings. Similarly, humans are inclined to animate non-human objects in order to create a greater sense of collective power. One of the motives for this is to break our sense of isolation as individuals, and to create a greater sense of power against the threat of death. Hence, humans at some level are attracted to large objects like trees, whales, clouds, sky and sun, but less to smaller objects in nature.

The Vikings worshiped trees as images of endurance, and they used to sit by the camp fire and pass around a large horse phallus wrapped in cloth. Similarly, we today are attracted to other bodies because of their strength—the stronger the better. Like the Vikings with trees, modernist Americans today idolize African Americans because of Blacks' imagined greater strength and size. And recall here that higher consciousness naturally wants to express "body ideals," and to view this as good, just, desirable and defensible, instead of repressing this impulse and its representatives. We shall return to Blacks' perceived strength later.

Because of our large emotional investment via dependent rank and resonance, the human figure has been central throughout most of art history. An ancient description of Daidalos, the mythical founder of Greek art, makes this clear:

> In the sculptor's art he so far excelled all other men that in after times the fable was told of him that the statues which he made were like living beings; for they saw and walked, and, in a word, exercised every bodily function, so that his handiwork seemed to be a living being. And being the first to give them open eyes, and parted legs, and outstretched arms, he justly won the admiration of men: for before his time artists made statues with closed eyes and hands hanging down and cleaving to their sides.[14]

Another innovation occurred during the Classical period of Athenian history. Sculptors started to portray the figure in *contrapposto*, in which the figure rests his weight on one leg. This resulted in an asymmetry with one hip being higher than the other. This created the impression that the figure was about to move, thus

---

[14] H. Stuart Jones, *Ancient Writers on Greek Sculpture* (Chicago: Argonaut, 1966) 3-4.

having greater dynamism. Egyptian sculpted figures have even or symmetrical hips, creating a more static image. The figures in our dreams are most frequently moving, and almost never standing at attention for long periods of time.

The ancients were detail orientated, and were concerned with the development and refinement of the figure. Roman author Pliny the Elder was the first art historian whose works have come down to us. The focus on the figure is visible in Pliny's observation of the sculptor Pythagoras, "He was the first to make the sinew and veins duly prominent and to bestow greater pains on the hair."[15]

Regarding the sculptor Lysippos, Pliny observed, "His chief characteristic is extreme delicacy of execution even in the smallest details."[16]

The ancients often strove to portray emotions. Regarding the sculptor Praxiteles, Pliny described how, "There are two statues by him expressing contrary emotions, a mourning matron and a rejoicing courtesan. The latter is believed to be Phryne. The sculptor's love may be read in the whole in the statue, and Phryne's satisfaction is depicted on her face."[17]

The human figure was central in the ancient imagination from about 600 BCE to about 500 CE, a duration of more than a thousand years. After Christianization, sculptures were believed to be possessed by demons, and often defaced and destroyed as pagan idols or expressions of the sinful body and the mortal world. They were replaced by flat and lifeless Byzantine icons, and this style dominated art until the Italian Renaissance of about 1300.

At that time, the fleshed-out figure in painting began to reoccur in the work of the Italian painter Giotto. By 1400 the figure in both sculpture and painting became more volumetric. The sculptor Donatello made several of his works with *contrapposto*. The painter Masaccio made the most realistic figure up to that time, improving over Giotto, but his figures were still crude and clumsy by comparison with what was done later in the century. Nevertheless,

---

[15] Pliny the Elder, K. Jex-Blake, trans, *The Elder Pliny's Chapters On The History Of Art*, Kessinger Publishing. reprint of (New York: The Macmillan Co, 1896), 49.
[16] Ibid., 53.
[17] Ibid., 57.

he did achieve a certain weight that is an important component of realistic art.

By the late fifteenth century, in the painting of Botticelli, there started to be real beauty and grace. Artists by this time had begun to use shading and curvilinear forms. The fifteenth century is commonly called the Middle Renaissance.

But, according to Vasari, the contemporary art historian of the sixteenth century, figures still lacked volume, and compositions were overly schematic or harsh. He also said that figures during this whole period lacked freedom, which is another way of describing the overly schematic character of the painting style. Another flaw of this period was that paintings were too busy, or detailed with an overabundance of objects, which detracted from and weakened the human figures.

The breakthrough in art, when it again achieved the perfection of antiquity, occurred at the hands of the triumvirate: Leonardo Da Vinci, Raphael and Michelangelo. With these artists, painting and sculpture achieve a monumentality and idealization that defines the High Renaissance. Leonardo was the first to create a monumental figure and compositional type, around 1480, with Raphael and Michelangelo maturing around 1500.

Together they brought true freedom to the figure and composition, and removed the harshness. One way that they achieved this was by omitting excess objects, like the trees and bushes that had cluttered the paintings of Botticelli and others from the earlier century.

Now the figure, like Michelangelo's *David*, strode forth in singular glory, grandeur and heroism. Raphael, in his flowing, pyramidal figure groups, achieves *sprezzatura*, or studied casualness.[18] Raphael, with his flowing elegance, is the Mozart of art,[19] while Michelangelo, with his muscular heroism, is the Beethoven of art. Raphael and Mozart, who minimize conflict, are more utopian, while Michelangelo and Beethoven, with their heroism, have more

[18] Pierluigi De Vecchi, "Difficulty/ease and studied casualness in the work of Raphael," *Raphael: Grace and Beauty* (Milano: Skira, 2001).
[19] Patrizia Nitti, Marc Restellini, and Claudio Strinati, Ed. *Raphael: Grace and Beauty* (Milano: Skira, 2001).

engagement with the world. Notice the furrowed brow of David, as if he is readying himself for the action of battle rather than being portrayed as triumphant.

A critical observation by Vasari is that those artists achieved perfection by only portraying the beautiful. They did this by using the most beautiful examples of the human body or nature. In this way, they achieved idealization or perfection of both body and nature.

In fact, Vasari goes so far as to say that Michelangelo was so wedded to the idea of perfection that he had a policy of never doing a portrait of a living person. This would have been descending away from the ideal in the "mind of God" or the human mind, and losing himself in the particular or the empirical.

Michelangelo's faces are described in earlier scholarship as "idealized." Modern scholars use the term "generalized." Both names contain an element of truth. Newborn babies have an innate ability to recognize the human face.[20]

They do not respond to other figure types, but they do respond to the human face. Apparently, babies have a general face-type hardwired into their brains. So the term "generalized" is accurate.

Yet, because all babies have this pattern, it could also be described as "idealized" due to its universality. In addition, there is a certain nobility in the generalized face, which helps create the sense that it is ideal.

Seeing the face that is in the mind takes the viewer above or out of this world and into the mind, the most powerful and noble part of our bodies. Michelangelo also responded to this nobility, suggesting why he never did portraits in either painting or sculpture.

Let us now revisit the body imagery psychology described at the beginning of this chapter. What the High Renaissance triumvirate achieved is a beautiful or ideal figure type, which adheres to our expectations or ideals, and a very wide spectrum of human expression: from the dark languor of Leonardo, to the

---

[20] Vicki Bruce and Andy Young, *In the Eye of the Beholder* (Oxford: Oxford University, 1998).

beautiful elegance of Raphael and the monumental heroism of Michelangelo. Vasari describes how in the fresco *The Last Judgment*, Michelangelo portrays a wide spectrum of emotion to which people have responded for centuries. Many respond today. The High Renaissance triumvirate set the standard. The supremacy of these artists was unquestioned until the mid-nineteenth-century rise of modernism.

The triumvirate achieved the perfect balance between art, form or mind, and nature. The body needs to be controlled or encased in an artistic or slightly geometric media to be raised above itself, to be projected into the mind and thus to be idealized, aestheticized or experienced as art. We saw this with the experience of the idealized face type. Real people are too animated and have too many imperfections.

When viewing a real person, your attention is drawn too much to their details and movement, and less to the experience in the ideal of the face and body in the mind. There is a similar contrast between the experiences in the mind of seeing a beautiful person as opposed to an average person. A Hollywood film from the 1930s shows the importance of a large degree of stillness for art. In the film *Marie-Antoinette* (1938), with Norma Shearer and Tyrone Power, the queen is beautifully dressed and surrounded by her courtiers. A man looks at her and says, "In repose you are a statue of beauty." Almost all later artists have lost the balance between mind and nature, either emphasizing details or nature in excess, or overly emphasizing art or artifice.

One popular idea during the Renaissance was to transform your life into a work of art. This can be seen in the life of the actress Audrey Hepburn. She studied ballet as a child and went on to become the embodiment of grace and beauty during the 1950s and '60s. Her beautiful personality is well described by film critic David Thomas. Here are some excerpts from a longer description:

> [She] moved to Hollywood, where she was a fairy queen for some fifteen years…She seemed English; she had a sense of manners and kindness that came close to grace…She was never happy with men her own age; she made them seem older and crude. There was always an

untouched glory in her...Her Oscar [for *Roman Holiday* (1953)] was generous, but it showed how far Hollywood had been swept off its democratic feet by her outrageous purity...Hepburn was a creature of the fifties: she was sustained by the real-life royalty of Princesses Margaret and Grace (neither of whom matched the actress's perfection.)...Hepburn largely ignored and smoothed away the ironies and awkwardness in Capote's women... The feeling of public loss at her death spoke to how fondly her look and her benevolence were remembered. Retrospectives had standing room only, and Audrey— in eyes, voice, and purity—rang as true as a small silver bell. The great women of the fifties had a character that is in short supply now.[21]

Hepburn's personality was not an accident, but the result of centuries of cultural pressure in the West to be virtuous, guilt-ridden, and self controlled, like a ballet dancer or a work of art. Of course, since the sixties, as Thomas has noted, there has been regression to savagery—with the West's exposure to a violent world, recent trends in sexual selection, and the extension of negative rights, the excuses that allow some to think that rape, murder and theft are acceptable.

These excuses, as we shall see, are in place to help facilitate the new inverted justice, and "brotherhood." We will see the aggressive drives in full force and their effects on thought and ideals in our discussion of the state of nature.

Most thinkers of the seventeenth and eighteenth centuries took a dim view of raw nature. According to Robert Greenberg, an unnamed seventeenth century scientist wrote, "The visible world would be more perfect if the seas and lands made more regular features; if the rains were more regular; if, in a word, the world had fewer monstrosities and less disorder."

A French missionary described Niagara Falls as "falling from a horrible precipice, foaming and boiling, after the most

---

[21] David Thomson, *The New Biographical Dictionary of Film* (New York: Knopf, 2010), 439-40.

hideous manner imaginable and making an outrageous noise, a dismal roaring, really more terrible than thunder." An English explorer described the Alps as, "Hideous, uncouth, monstrous, excrescence of nature."

Commenting on these quotes, historian Frederick Art said that, "In the age of the Baroque, they evidently wanted to smooth and regulate all nature and make, as it were, domestic pets of the rivers and mountains."[22] Winckelmann, the eighteenth century theorist of Classicism, succinctly described the import of nature as "vulgar nature."[23] As unformed, it is simply "too much," crude, confining and claustrophobic.

Nature's crudeness did not become an artistic ideal until the mid nineteenth century. The contrast between the two views of nature clearly resulted from the two different versions of Platonic justice. With the old mind-based system or bias, nature was perceived to be unformed, crude, base, inferior, an injustice and so unattractive. With the inverted Platonism, now crude nature is high, good and so beautiful. As we shall see, as democracy progressed, this aesthetic bias only became more extreme creating the vulgarity common today. Westerners once embraced the distinction between nature and culture. Nature *per se* was viewed as vulgar and disgusting, while refined culture was viewed as beautiful and a relief from vulgar, oppressive and confining nature. Eighteenth century artist and theoretician Sir Joshua Reynolds wrote:

> The same local principals which characterize the Dutch school extend even to their landscape painters... Their pieces in this way are, I think, always a representation of an individual spot, and each in its kind a very faithful but a very *confined* portrait [emphasis added].

> Claude Lorrain, on the contrary, was convinced, that taking nature as he found it seldom produced beauty.

---

[22] Quotes on nature from Robert Greenberg, *How to Listen to and Understand Great Music*, 3rd Edition. DVD lecture series (Chantilly VA: The Teaching Company, 2006).

[23] Johann Joachim Winckelmann, Harry Francis Mallgrave, trans., *History of the Art of Antiquity* (Los Angeles: Getty, 2006), 133.

His pictures are a composition of the various draughts [drawings] which he had previously made from various beautiful scenes and prospects.[24]

Reynolds sensed a certain constricted or claustrophobic feel to the naturalistic or unformed landscape. The mind gets caught up in the vulgar details or confining clutter instead of flowing smoothly over a lucid form, as in the idealized landscapes of Claude. We also saw this in Michelangelo's preference for the idealized face type. Outside of the control of the mind, random nature is cluttered and an imposition.

As some experience their own body image as intrusive and confining, as we saw with homosexuals, we can experience unformed nature in this way. For both Winckelmann and Reynolds, raw nature is too much or oppressive.

The theme of claustrophobia and oppression will recur in our discussion of modernism, in both art and politics. To anticipate, this aesthetic of confining oppression will be displaced from nature to seeing high art formalism itself as confining or imposing, then further displaced to oppose the confining upper class during the French Revolution.

Such perceived confinements will be the primary element thrown off or rebelled against, to create the new moral and political or hierarchical and aesthetic priorities of modernism. People started to feel that form itself and the traditional hierarchies were confining or oppressive, instead of nature.

Put another way, the metaphors we formally used to understand our bodies and nature were displaced to the social sphere. So instead of the body being evil and threatening, suddenly the formalism of the classical tradition was evil and oppressive, and, in terms of social relations, the upper-class started to be viewed as evil and oppressive.

As the body was viewed as a trap, now "society" is viewed as a trap. Instead of the body being a disgusting pollution to be purged, suddenly beauty and the upper class became disgusting

[24] Sir Joshua Reynolds, *Discourses* (New York: Penguin, 1790/1992), 130.

or an "outrage" that needed to be purged. The traditional heroic anger against our fallen selves and "outrageous" nature, was turned outward to the public sphere, in both art and politics. With a new sense of justice, instead of needing to escape from "the world" suddenly we felt the urge to escape from human and aesthetic control and hierarchy, this form of entrapment, this new form of infringement or injustice.

So instead of looking at social control on the evil body as a just good, suddenly we started to see it itself as an evil or an injustice that needed to be escaped through ideals of individual expression and "self realization." This of course is consistently conceived as in opposition to the needs of group conformity, taming of the individual, low crime or peace.

Hence we have more crime today and promiscuous socializing that promotes crime and cultural debasement. With the traditional sense of justice, all of this was experienced to be dangerous, and so parents, for instance, controlled who their children socialized with. Bad *people* were the problem, not bad "society." As we were alienated from bad people, now we are alienated from bad society.

If one reads modern culture from this perspective, it is a very tight unity, as is evident even in this short summary, and modern culture turns out not to be a disparate jumble of volitional actions, as many claim.

We are as hierarchical today as we were during the *ancien regime*, we now simply think that the individual, the low, the emotions and the body should rule or be the ideal for the group and the upper class, instead of the traditional model of socially induced virtue or self control from elites, which had been case for centuries with the old justice. Instead of moving from the public to the private, high to low, we started to move from the private to the public or from low to high.

This new logic creates the ACLU. As we traditionally wanted freedom from our evil bodies, now we want freedom from evil "society" or the social body, as I will refer to it in this study. We now want to "purge" society, like race, gender and class, this being the new offensive "low."

How this "problem" is defined, or where this evil spirit is situated in our social life, varies from group to group and era to era, but the desire for freedom from evil does indeed unify both the left and most of the right today.

As the body was commonly viewed as dangerous, now society is commonly viewed as dangerous. As physically stimulating jazz music was viewed as suspect and dangerous, now controlled and controlling classical music is viewed as suspect and dangerous: meretricious. As popular culture was viewed as illegitimate, now high culture is viewed as illegitimate.

Let's consider the term *meretricious*. Older definitions refer to the body and sex, and prostitutes, as being a fake pleasure. Modern definitions refer to fancy objects like limousines as a being a fake pleasure or temptation. This of course is a good example of the displacement of evil and metaphors we had about the body. The meaning of words, how they are used and how they change speaks volumes about how values and perceptions change.

This is, at root, an inversion of Platonism played out in all aspects of life from how we raise our children, to Hollywood film, to the most refined theories in art history. Several scholars during the last three centuries have noticed inversion at work in the culture, but none, as far as I am aware, have applied it systematically and broadly to all aspects of culture, both high and low.

To continue with our discussion of art, according to Reynolds, the Dutch artists emphasized dark, cluttered, and grimy nature. The Rococo, as in the work of Boucher, emphasized an overly stylized eroticism.

Nevertheless, Vermeer was a master of light, and this has a certain, limited, appeal. In the Baroque, like Rubens or Bernini, the figure was over-animated. There was too much movement, with figures vibrating and tumbling here and there and drawing to much attention to themselves and not allowing the image to be really felt in the mind, as we saw earlier. What is evident in art history is that most artists either expose the viewer to too many details in the object portrayed, as in the Baroque, or they take the viewer too much into the mind as in medieval art. Classicism strikes the balance between the form-creating faculty of the mind and observed detail.

Pornography is not art because it stimulates the lower emotions and appeals not enough to the form-giving faculty of the mind. The mind is overwhelmed by the body and emotion. Perfect art strikes a balance between mind and body or emotion, while porn places too much emphasis on the body and emotions. It is simply vulgar to refined sensibilities before the twentieth century. A Classic Venus is art because it strikes a balance between the lucid form of the body and a slight charge of erotic emotion. We saw this in the comment about Marie-Antoinette.

Pornography shows that we are hardwired to have strong emotional responses to the body, and so we don't have those responses to much of nature, like small rocks and frogs. From an artistic perspective, the body and inert material like stone and metal pose fundamentally different challenges. The body needs control, while inert material needs animation or to be formed into body like or animated objects. The sculpted figure is the best example of this, but so is the fact that baroque decorative arts, with their greater curves, are more engaging than the more subdued styles like rococo and classicism. So inert material needs animation, while the figure needs control.

What varies from period to period in art history are the perspectives on the body and how it is controlled. For instance, on an episode of *Friends* Joey gives Chandler a heavy gold bracelet, and Chandler does everything he can to not wear it, and at one point yells that it comes from "the Liberace house of crap!" Obviously our perspectives have changed, and we will see the reasons during this study.

Vasari said that the Venetians artists could not draw, and this was evident today in their amorphous forms. In order to create a solid figure, the brush strokes must be perfectly blended or invisible, as in the neo-Classical paintings of Ingres. During the seventeenth century there arose an interest in still-life and landscape, but these were viewed well into the nineteenth century as being of lower import than history painting or portraits.

Hundreds of books have been published on art history over the past 150 years. Many describe how artists treat the figure, and the influence that religion, politics and science have had on artists' perspectives. The preceding discussion has been a psychological perspective on why the figure so dominated art history before the twentieth century, and why, in the modern period, the Italian High Renaissance was unique and perfect in its treatment.

Regarding further reading, on Greek sculpture, *The Greek Miracle: Classical Sculpture from the Dawn of Democracy* edited by Diana Buitron-Oliver is an excellent short collection of essays on the subject. On Italian Renaissance art, *Classic Art* by Heinrich Wolfflin is itself a classic. A good general survey of art is an early edition of *History of Art* by H. W. Janson. Another useful work is *The Nude* by Kenneth Clark.

Chapter Two: Violence and the State of Nature

The northern tribes are spirited.

—Plato

Before we proceed in analyzing the inversion of the culture, we need to stop and get a tangible sense of the state of nature because a larger point that his book will try to make is that modernism, with the inversion, represents a sliding back to natural behavior and more natural cultural ideals of emotional expression and romanticizing violent behavior. In addition, I will try to prove that the cultural and political institutions of the early modern era, like church discipline, were constructed to create peace and beauty out of behavior that naturally tends to be conflicted, disharmonious and ugly. As beautiful Raphael paintings don't grow on trees, neither does extremely virtuous behavior as we saw in the discussion of Audrey Hepburn. Her personality grew out of an unnatural definition of justice. Put another way, if one looks at anthropology and history, it is clear that being very inhibited is not natural, but emotional expression, conflict and violence are; we saw this with the fact that 70% of dreams are negative. In a state of nature, "Self-help" is more the norm in the absence of a judicial system.

At least since the seventeenth century, a basic debate surrounds the question of how much violence there is in the state of nature or among tribes. Thomas Hobbes believed that life in nature is "nasty, brutish and short," while John Lock believed that it was Paradise. Lock was very influential among the left during the last three centuries in their rush to condemn modern institutions as "unnatural" and evil. Jean-Jacques Rousseau is a good example of this. Fortunately we no longer have to rely on speculation, or even well informed anthropological and historical descriptions, but hard data. Harvard psychologist Steven Pinker, in his recent *The Better Angels of Our Nature: Why Violence Has Declined* presents a very large amount of data representing the high rates of violence among tribes. If one combines this with psychological, anthropological and historical descriptions, it settles the question: life among tribes is indeed nasty, brutish and short, and in short, "primitive," as it used to be called.

It is clear that high degrees of virtue or inhibitions are not natural, but result from conscious constructions from "unnatural," or top heavy political and cultural institutions, as is evident in the beliefs and practices of early modern history. Of course to argue today that the old institutions were morally justified, even to some extent, tends to upset most people for all ethical reasons so far outlined regarding the inversion of Platonism.

Pinker reports that the death rate among non-state groups from war is about, on average, 600 per 100,000 population. The rate for Europe in the last century was a fraction of that, including Russia and Germany taken by themselves. Regarding homicide, the average non-state societies' average is 700 per 100,000 population. In Europe during 1300 CE it was about 80. Between then and now it dropped to almost zero because of cultural pressures from Church, state and elites.

Though it needs to be said that it is common for historians to report that Europe was much more peaceful during 1300 than year 500 when more people, at least in central Europe, lived in a state of nature or close to it. During the Dark Ages, murder was so common that the church only outlawed it on Sundays and Christmas. The data for the non-state societies are from recent decades or are historical reconstructions. Commenting on this data, Pinker said, "Macho violence among male acquaintances [as opposed to violence within families] is fueled by contests of dominance that are more sensitive to circumstance. How violent a man must be to keep his rank in the pecking order in a given milieu depends on his assessment of how violent the other men are, leading to vicious or virtuous circles that can spiral up or down precipitously."[25] So the "circumstance" that he refers to is the nature of the kinds of social promoters or inhibitors of the hostile emotions that boys and men are raised with or surrounded by.

Another factor is the kind of men that we are exposed to and that women marry. This peer pressure determines if whether men turn out to be naturally vicious or unnaturally virtuous like Audrey Hepburn.

If modernism turns out to be romanticizing or supporting the emotions that promote conflict, and undifferentiated human socializing, then it is implicated in the recent cultural degradation that much of this study will document, and implicated in the increased crime in the West since the 1960s.

Regarding the state of nature, let's now examine some qualitative descriptions, both in the third world and early Europe. The *Dictionary of Black African Civilization*, under the entry for "fertility," describes how African boys engage in "crude horseplay and tough physical ordeals that may prove fatal..., and receive professional training" for hunting and war.[26]

These values are perceived to the good, in part, because they feel good. And recall here that 70% of dreams are negative. The cultural status of male physical fertility, heroism, or dominance is further illustrated by the following African tribal incantation:

> Become a big man of crowds, a hero in war, a macho man with women, rich in children, and in many objects of wealth.... Let toughness and fame be with you.... Become macho and dominant, a great man.[27]

---

[25] Steven Pinker, *The Better Angels of Our Nature: Why Violence has Declined*, (New York: Viking, 2012), 64.

[26] Georges Balandier and Jacques Maquet, *Dictionary of Black African Civilization* (New York: Leon Amiel, 1974), 189.

[27] Jan Vansina, *Paths in the Rainforests* (Madison: University of Wisconsin Press, 1990). pp. 73-74.

Clearly, humility is not part of his ethical tradition as we saw with Audrey Hepburn. In the Hebrew Bible, a man wins honor on the battlefield, and a woman wins honor through childbirth.

Two recently televised documentaries on African tribes portrayed the men heroically fighting their peers for the twin purposes of earning glory, respect, and honor from other men and sexual favors from women. A husband and wife were interviewed separately, and both stated explicitly that their marriage was based on the man's heroic ability. They talked about it with glee—it clearly was not a hardship.

In one of the documentaries, it first showed the males of a gazelle like creature fighting for mating rights, and then the film cut to African men engaged in ritualized fighting to earn the respect of male and female peers.

This perspective of macho heroics is brought over into African and Latin American village and urban life, and results in high "crime" or heroism rates for these regions[28] and for their populations in the modern West. In *Savage Africa* (1967), nineteenth-century English explorer Winwood Read, the first European to set eyes on certain African tribes, reported witnessing just such primitive values. Other scholars have found that tribal values of fertility predate contact with European colonists.[29] And Lawrence H. Keeley in *War before Civilization* noted that prehistoric warfare was more frequent and ruthless than modern war.[30]

Male dominance in terms of macho prowess can be seen in the following description by Obaharok, an aspiring New Guinea warrior and leader:

> I knew I was meant to be a *kain* ["leader"]. My father told me. But everyone said I couldn't kill because I was

---

[28] Dane Archer and Rosemary Gartner. *Violence and Crime in Cross-National Perspective,* (New Haven & London: Yale University Press, 1984).

[29] David M Buss, *Evolutionary Psychology: The New Science of the Mind* (New York: Alan and Bacon, 1999). Martin Daly and Margo Wilson, *Homicide* (New York: Aldine De Gruyter, 1988.) Richard Wrangham and Dale Peterson, *Demonic Males* (Boston: Houghton Mifflin, 1996).

[30] Lawrence H.Keeley, *War Before Civilization*. (Oxford: Oxford University Press, 1997).

too young. I began by stealing a pig. I succeeded and so I stole and again and again. Each time I succeeded. The *braveness* in my heart grew bigger. I felt myself a brave man. Quietly, I tried to kill a man. I returned home with that *victory*. I wanted to go to war and fight with the others, but they still considered me to be a child. I felt so angry. I went, anyway. With bows and arrows in my hand, I killed the enemy one by one. I killed and I killed until many enemies were dead. I have killed many, many people. In the end I was accepted by the people as *overlord*. I am not *afraid* of anybody [emphasis added].[31]

This is all about *me, me, me!* In addition, our hero keeps track of his kills, as children do while playing video games, but the real thing is clearly more exciting. UCLA professor Jared Diamond recently said that you stood a better chance of surviving Poland during World War Two, than life today in a New Guinea village.

This is consistent with the crime data provided by Pinker. Notice in the first sentence the direct equation between killing and leadership. So for him, and most other groups in a state of nature, what determines dominance, governance or justice are body based values, those of course we have seen develop in the West with the inversion and increased crime.

At the University of California at Berkeley, a Black African professor stated that the cultural or behavioral characteristics of African-Americans are largely derived from their native societies. Anthropologist Melville J. Herskovits drew the same conclusion.[32] This fact has been known by anthropologists at least since the 1950s.

A more flamboyant expression of these values of heroism and hierarchy comes from a male resident of Mexico City:

Mexicans, and I think everyone in the world, admire the person "with balls," as we say. The character who

---

[31] W. Sargent, *People of the Valley* (New York: Random House, 1974). p. 178, italics added.

[32] Melville J Herskovits, *The Myth of the Negro Past* (Boston: Beacon Press, 1958).

throws punches and kicks, without stopping to *think*, is the one who comes out on top. The one who has guts enough to stand up against an older, stronger guy is more *respected*.

If someone shouts, you've got to shout *louder*. If any so-and-so comes to me and says, "Fuck your mother," I answer, "Fuck your mother a thousand times." And if he gives one step forward and I take one step back, I lose *prestige*. But if I go forward too, and pile on and make a fool out of him, then the others will treat me with *respect*. In a fight, I would never give up or say, "Enough," even though the other was killing me. I would try to go to my death, smiling. That is what we mean by "macho," by being *manly* [emphasis addes].[33]

Again, *me, me, me!* He is strongly inspired by a spontaneous sense of justice. Notice how similar these attitudes are to those held by a group of eight-year-old boys. What is interesting about this last example of hierarchy and honor is its informal nature in comparison to the New Guinea example.

For Obaharok, official political hierarchy is negotiated by heroism, while for this Mexican youth, hierarchy and primitive values of heroism spring spontaneously from the body and structure informal peer relations.

All men automatically measure their mental image of their own body against that of their male and female peers, and so are socially stratified by how weak or strong they are. This is the point that Pinker makes in his quote. Unless frustrated by some form of group pressure, this desire compels men to form a dominance hierarchy in more primitive terms. Essentially, fear is retraction or smallness. It is of low value in a state of nature.

African-Americans' pursuit of their native cultures manifests itself in a nonliterary, oral tradition and in a tribal-influenced vocabulary and syntax.[34] For instance, the phrase "you

---

[33] O. Lewis, *The Children of Sanchez: Autobiography of a Mexican Family* (New York: Random House, 1961), 38, all italics added. Quoted in Daly & Wilson.
[34] Melville J. Herskovits, *The Myth of the Negro Past* (Boston: Beacon Press,

all" is derived from the west African language Twi, in which it is spelled *mo nyina*.[35] Other cultural traits that Blacks have retained include: ritual songs and dances; polygamy; extended families; units of time; religious chanting; war; male avocational and vocational fraternalism (gangs); childbirth as a fertility ritual for peers (exploding rates of illegitimate births); religious concepts; sacred and secular narratives and rituals; secret societies; political forms; body decorations; customary body language; working patterns; and motor behavior.[36]

These priorities are retained by the process of syncretism. For instance, the African immigrants experienced Christian icons as they did their native icons,[37] and this was a vehicle for them to retain narratives and values. The African-Americans have also maintained the gender ideals of physical prowess for men and the absence of a work ethic.

Of course these are just trends, especially among the lower classes, but are not universal. In much of Africa, the natives only work about three hours a day. In their spare time, many groups enjoy themselves by taking drugs. And just as they spend much of their time debating cultural and political issues among themselves, their American cousins tend to gather on the front porch or street corner to talk things over.

As Herskovits noted, that American Blacks believe that "no dichotomy exists between good and evil in the realm of the supernatural, but that both are attributes of the same powers in terms of predisposition and control, is characteristically African".[38] Power is both good and evil, and if it works in one's favor, then it is better, more fertile.

African-born basketball player Menute Bol was required to kill a lion for his puberty rites, so he strongly identifies masculinity with the willingness to aggressively assert himself.

1958). Salikoko S. Mufwene, ed. *Africanisms in Afro-American Language Varieties* (Athens, Ga.: University of Georgia Press, 1993).

[35] Ibid.

[36] Leon Dash, *When Children Want Children* (New York: Morrow, 1989). Melville J. Herskovits, *The Myth*.

[37] Melville J. Herskovits, *The Myth*.

[38] Ibid., p. 242.

A documentary on beauty reported that in Venezuela, 40 percent of men and 60 percent of women think about their physical appearance *constantly*. This extreme self-absorption with their animated faces often results in a beaming quality or serious, brittle intensity to the personalities of these macho men. This is seen in history. Homer sometimes described his heroes as "shining".[39] Human males are indeed prone to swagger to be impressive, and to expand their proportions and egos.

Recall in the dream psychology I described how desire always want to expand outwards because of resonance with self and others. Among chimpanzees, the dominant male swaggers to show off his virility and high status.

So what we have been seeing here is that men, and women, tend to use the self and its lower aspects to define justice: "I want" etc. On the other hand, in a state of nature, humility doesn't get you very far; this is something that everyone has to agree upon and impose upon the young as we did before the twentieth century.

When northern Europeans lived in nature, men competed and aspired to power over each other or enforced their will by strength. This was considered a male gender performance ideal, a way that men earned social status among peers.

The following excerpt from the Nordic *Saga of the Volsungs* illustrates how northern Europeans competed individually in terms of physical strength to earn social status:

> Then Hogni fought on gallantly and courageously, killing twenty of King Atli's greatest champions. He flung many into the fire that had been built there in the hall. All were agreed that such a man had hardly ever been seen before. Nevertheless, at the end, Hogni was overpowered and made prisoner.
>
> Now, at the urging of King Atli, they seized Hogni and cut out his heart. Hogni's strength was so immense that he laughed while he suffered this torture. Everyone wondered at his courage, and it has been remembered ever since.[40]

---

[39] e.g., *Iliad*, 7.48.
[40] Jesse Byock, trans., *The Saga of the Volsungs*, p. 102.

This scene represents values that are still alive today. For example, James Cagney once portrayed a young criminal on death row. The day before he is to be executed, he says to a friend: "They think I'm scared. I'm gonna laugh when they take me to the chair!" The Saga glorifies technology that is an extension of men's bodies:

> When the battle had gone on a very long time, Sigurd advanced past the standards, holding in his hand the [invincible] sword Gram.[41]

This is a tool of ultimate physical power and, like guns for Black men, a symbol of Sigurd's manly willingness to be violent.

These fertility values are evident in the expectations of boys during puberty:

> After a time, Signy gave birth to a son. This son was called Sinfjotli. And when he grew up, he was both large and strong, handsome of appearance, and very like the Volsung stock.
>
> He was not quite ten years old when Signy sent him to Sigmund in his underground shelter. Before sending her first sons to Sigmund, she had tested them by stitching the cuffs of their kirtles to their hands, passing the needle through both flesh and skin.
>
> They withstood the ordeal poorly and cried out in pain. She also did this to Sinfjotli; he did not flinch. Then she ripped the kirtle from him, so that the skin followed the sleeves. She said that it must certainly be painful for him. He replied: "Such pain would seem trifling to Volsung."[42]

Women determine the social status of men by the men's ability to dominate other men physically. A good example of this in the Saga is the scene in which Brynhild announces to Gunnar the powers that her future husband must have:

---

[41] Ibid., p. 62.
[42] Ibid., p. 43.

"[Odin] also said that I must marry. And I made a counter-vow that I would marry no one who knew fear...."

[Gunnar replies,] "I shall pay a generous marriage settlement of gold and precious treasures in return for your hand."

She answered gravely from her seat....

"Gunnar," she said, "do not speak of such things to me, unless you surpass every other man, and you will kill those who have asked for me in marriage, if you have the courage to do so. I was in battle with the king of Gardariki, and our weapons were stained with the blood of men, and this I still desire....

"So it happened that I betrothed myself to the one who would ride the horse Grani with Fafnir's inheritance, to that one who would ride through my wavering flames and would kill those men who I decided should die. Now, no one dared to ride except Sigurd alone. He rode through the fire because he was not short of courage for the deed. He killed the dragon and Regin and five kings—unlike you, Gunnar, who blanched like a corpse. You are neither king nor champion. And I made this solemn vow at my father's home that I would love that man alone who is the noblest man born, and that is Sigurd."[43]

Killing men, demonstrating physical power, aspiring to power over other men with violence, brings Sigurd social status and the admiration of the heroine. Recall here the African man and wife that said that their marriage was based on the man's fighting ability. Her natural desires are what defines goodness, right action and justice.

Females' preferences for violent men are alive in our own folklore. After the deaths of Clyde Barrow and Bonnie Parker, police investigators found six notches cut into the stock of Clyde's shotgun—notches that certainly must have warmed Bonnie's heart.

---

[43] Ibid., pp. 67, 81, 85.

Man is one of the mammals, and this is obvious when one compares his patterns of aggressive behavior to that of other mammals. For example, during the mating season of the African wildebeest, the adult males run and jump around, and snort and ram other males to show off their virility. The young males imitate them. Recall that among chimpanzees, the dominant male swaggers. Chimpanzee interpersonal relations tend to be antagonistic.[44] What differentiates man from the other mammals is his mind's ability to control his behavior with religion or other social ideals. Compared to traditional Christian standards, Bjorn is very prideful and has a poorly developed sense of guilt.

For Dante, to sin is to succumb to bestiality. And historian Simon Schama reported in his *A History of Britain*, that this association of violence with bestiality was also the norm during the eighteenth century. One medieval writer noted that "you can tell a sinner by his gait." Of course, we today have lost those high moral standards of behavior, and so lost this kind of sensitivity and revulsion to bad people. Recall that today we think that society is bad, not people. In earlier centuries people associated good behavior with refined culture, and bad behavior with vulgar, bestial nature. With the inversion, we have reversed this. To be controlled is now suspect and evil, while to be emotional is seen as good and exciting. We will see this inversion repeatedly in film, culture, and social and political theory. In a state of nature, self help is the norm. For instance:

> One summer, Thorgils Maksson found a whale at the Almenningar and went out at once with his men to cut it up. When the two foster brothers heard of it, they went there, too, and at first it seemed as if matters would be settled peaceably. Thorgils proposed that they should share equally that part of the whale which was yet uncut, but they wanted to have all the uncut part or else to share the entire whale. Thorgils positively refused to give up any portion of what had already

---

[44] Jane Goodall, *The Chimpanzees of Gombe* (Cambridge Mass: Harvard University Press, 1986).

been cut. They began to use threats and at last took to their arms and fought. After a long and furious battle, Thorgils fell, slain by Thorgeir....

The foster brothers took possession of the whole whale.[45]

These "heroes" are just big kids. "It's mine!" they shout. Again we see how the self is used to define justice. Of course, as Pinker does a good job of demonstrating, the modern judicial system has replaced the "self help" of interpersonal violence. But I will try to show in this study, at a deep level, we like the primitive way. This is a temptation.

There is a recent example of using the self as a standard of justice. After raping and murdering 33 boys during the 1970s, John Wayne Gacy said, "I see myself more as a victim than as a perpetrator...I was cheated out of my childhood." He complained that the media were treating him like "an asshole and a scapegoat."[46]

Obviously he got his good ideas in part for his teachers, but as will became increasingly clear this way of thinking defines popular and academic culture, and is a clear example of how desire has refashioned ethics or inverted it. What defines goodness, justice and ultimately "reason" is his desire, and "society" is the enemy, the evil one. He is good and society is evil, which is a straight inversion of what people believed for centuries. All of this will become increasingly clear as we see this logic in many aspects of high and popular culture. We saw this external view of evil with the Vikings and the other tribes. For them, the self is good, and this is natural. Israel Keyes confessed to killing 8 people, and this is how an investigator described his motive: "He enjoyed it. He liked what he was doing," the investigator said. "He talked about getting a rush out of it, the adrenalin, the excitement out of it." The investigator also reported that Keyes liked to brag about it and enjoyed describing the killings. So again we see how emotion automatically creates articulated values and higher order thought. It was a good. Body

---

[45] Ainslie Hight, trans. *Gritter* pg. 70.

[46] Jonathan Gottschall, *The Storytelling Animal: How Stories Make Us Human*, (Boston & New York, Houghton Mifflin Harcourt, 2012), 171.

image resonance, in the context that 70% of dreams are negative, seems to play a role here.

This compulsion to conflict is reproduced in other animals. For example, Eibl-Eibesfeldt noted that monkeys and rats with electrodes implanted in the area of their brains that stimulates the feeling of aggressive threat will continue to stimulate themselves in this way after the electric charge is turned off.[47] The Greek hero Theseus craves danger for the sake of danger. And Athena rejoiced in the war cry.

As the Vikings were highly patriarchal, and male power was based on physical aggression, so are chimpanzees. Goodall found that only in captivity, never in the wild, do female chimpanzees occasionally put males to flight.[48] As among the Vikings, male physical aggression reigns supreme among the chimps when they are in the wild.

In *Savage Africa*, nineteenth-century British explorer Winwood Read noted that one West African tribe did a "Gorilla Dance." The dancer imitated the "uncouth movements" of the gorilla and had the "vacant expression of the brute".[49] Read noted that the imitation by the dancer was so good that nothing short of seeing a real gorilla in its wild state could have given him so good a clue to the animal's real habits. The dance was not a show for Read's entertainment, but a great religious ritual. The gorilla was an integral part of the tribe's cultural conception. This is what they conceive to have real value. Read finds it curious that a man should devote himself to emulating a gorilla. The tone that this English gentleman takes toward the hyperphysicality of his African subjects and the physical demands of the jungle is one of repugnance. He clearly wanted to distance himself from bestiality. We saw this with the disgust that people had in response to nature.

Several times we have seen how females play a role in male fertility. Women then and now do indeed have a natural emotional investment in male violence. In *Notes of a Feminist Therapist*,

---

[47] I. Eible-Eibesfeldt, *The Biology of Peace and War* (New York: Viking, 1979).

[48] Jane Goodall, *The Chimpanzees of Gombe*.

[49] Winwood W. Read, *Savage Africa* (New York: Harper and Brothers, 1967), 164.

Elisabeth Williams described how Barbara, like many normal women, enjoyed rape fantasies during sex. She imagined herself as a resisting victim of a man's sexual aggression. She envisioned herself strapped to a mast and raped by a handsome, rugged pirate, or as an old-fashioned, naive young servant sexually assaulted by the master of the estate. Sometimes she would be violated by a burglar who broke into her apartment. In each instance, she "found" someone raping her, but it wasn't her "fault"; he would "overwhelm" her weak resistance, and she would be passively enjoying it—coming all over the place.[50] The study *A Billion Wicked Thoughts* reported that men have rape fantasies that are even more violent. One study found that about 30% of white couples who advertised for a sexual partner requested a black man.[51] Now about 30% of black men will eventually spend time in prison, and black male offender rates are about 10 times higher than white men. With the inversion these spontaneous desires define which men are attractive, lovable and so good. Supporting these men is what defines good and just social action and we saw this among the Viking and tribal women.

This female sexuality influences patterns of sexual selection and social values, in that women are attracted to high crime groups, like black and Hispanic men. For instance, I've heard women say, "Latin men with switch blades are sexually exciting," "I want a dangerous man," "I think thugs are sexy" and "Black men are *real* men." And a female journalist once asked, "Why is dark skin so attractive?" As innuendo and righteous politics these attitudes and preferences are very common. Woody Allen's film *Everyone Says I Love You* (1996) is about an upper class white woman who dumps her uptight white fiancé, and pursues a convicted criminal who has a vicious look on his face, and Allen makes this point about female sexuality in several of his films. I've never heard a woman say, "Beethoven is a *real* man" but several times I've heard things like black men are real men, and the nineteenth century understood this about women. They understood that we need to give form to our

---

[50] Elizabeth Friar Williams, *Notes of a Feminist Therapist* (New York: Praeger, 1976).
[51] Ogi Ogas & Sai Gaddam, *A Billion Wicked Thoughts: What the World's Largest Experiment Reveals About Human Desire*, (New York: Dutton, 2011).

energies in historically constructive terms, like through conceptions of class, being high minded and inhibiting virtue. Merle Streep once said "It's the same everywhere: women want to be pretty, and men want to be powerful." Just think how much better the world would be if the "professors" traded in their Ph.D.s for this fact.

Notice that this is the same sexuality exhibited by African and Viking women, but of course between then and now women went through a period of repression, which have come down as we "go back" because of our new, modernist or inverted ideals of placing body over the mind and social controls. Put another way, social controls now enforce freedom and unlimited socializing. That this results in increased sexual gratification, for both white women and men, is not an accident as we saw with the self reporting of John Wayne Gacy.

The recent work, *A Billion Wicked Thoughts* is one of the largest empirical studies conducted on sexuality. It drew mostly on internet pornography and romance novels to determine people's preferences. And its authors, like Williams, also report rape fantasies, and, in general, it is clear that violence is sexualized for people. They quote a gay man on black men in general: "Black guys are hot," explains Rocco. "They're the ultimate in 'you're going to suck me off', the ultimate in 'I'm going to throw you down and manhandle you'. They're the ultimate in tops. Big, strong, dominant with a huge dick."[52]

Similarly, paranormal romance novels are popular with women, and they typically portray women being attacked by monsters like Werewolf and Dracula.[53] The Andrew Sisters were a popular music group and their song "Rum and Coco-Cola" is all about how hot and sexy the Caribbean is. The Beach Boys on their CD, *20 Good Vibrations, The Greatest Hits* (Volume 1) is the song "Good Vibrations" which is all about how hot and sexy the Florida Keys are. Printed on the label of *Old Spice: Aqua Reef* deodorant is "Aqua Reef gives your armpit that fresh Caribbean feeling it craves." Apparently, that association is pervasive in pop culture. These are just the examples I've noticed recently. The body does rule today.

---

[52] Ogi & Gaddam, p. 183
[53] Ibid.

The Barry Manilow song *New York City Rhythm* (on his greatest hits CD) includes the line, "Funky dives on the old west side... there's always something going down." We do want to get down and dirty today, and this inspires who we associate with.

This is evident in recent patterns of interracial marriage and cohabitation in the United States. 20% of married or cohabitating black men are doing so with white women, or 1.1 million. Asian men are less popular, and white men have little interest in black women[54] for the same reason that white women are interested in black men: aggression. And one has to consider that this figure does not represent white women who were formally married or cohabitating.

The divorce rate for the white women/black man couple is twice that of the white/white couples. So white women's excitement is clear. In *Hellfire Nation: The Politics of Sin in American History*, Morone says that it was common knowledge during the nineteenth century that "amalgamation" with blacks, as it was referred to at the time, would result in the debasement of whites. Recall that the dominant male chimpanzee swaggers through the jungle to show off his high status. Similarly, lower-class black men and now some white men swagger through the urban jungle and land in prison.

Women's sexuality forms a template to help to inspire gender, social and cultural ideals. We will see this process through out this study, but in particular when we examine film. Though it should be observed here that the nineteenth century proves that women can internalize and promote constructive social ideals and behavior.

Primitologist Jane Goodall reported seeing a male chimp ascend to the rank of dominant male by throwing a kerosene can, and so impress members of the troupe.[55] This is a good example of

---

[54] Swanbrow, Diane (2000-03-23). "Intimate Relationships Between Races More Common Than Thought".University of Michigan.http://www.umich.edu/news/index.html?Releases/2000/Mar00/r032300a.Retrieved 2008-07-15. For a general discussion of many aspects of interracial sex see: http://en.wikipedia.org/wiki/Interracial_marriage_in_the_United_States#Interracial_marriage_versus_cohabitation

[55] Jane Goodall, *The Chimpanzees of Gombi* (Cambridge, Mass: Harvard University Press, 1986).

the power of charisma and natural justice. This is often a factor in human life and values, as we saw in inter-racial marriage and the perception of goodness and justice.

The power of charisma can also be seen in high society. Angela Gheorghiu and Patricia Racette are world famous opera singers, and who recently performed the lead role of the opera *Tosca*. Here is how an article in the program on their performance starts: "For any other singer it might have been a surprising turn of events. But when it comes to Angela Gheorghiu, the high-profile diva who has a flare for making news, big-impact drama is more or less routine.

Before she had ever sung the role on stage, the Romanian-born soprano made her debut as Tosca in a striking, high-concept 2001 with film by Benoit Jacquot... That, it turns out is only the first act. In 2011, Gheorghiu's Royal Opera, Covent Garden performance in *Tosca* was seen in some 700 movie theaters around the world. "I believe in cameras and microphones, and I believe in everything recorded," Gheorghiu said in an interview with Bloomberg News, "Because this is the only way to leave a testimony. Magnification, for Gheorghiu, comes naturally. Patricia Racette... may not embody that kind of grandeur writ large. But she's every bit as potent on her own terms."[56] If this is what it is like the polite world of opera, the thrills, you can imagine what it's like among the bottom half of the population and in the state of nature. I think the point is clear. We have strong impulses to go back and to have idiomatic ethical and cultural ideals.

But how did we get out of the state of nature or natural values? Pinker emphasizes the development of the modern state, pressure from elites, the judicial system and the manners revolution. He does mention religion but does not dwell on it. In the *Religion of Macho*, London and Smith place a greater emphasis on religion. They say that the fertile Vikings eventually turned into the angelic Swedes, but only after centuries of terrifying visions of damnation, or prohibitions against being inflated and shinning. For instance, in sixteenth-century France, Agrippa d'Aubigne confessed:

[56] Steve Winn, "Angela Gheorghiu & Patricia Racette on Tosca", *San Francisco Opera Magazine* (Seattle: Encore Media Group) November, 2012, Volume 90, No. 3, p. 43.

My head has a great many less hairs than sins…. My dreadful transgressions horrify me…, growl in my ears, hiss like serpents in the night, constantly appear before my eyes like so many fearful specters, accompanied by the hideous image of death. Worse still, these are not the vain smoke of dreams but rather the living portraits of my very own deeds.[57]

So the heroic energy that was directed outward to others in the state of nature here is directed to conquering herself. She is evil, not others. The heroic tradition will change again in the modern world with the directing of anger back out to destroy the sinful upper-class and the classical tradition in the arts, and ultimately any idea of social standards, creating the ACLU.

Keep in mind that she strongly associates sinful feelings or evil with a snake, as this dehumanized image will recur in our studies of what could be described as political ethics.

Instead of finding the low to be an evil monster, like for this woman, we now today find the high and the traditional social controls, "society," like big business, to be evil monsters. The above quote appeared in *Sin and Fear: The Formation of a Western Guilt Culture* by historian Jean Delumeau, who also wrote that "no civilization had ever attached as much importance to guilt and shame as did the Western world from the thirteenth to the eighteenth centuries."[58] As we saw among the Vikings, this is not natural.

In the twentieth century, the children of the conservative Hutterite denomination are taught the terrible fear of God, self-discipline, self-awareness, diligence, and the fear of the strap. This was typical of Western education before the 1960s. People lived in a state of theological terror, which severely constricted them emotionally and made them circumspect. Our inhibited personalities today are not natural.

The Vikings and other primitive tribes have more naturally expressive, loose and swaggering personalities and white women

---

[57] Jean Delumeau, *Sin and Fear: The Formation of a Western Guilt Culture* (New York: St. Martin's Press, 1990) p. 2.
[58] Ibid, p. 3.

today like these characteristics, as we saw among the Vikings and with inter-racial sex.

By mentioning the factor of religion, I am not trying to advocate its practice; but if we are to understand the historical process and the psychology underlying it, we need to know precisely what happened. We will then be able to formulate an ethic that will really work without negative side effects, like witch hunts, and that we can all agree on, both secularists and religionists.

Regarding the old virtue ethic, though, today we are abandoning it and going back to a more natural ethic, with our new pro-emotion value system, like romanticizing anger and crime, sexualizing high crime populations of men, and other forms of destructive conflict, as we will see frequently in subsequent chapters on modern cultural values.

For a good description of the kind of community pressure on people in Puritan England, see "Death, Life and Discipline," in *The Reformation* by Diarmaid MacCulloch, an Oxford professor. For a discussion of more recent ethical history, see *Hellfire Nation: The Politics of Sin in American History* by James Morone. It is clear from their discussions of the intersections of religious ethics and history, that "sin" was not an arbitrary construct, but was an attempt to come to terms with and control the bodies' natural orientation toward exciting conflict or evil; the kind of conflict we saw among the Vikings and others in a state of nature. The old sarcastic saying was "The Devil looks good." Of course, today we believe that the devil looks *really* good because of our inverted values.

Chapter Three: The Race to the Bottom of the Cave — The Modernist Revolt In Life and Art

Greece was barbarian, and will become so again from
foreign influence and from Nature herself. She is always
younger and has a beginning in reference to us.
— Ancient Greek Philosopher (Ocellus)
On the Nature of the Universe
But every person, surely, is his own god…
— Ovid

Anointed sovereign of sighs and groans.
— Shakespeare

Ornament is a Crime.
— Adolf Loos, Architect

The bio-determinism described in Chapter One was common sense to almost everyone before about 1825. By the early to mid-century, though, perspectives started to change with the rise of relativism and particularism, and the Classical tradition in the arts fell under assault from many of the educated young because they experienced its rationalism as unjust, and so confining and oppressive.

This is a moral and aesthetic expression of how people were experiencing the upper class. By about 1720 the French aristocracy abandoned the triumphalism of the Baroque style and grand ritual, and contracted to the more modest Rococo style and more modest social behavior.[59]

The aesthetic and philosophy of the nineteenth century emphasized nature, and nature as it actually was, not as it was arranged or perfected by the mind, the latter being seen in the Classical landscapes by Claude. Raw, vulgar nature erupted into fashion as people sought freedom from the traditional formal confinements. Landscapes became the greatest expression of human emotion.[60]

The Salon of 1824 saw the introduction of the Romantics, and the painting *The Massacre of Chios* by Eugene Delecroix. Commenting on this Salon, art critic Adolphe Thiers wrote:

> The cry for independence [from being confined] has reached the ears of the artists. Each has taken his own path. One loves the handsome form of *Romulus* and of *Leonidas*, or the grandeur and profundity of the painting of the 16th century; another prefers our everyday lives and does not scorn our customs; and each, following his personal inclination, indulges his own taste, offering us different styles and genres... Nothing is more pleasing than the variety that characterizes the present-day school...[61]

...because of its freedom or lack of confinement.

Artists were beginning to find beauty and greatness themselves to be confining, and sought escape into the chaos and irregularities of nature and personal experience. This defines relativism, particularism and the decline of standards. This became a great moral priority with the inversion of justice. The statement could have been made by almost any art history professor today. Though it is probably not radical enough for most. And Manet's

---

[59] Marc Bascou, Michele Bimbenet-Privat & Martin Chapman. *Royal Treasure from the Louvre: Louis XIV to Marie-Antoinette*. Munich, London & New York: Delmonico Books, 2012.

[60] Richard Bretell, *Museum Masterpieces: The Metropolitan Museum of Art*, DVD lecture series (Chantilly VA: The Teaching Company, 2007).

[61] Manuel Jover, *Ingres* (Paris: Terrail/Edigroup, 2005).

portrait of a reclining, nude woman, *Olympia*, shocked most people who regarded its frank sexuality as hubristic vulgarity.[62]

Gustav Courbet was accused of vulgarity for the low emotional tone in his painting *The Stone Breakers*.[63] But this was viewed as "righteous" by many because of the new definition of low justice.

In literature, it was the time of the romantic and realistic novel, such as by Flaubert and Zola. Western culture was descending from the form-giving faculty of the mind to the worst, vulgar expressions of the body, as in the lower-class taverns, dancers and whores of Toulouse-Lautrec. Lautrec had no interest in being confined to mere beauty. He had a more expansive agenda; namely, all of nature, the good and the bad, though mostly the bad and the ugly.

When the French nation accepted a donation of Impressionist art, Jean-Leon Gerome wrote, "For the Government to accept such filth, there would have to be a great moral slackening."[64] The form-giving and elevating aspects of the mind were losing their grip on the naturally base body. But why?

The answer lies in the developments of contemporary political philosophy/psychology. The theory of natural rights promoted a sympathetic view to the empowerment of the individual, the body, and the subjective emotions and raw nature as resonating objects. The traditional confinements, which came from above in the social hierarchy, the educational system, and the mind, started to be questioned and attacked.

Instead of artists, like Reynolds, being critical of confinements from raw, unformed and cluttered nature, and looking to the mind for liberation and righteousness, they started to embrace raw nature as liberating: liberating from the beauty of the human figure and from formalized nature, as had been seen in the Classical landscapes of Claude and the Classical figures of Michelangelo.

---

[62] Ian Chilvers, *The Oxford Dictionary of Art* (New York: Oxford University, 2004).

[63] H.W. Janson, *History of Art* (Englewood Cliffs NJ: Prentice-Hall, 1969).

[64] Chilvers (2004), 356.

It was very common to accuse people, like the upper class, during the nineteenth century, of "fighting against freedom." We saw were this impulse for "freedom" comes from among the Vikings. Put another way, starting during the nineteenth century, people started to apply the idea of political freedom to social and cultural issues. Or, as we saw the old top heavy governments to be evil, so we started to see the old top heavy definitions of beauty and moral goodness to be evil. The slide to the body and nature was done in the name of liberating raw emotions from the tyranny of reason, which had dominated the West for centuries.

When businessman J. Paul Getty was a child in turn of the century America, he was given a beating if reason and reasoning did not dominate his life.[65]

In about 1860 an American college president said "Democracy is about intelligence." (Even most Republicans today would have difficulty making that claim.) Nineteenth-century German physician Theodore Billroth believed that moodiness "was a form of stupidity."[66]

In the nineteenth century, it was felt that emotions cloud the mind. And in the nineteenth century novel *Les Miserables*, a character tells a man who is melancholy, "I see that you have been nothing but an animal."[67] In ancient Greece sex was seen in a somewhat negative light because it suspended reason. And recall that, for Dante, to sin is to succumb to bestiality.

In *The Golden Legend*, a medieval anthology of saint's lives, at least twice reason is valorized and cast in opposition to the sinful emotions. And Simon Schama reported, in his *A History of Britain*, that during the eighteenth century the standard interpretation of sin and the emotions was that they were bestial or anti-reason and invited damnation or punishment. We saw this with Getty. As we saw with John Wayne Gacy, though, today we want to be free to be animals. But this is natural and just as we saw among the Vikings.

---

[65] J. Paul Getty, *As I See It: The Autobiography of J. Paul Getty* (Los Angeles: Getty, 2003).

[66] Peter F. Ostwald, "Johanness Brahms, Solitary Altruist," Walter Frisch, Ed., *Brahms and His World* (Princeton: Princeton University, 1990), 32.

[67] Victor Hugo, Charles E. Wilbour, trans., *Les Miserables* (New York: Modern Library, 1862/1992), 629.

Some examples of this traditional perspective on the lowly status of the body can be found in the history of dance.

During the nineteenth century, young dancers at the Paris Opera Ballet were referred to as "little rats," and during the 1940s, at the Metropolitan Opera, the ballet section was referred to as "the animal act."

Obviously, ballet lovers had a higher opinion of ballet, but compared to opera, it is a more physical art form. Similarly, in the hierarchical organization of the military, during the 1940s, privates were sometimes referred to as "dog faced privates." These priorities are rooted in Platonist psychology.

As Plato described in his dialogue *Republic*, justice is achieved when the mind and reason use the will to dominate the appetites or the lower emotions. Similarly, he argued that social justice is achieved when the educated upper class dominates or controls the ignorant, over-emotional lower class. We saw this when Louis the 14th said that he was "under control." Plato's hierarchy implied a value judgment, with the upper classes being wise, rational, and under control, and the lower classes being foolish and tending toward emotional indulgence. One can often see this today on the street and any number of bars.

This was the concept of class in the West for most of the early modern period. After the Bible, Plato's *Republic* is the most influential book in the history of the West. It, combined with Christian strictures, created a generally ascetic culture. For instance, Thomas Jefferson once wrote to one of his daughters that she should never "regret of having eaten too little." And a Czech proverb says, "Expect nothing, and you won't be disappointed." People of the time believed in rising above or transcending the body by climbing up the divine hierarchy through an active or form-creating mind. Acting like a pig was stigmatized, while acting like an angel and religious observance were encouraged. "Mind over matter" was a popular idea at the time.

Manners were valued and taught. We saw this moral perspective in the discussion of Audrey Hepburn. People saw moral lessons in the elaborate, beautiful, or formal decorative arts of the time. They thought that confinement of the body by the mind, or of the individual by the group, were good and created social order. They were very conformist orientated. This was just after the Great Chain of Being was the dominant philosophy, in which everyone understood their nature and place in the social and natural hierarchy. Like most of Europe and the world, in England sex came under very strict control before the eighteenth century, because the poor and their illegitimate children had to be taken care of by the church congregation.

So sex was heavily policed and fornication punished. As a result, during 1650 the illegitimacy rate was only 1%. By the early eighteenth century, sex stopped being policed, and by 1750 the illegitimacy rate rose to 25%. So the old system was felt and impacted behavior.[68] Recall here that crime started to skyrocket during the 1960s with our new definition of justice and freedom.

While hierarchical and rationalistic perspective dominated popular culture of the middle class and clergy during the nineteenth century, it was eventually eclipsed among the urban poor and the many of the educated, especially the young artists. Historicism, a form of relativism that displaced natural law, began to dominate college curricula by the mid to late nineteenth century, while Freud argued that the unconscious is in control of the mind, and Darwin presented evidence that humans were just fancy apes and that there was nothing divine about us at all.

The nineteenth century immediately followed the French Revolution, with its bottom-up politics of natural rights and equality. The ideal of modernism was that instead of reason and the upper class controlling the appetites and the lower class, respectively, the reverse should be the case.

In order to achieve justice and goodness, the appetites, nature and the lower orders should control the mind, the upper class, and the government. Instead of the high confining the low, the low should confine the high. Hence, we see the righteous lower-class whores of Toulouse-Lautrec, and an expansion of suffrage starting during the early nineteenth century based on nothing more than being alive.

---

[68] Faramerz Dabhoiwala, *The Origins of Sex: A History of the First Sexual Revolution*, (New York: Oxford University Press, 2012).

Many people were becoming fed up with the traditional confinements. The redemption of the emotions explains why obesity, and hence gluttony, became a growing problem in the modern West. Nineteenth-century composer Richard Wagner said, "the emotions are the beginning and end of the intellect."[69] And Hume famously said that the passions should control reason. And Blanning's characterization of Rousseau and the other Romantics is helpful: "Indeed, it might be said that romanticism was institutionally erotic."[70]

So things were starting to change in terms of how we thought about and reacted to our emotions. Herder described Fuseli, a romantic artist: "The wildness of the warrior—and the feeling of supreme sublimity!...His spirits are storm wind, his ministers flames of fire! He goes upon the wings of the wind. His laughter is the mockery of hell and his love—a deadly lighting flash."[71]

This sounds like a description of the Vikings. And Blanning said of Fuseli that, "Naturally, too, he venerated all the rough and ready rule-breaking geniuses of the past, especially Shakespeare: that is to say the Shakespeare of violence, the occult, and dreams, of Macbeth's witches and Titania's erotic fantasies. It was those irregular characteristics of Shakespeare that appalled the classicists the appealed to him most.

As he put it...'Shakespeare is to Sophocles as the flashes of lightning of a stormy night are to daylight.' The academic artists from around Europe he encountered in Rome he dismissed as 'vermin.'"[72] So as we will see repeatedly, the high is now "low," subhuman and even monstrous, like in the film *Alien*, to be analyzed later. This is the new perception and just conclusion. This is what we rebel against, this new evil.

Plato and his theory of justice were inverted or turned on their heads. Like with the low in art, the lower class came to be viewed as righteous, good, and wise while the upper classes started

---

[69] Ulrick Muller and Peter Wapnewski, *Wagner Handbook* (Cambridge MA: Harvard University, 1992), 594.

[70] Tim Blanning, *The Romantic Revolution: A History* (New York: Modern Library, 2011), 65.

[71] Quoted in Blanning, p. 62.

[72] Ibid, p. 62-63.

to be viewed as mindless, hubristic, and evil. This is evident in operas of the time, as we shall see.

The nineteenth century also saw the rise of nationalist movements that focused attention on a bottom-up perspective. Johannes Brahms complained that Tchaikovsky's was elite "parlor music" while his own "came from the soil."

This logic generated Marx's economic determinism and his notion of the dictatorship of the proletariat. Marx's ideas have a family resemblance to the Enlightenment idea of popular sovereignty. As eighteenth-century poet Schiller wrote:

> In the work of the Divine Artist, the unique value of each part is respected, and the sustaining gaze with which he honors every spark of energy in even the lowliest creatures manifests his glory not less than the harmony of the immeasurable whole. Life and liberty to the greatest possible extent are the glory of the divine creation; nowhere is it more sublime than where it seems to have departed most widely from its ideal.[73]

This exemplifies the particularism and the bottom-up perspective that inspired the Romantics and the lower-class revolutionaries. Life and liberty can be interpreted as no more confinements. Who would want to stop justice? There is a recent film called, *The Elegance of the Hedge Hog*.

The nineteenth-century anarchist Bakunin said, "To the destruction of all law and order and the unchaining of evil passion."[74] One cannot get more blunt. This would certainly redeem the lower classes since they commit most violent crimes. In the traditional ending of the ballet *Swan Lake*, good triumphs over evil; in the Nureyev choreography from the 1960s, evil triumphs over good. Regarding the leftist movement Syndicalism, Stoddard noted:

> Syndicalism is instinctively hostile to intelligence. It pins its faith to instinct—that "deeper knowledge" of

---

[73] Arthur O. Lovejoy, *The Great Chain of Being* (Cambridge MA: Harvard University, 1964), 299-300.
[74] Lothrop Stoddard, *The Revolt Against Civilization* (New York: Charles Scribner's Sons, 1923), 159.

the undifferentiated human mass; that proletarian quantity so much more precious than individualistic quality...[and] art is "a mere residuum bequeathed to us by an aristocratic society.[75]

As leftist leader Georges Sorel put it, "Man has genius only in the measure that he does not think"[76] Today's bias against the mind is evident in the findings of a study done on the public opinion of eugenics. As Prof. Glad found:

> When asked if persons suffering from genetic illnesses should have children, the response was neutral, but when asked if persons of high intelligence should have more children than persons of low intelligence, the response was moderate to strong disagreement with such an assertion.[77]

This exemplifies modern resistance to being confined and denigrating rationalism. That the West was inclined to invert the traditional Platonic hierarchy was sensed by eighteenth century artist and theoretician Sir Joshua Reynolds; he wrote, in his Discourses, that:

> The mind is apt to be distracted by a multiplicity of objects; and that scale of perfection which I wish always to be preserved, is in the greatest danger of being totally disordered, and even inverted.[78]

Reynolds, as president of the Royal Academy, gave the annual lectures to the incoming freshmen, and these became his *Discourses*. Similarly, Gill identifies elements of Renaissance thought that contain seeds for inversion. She noted that Augustine and Michelangelo:

> saw a potentially ineradicable divide between the corporeal and the incorporeal realms, and both describe

---

[75] Ibid., 174.

[76] Ibid., 175.

[77] John Glad, "Eugenics and the Public," *The Mankind Quarterly*, Fall-Winter 2009, Volume L, no. 1 & 2, 120.

[78] Sir Joshua Reynolds, *Discourses* (New York: Penguin, 1790/1992), 136.

spiritual love in a language that draws its impact from earthly analogies.[79]

We have certainly seen the impact of the earth during the past two centuries. The connection in this quote is such that the traditional hierarchy could be inverted and notions of proper justice and morals could be used to empower the lower orders or realms.

Translating the terms of today's debate into that of ancient Greek philosophy, what we have seen during the last two centuries is the gradual triumph of Heraclitus' flux and particularism over Parmenides' *One* and Platonic realism or theory of forms.

Everyone today praises diversity and inclusiveness, instead of the traditional divisions and hierarchy that directed life and art to the ideal in the mind. As people once praised "racial" uniformity, now they praise diversity and anything else that drives towards particularism and disrupts the norms in the mind like heterosexuality.

Rebellion has become worthy and romanticized, rather than conformity to the best, most constructive and natural ideals from a perfect blending of mind and body. Gender and racial solipsism come to mind here.

The attack started early. In the film *The Philadelphia Story* (1940), Katherine Hepburn is engaged to an upright man, and he says to her, "We are going to represent something fine and straight. You are cool and a queen and so much your own. You have a beautiful purity, like a statue." Hepburn protests that she just wants to be loved.

The man embraces the nineteenth century norm of human beings striving towards ideal behavior, while Hepburn is more focused on the raw desires of the body and is resistant to being confined to being a mere statue. (She eventually dumps her fiancé and marries a drunk who would never confuse her with a statue.) It is interesting to note here that Audrey Hepburn was raised in Europe, and her mother was an aristocrat, while Katherine Hepburn was raised in a liberal home in the more cool continent of North America.

---

[79] Meredith J. Gill, *Augustine in the Italian Renaissance: Art and Philosophy from Petrarch to Michelangelo* (New York: Cambridge University, 2005), 3.

Today, of course, is there anything worse than being straight or square? These are figures that create form. Nineteenth-century novelist Victor Hugo opposed clear and straight thinking. He wrote:

> A certain amount of reverie is good, like a narcotic in discreet doses. It soothes the fever, sometimes high, of the brain at work and produces in the mind a soft and fresh vapour which corrects the too angular contours of pure thought, fills up the gaps and intervals here and there, binds them together, and blunts the sharp corners of ideas.[80]

As the ideal was to be straight or heterosexual, now the ideal is be a rebel against being straight or confined, to romanticize rebellion and be radical or gay. This is what defines justice and righteousness today. A fast food chain sells a brand of ice tea called *Fuze*. As stores during the 1950s would sometimes have a picture of Jesus in their windows to show they are with it, now they sell *Fuze*, a similar exemplar.

The inversion or debasement described by Hugo has made its way today into popular culture and advertising. The screen-saver for a Samsung DVD player reads: "Samsung, Digit*all*: Everyone's Invited." There is the ever popular "One World" and "One Love." A billboard advertisement for a car reads: "United by Individuality." Another advertisement includes the phrase, "Unlimit Yourself." These are examples of rebelling against confinement, and being unlimited like God. They are the norm today. As God was all powerful, so now are "the people." So when they were empowered, this inverted the culture with primacy given, naturally, to the low and particularisms over the high and the mind.

As God was a unity, this then was perceived as a good. Now that the people have power, and they are a diversity, as it was always understood, now this is perceived to be good. So we see inversion and the movement from unity to diversity. Such advertisements point down to the body instead of up to the form-giving, unifying, confining, and hierarchical faculty of the mind.

---

[80] Victor Hugo, Charles E. Wilbour, trans., *Les Miserables* (New York: Modern Library, 1992), 744-45.

A shift in political thought during the last three centuries was the transference of governmental sovereignty from the king to the people via natural rights.

Following this, divinity, wisdom, and goodness were also transferred from god and the king to the people. As the king had legitimacy via God and ruled by divine right, now the individual had natural rights that were also divine and had legitimacy via reflecting Jesus.

Everyone suffers today or is a victim, as Jesus was a suffering victim. And everyone is good and wise today, just like Jesus. John Wayne Gacy saw himself as a good and victimized person.

This is how French revolutionaries portrayed the people in ritual demonstrations.[81] For instance, Robespierre said, "There shall be instituted fetes in order to remind man of the Divinity and of the dignity of his being—these fetes shall take their names from the glorious events of our revolution."[82]

And Carl L. Becker, in his study *The Heavenly City of the Eighteenth Philosophers*, characterized the thinking of the period as establishing a "religion of man" (and Chartier makes the same point in *The Cultural Origins of the French Revolution*). Becker quoted Robespierre above, and he also makes the point that people started to invoke posterity instead of God as issuing punishments and rewards for behavior. So man, and no longer God and his elite representatives, was to be the judge.

Man was now the standard and defined virtue. The first thing to go from the ideology of the revolution was the belief in the intrinsic depravity of human nature, the one vividly illustrated in the chapter on the state of nature.

This denial started the process of idealizing the lower classes. The traditional perspective was that people were evil and could not be trusted. We saw where that perspective came from with a Platonist perspective on our animal nature. For the traditional king, power derived from God.

---

[81] Jennifer Homans, *Apollo's Angels: A History of Ballet* (New York: Random House, 2010).

[82] Carl L. Becker, *The Heavenly City of the Eighteenth-Century Philosophers*, Second Edition. (New Haven & London: Yale University Press, 2003), 157-158.

For people, rights are natural or spring spontaneously and naturally from their bodies, and so this greater stature, in comparison to an endowment, gives them divine status over the king and government. Chartier describes how during the French Revolution, there was an inversion in the legal system resulting in power shifting down.[83]

Kings were the servants of God, so they felt a pressure to be conscientious and do a good job and be just, while people feel no such pressure and so are rather prone to just have a good time and tyrannize over anyone who gets in their way as we saw among the Vikings.

This is vividly clear in our "modern" ideas about "diversity" or race on campus. If "nature rules," as we have seen, then so should human nature. And as God was good, then so are people. As the king, in certain contexts, resisted confinements of his power, people today resist confinements and want to be unlimited and tyrannical. One political commentator observed that the Left have a problem with the idea of limits.[84] And a social scientist objected to bio-determinism because it implied that people are limited.[85] As nineteenth-century writer Frederick Schlegel described:

> It is precisely individuality that is the original and eternal thing in men...the cultivation and development of this individuality, as one's highest vocation, would be a divine egoism.[86]

Woodrow Wilson observed the tendency of natural rights to promote selfishness:

> It is a perilous attempt to train the unlearned and the undisciplined to "live and trade each on his own private stock of reason." Its success is due to the fact that it uses

---

[83] Roger Chartier, *The Cultural Origins of the French Revolution*, (Durham & London: Duke University Press, 1991).

[84] Steven Hayward, *The Age of Reagan* (New York: Three Rivers, 2009).

[85] Carl N. Degler, *In Search of Human Nature: The Decline and Revival of Darwinism in American Social Thought*, (New York: Oxford University Press, 1991).

[86] Quoted in Arthur O. Lovejoy, *The Great Chain of Being* (Cambridge MA.: Harvard University, 1964), 307.

these theories of natural right which chime in with selfish desire and so establishes passion at the same time that it overthrows habit."[87]

This is precisely what has happened during the last two centuries. For John Stuart Mill, the individual was above the state and to be served by the state.[88] If the individual reflects the unlimited God, then who could come to any other conclusion? Today, hippies who strive toward the natural indeed look and talk like their imagining of Jesus, complete with ideals of love, peace, humility, brotherhood, and poverty. The original idea of Christian brotherhood was secularized into the social and political brotherhood of the Romantics, the early Progressives, and later Leftists. We saw this in Becker's characterization of the revolution as establishing a religion of man.

We now define man as expressing a divine and exciting diversity, and we especially saw this excitement with white women. There are different styles of counter-culture today, but being a hippie, the literal imitation of Jesus, is still one of them. A recent book is titled, *The Culture of Complaint*. Jesus had reason to complain, and people try to imitate Him as a high status figure. Westerners today complain about feeling confined. Today, all are the "anointed sovereigns of sighs and groans," as Shakespeare wrote. This is how people respond to being confined or limited.

It is a small step from the imitation of Christ to fantasizing that one is Jesus. For instance, an American man who is a graduate student in science at UC Berkeley, and is a conservative Protestant, said that some people say, "I'm God." And I once saw on television a girl being auditioned for a part in a commercial. During her rehearsal she kept making mistakes reciting the lines. A judge said that while watching her it was clear how nervous she was, and that she was clearly suffering.

He had a look of pity on his face as he said this, and the girl kept wiping tears from her face as he described how much she was

---

[87] Ronald J. Pestritto, *Woodrow Wilson and the Roots of Modern Liberalism* (Lanham MD: Rowman and Littlefield, 2005), 52.

[88] J. Rufus Fears, *Books That Have Made History*, Audio-tape lecture series (Chantilly VA: The Teaching Company, 2005).

suffering. This is very common today. For instance, during 2012 on the website for the Pulitzer Prize, there was a picture of a black baby with medical bandages covering half its face. And the news reports love these kinds of stories, and characterize them in this way or in such a way as to have this kind of reference or resonance. A mother recently said that, of all her children, she preferred her retarded one.[89] This is so because it suffers and is pitiable. This kind of sentiment is common today, and contrasts with how people in the past responded to defect, abnormality and deviance.

In addition, it is a small step from the priesthood of all believers to the godhood of all people. This helps to explain why it is Protestants who tend to suffer from modernism a bit more than Catholics.

Dabhoiwala, an Oxford historian, describes in his study on sex that it was the expansion of the public sphere during the eighteenth century that contributed to the process of loosen up social controls on sex. And he says that this public sphere in turn resulted from the disintegration of centralized religious authority with the Reformation.[90] It is easy to see how all of this, combined with increasing popular sovereignty, resulted in the deification of man and the drive toward diversity.

If everyone is Jesus, then the obvious ethic would be universal love. What could be simpler and even simple minded. No inconvenient facts about people are allowed the break the constant love that whites have to exhibit toward non-whites. And this is the law, just like there was the tyranny of love during the nineteenth century. Like at that earlier time, whites today achieve redemption through love. If one stops loving one becomes guilty of "hate." This is the criteria for science and scholarship.

Like our suffering, crying, Jesus-like girl, others in similar position conjure up the same imagery. That there is rampant self-pity today is obvious. It is a powerful force in academic thought.

---

[89] Anne Fernald, "Human Maternal Vocalization to Infants as Biologically Relevant Signals: An Evolutionary Perspective," Jerome H. Barkow, Leda Cosmides & John Tooby, ed. *The Adapted Mind: Evolutionary Psychology and the Generation of Culture.* (New York & Oxford: Oxford University Press, 1992).
[90] Faramerz Dabhoiwala, *The Origins of Sex: A History of the First Sexual Revolution* (New York: Oxford University Press, 2012).

Each academic department studies its own victim on the cross, and often they swap notes because of their similarity. A sports clothing store had a hand painted sign in the window that read, "Your body is a temple, but only if you treat it as 1."

Notice that the body here is divine and "number 1." As temples contain God, so now do bodies. It is no wonder that everyone sees themselves as wise, good, and smart today. Another clothing store had a picture in the window of a man and woman facing each other, and below the picture was written, "Republic of Us." For Ralph Waldo Emerson, people were gods, and everyone should be free and equal.[91] No confinements here. Emerson once said, "Build your own world."

The mother of Louis the 14th encouraged her son to do the same. Today, it is hard to get people to do anything else. This is evident in the subjective bubbles young people build for themselves on the internet.[92]

Recall here that instead of moving from the high elites and the public to the individual, now we move from the low and the individual to the public and elites. This moral individualism is what is perceived to be just and righteous. And this generates diversity and the ACLU. Today's emphasis on unfettered individuality recalls the traditional intersection of saint and social policy:

> The image of the holy person is a measure of ideals. The saint is a privileged focus of spiritual aspirations and imaginative creative strategies. As depicted by artists, and by humanists, patrons and religious orders, the saint functions as an exemplar. In spiritual terms, he or she is the paradigm of otherworldliness, the privileged connection between earthly things and the mysteries of the divine. In intellectual terms, the saint is the conduit between the past and the present, the mortal life bringing with it a message of philosophical universals. More concretely, the saint can be the polemically bound

---

[91] Ashton, Nichols, *Emerson, Thoreau, and the Transcendentalist Movement*, Audio-tape lecture series (Chantilly VA: The Teaching Company, 2006).
[92] Mark Bauerlein, *The Dumbest Generation: How the Digital Age Stupefies Young Americans and Jeopardizes our Future* (New York: Penguin, 2008).

embodiment of institutional strategy, the vehicle of the order that claims him or her as founder.[93]

Almost every sentence in our definition of modernism expresses these institutional aspirations for a deified, exemplary and unlimited individualism. This is what the "savvy" subscribe to. Diversity is now a "philosophical universal" just like God, and its representatives in the past, like the abolitionists, are the conduits between past and present. The hippie agenda has been implemented.

It is common for professors today to romanticize leaders and writers in earlier centuries who turned out to be most "relevant" or like us today. These are the "saints," the "conduits between past and present," like John Brown and other abolitionists, and Thoreau and Emerson. Wilhelm Muller was an early nineteenth century poet, who wrote the poems that Schubert set in the song cycle *Winterreise*.

At one point the hero says, "if there are no Gods on earth to be found, at least he can be one."[94] Victor Hugo, in his mid-nineteenth century novel *Les Miserables*, has a man, who was a participant in the French Revolution, say:

> Justice has its anger...and the wrath of justice is an element of progress. Whatever may be said matters not, the French revolution is the greatest step in advance taken by mankind since the advent of Christ; incomplete it may be, but it is sublime. It loosened all the secret bonds of society, it softened all hearts, it calmed, appeased, enlightened; it made the waves of civilization to flow over the earth; it was good. The French revolution is the *consecration of humanity* [emphasis added].[95]

As the Vikings wanted to loosen all bonds, so do we. So as Christian anger against sin was a force for progress or purgation

---

[93] Meredith J. Gill, *Augustine in the Italian Renaissance: Art and Philosophy from Petrarch to Michelangelo* (New York: Cambridge University, 2005), 6.

[94] Tim Blanning. *The Romantic Revolution: A History* (New York: Modern Library, 2011), 71.

[95] Victor Hugo, Charles E. Wilbour, trans., *Les Miserables* (New York: Modern Library, 1862/1992), 36.

of the confining body and nature, now the same anger forwards the progress to popular sovereignty, the new vision of unconfined wisdom or virtue and the lower classes' control of the state. Hugo also describes a homeless child as God. He describes how:

> The two children, a little frightened, followed Gavroche without saying a word, and trusted themselves to that little Providence in rags who had given them bread and promised them a lodging.[96]

When *providence* is capitalized, it means *God*. Govroche is later described as being supernatural:

> The two children looked with a timid and stupefied respect upon this intrepid and inventive being, a vagabond like them, isolated like them, wretched like them, who was something wonderful and all-powerful, who seemed to them supernatural.[97]

This is a typical description of God. And Louis the 14th liked to portray himself as Apollo. In Renaissance portraiture it was common to portray people with a sign of a traditional virtue. So a woman might be portrayed with a dog, symbolizing fidelity. In portraiture during the seventeenth and eighteen centuries this became more extreme and people were commonly portrayed as either a pagan god or saint. So people, at least among the upper-classes, saw themselves as embodying or communing with the traditional divinities. In other words, the line was easily crossed.

The worst crime imaginable is to enslave God or beat Jesus, and this is how Hugo describes galley slaves, who are convicted criminals:

> At this moment the cudgeling, multiplied by a hundred hands, reached its climax; blows with the flat of the sword joined in; it was a fury of whips and clubs; the galley-slaves crouched down, a *hideous obedience* was produced by the punishment, and all were silent with the look of chained wolves [emphasis added].

[96] Ibid., 828.
[97] Ibid., 832.

Cosette [a young woman who is watching] trembled in every limb; she continued: "Father, are they still men?" "Sometimes," said the wretched man [who was a former galley slave himself].[98]

As the flagellation of Christ was a "hideous obedience" that evoked horror, so is this state in the modernist God of individualism. There is no clearer example of injustice and being confined. This creates the impulses to argue against the "horrible" death penalty. It is difficult to tell people what to do today, even with findings from science that clearly shows the biological basis of "sin," aggression or crime. Woodrow Wilson literally deified the electorate:

Wherever any public business is transacted, wherever plans affecting the public are laid, or enterprises touching the public welfare, comfort, or convenience go forward, wherever political programs are formulated, or candidates agreed on,—over that place a voice must speak, with the divine prerogatives of a people's will, the words: "Let there be light."[99]

Babeuf, a nineteenth-century leftist put it clearly:

You are the people, the true people, the only people worthy to enjoy the good things of this world! The justice of the people is great and *majestic* as the people itself; all that it does is legitimate, all that it orders is *sacred* [emphasis added].[100]

God is majestic, legitimate, and unconfined. No wonder modernists today think the common people are worthy of empowerment and wise. They claim that everything they do is legitimate. Like Louis XIV, they cannot err. For one Flemish populist, political correctness is "the end of critical discourse."[101]

---

[98] Ibid., 788.

[99] Ronald J. Pestritto, *Woodrow Wilson and the Roots of Modern Liberalism* (Lanham MD: Rowman and Littlefield, 2005), 155.

[100] Lothrop Stoddard, *The Revolt Against Civilization* (New York: Charles Scribner's Sons, 1923), 148.

[101] Paul Edward Gottfried. *Multiculturalism and the Politics of Guilt: Toward a Secular Theocracy*. (Columbia & London: University of Missouri Press, 2002), 35.

This is a good example of the tyrannical character in popular sovereignty and modernism. For Henry David Thoreau, the goal of life was self-knowledge gained through assimilation to nature.[102] This is certainly a vision of great power. Modernists could not agree more. A TV advertisement concluded with the phrase "Become a force of nature."

This is certainly charismatic just like running and throwing things. In Germany every year, about 8000 journalists and scholars are tried for voicing politically incorrect views, and thousands languish in prison. In fact, more people are in prison in Germany today than were imprisoned in communist East Germany.[103] If people become any more devoted to freedom we will simply have to put everyone in prison.

During the eighteenth century, people often tracked in their diaries the progress of their souls to God. Today, people monitor the progress of their souls to their so-called real selves, or the bestiality of the body that makes them happy. A school of modern psychology, by Maslow, is based on the idea of "self-actualization,"[104] and an opera production at Bayreuth had the goal of self-realization for the characters.[105]

Enya is a pop musician who has sold 70 million recordings; one of her songs is called Pilgrim (on the CD *A Day Without Rain*) and its lyrics include:

> Pilgrim, how you journey on the road you choose…the road that leads to nowhere, the road that leads to you… will you find the answer in all you say and do? Will you find the answer in you?…Pilgrim, in your journey you may travel far, for pilgrim it's a long way to find out who you are.

---

[102] J. Rufus Fears, *Books That Have Made History*, Audio-tape lecture series (Chantilly VA: The Teaching Company, 2005).

[103] Paul Edward Gottfried, *Multiculturalism and the Politics of Guilt: Toward a Secular Theocracy* (Columbia & London: University of Missouri Press, 2002).

[104] David Crystal, *The Cambridge Biographical Encyclopedia* (New York: Cambridge University, 1998).

[105] Fredrick Spotts, *Bayreuth: A History of the Wagner Festival* (New Haven: Yale University, 1994).

An ad for a website had the phrase, "Find your inner everything" and another ad read, "The web, myself and I." A medieval philosopher, Bonaventura, wrote a book called *Journey of the Mind to God*. Similarly, today thousands of books have been written that show you how to use your mind to get to yourself. This is what the savvy do.

These types of sentiments are considered to represent moral insight. As Jesus was singular, majestic, good and unique, and all-powerful, modernists believe that common people are singular, good and unique, and powerful rather than viewed as evil.

A major fast food chain has written on their drinking cups, "Made to order because we think you're special."

Another fast food chain had written on its cups, "Here's to YOU: A toast to your wisdom, clever drink buyer-you have selected a classic fountain beverage, precisely mixed for maximum refreshment." Everyone is portrayed as Einstein today and deserves power.

While playing Peter Pan on the New York stage in 1950, actress Jean Arthur said, "If I can get over the message that we should all try to be ourselves, to be free individuals, then I'm sure I'll have accomplished what [J.M.] Barrie wanted."[106]

As God was and should be authentic, so now should people. We should all be more natural as we saw among the romantics and in the state of nature, and reject unnatural institutions of control.

Since the Reformation, sincerity has become more popular. A television advertisement for a female skin product said, "Everything about you is unique." A recent book is titled *The Culture of Narcissism*, and a recent study on narcissism among the young has found higher rates in comparison to 30 years ago.[107]

As it was common knowledge that Jesus was all-wise and innocent, it is a common belief today that people are wise and innocent or good, and so worthy of sovereignty. The modernist quotations above imply that common people can do no wrong. This

---

[106] David Thomson, *The New Biographical Dictionary of Film* (New York: Alfred A. Knopf, 2002), 32.

[107] Mark Bauerlein, *The Dumbest Generation: How the Digital Age Stupefies Young Americans and Jeopardizes our Future* (New York: Penguin, 2008).

is their divine right and this tyranny represents justice just at it did under Louis the 14th. With this kind of cultural power at work, it is easy to see how the West collapsed into unlimited particularism and inverted the traditional hierarchy.

Now the lower classes are good and wise, while the upper are evil and mindless. We will see more examples of this when we examine operas and film. What was low has become high, and vice-versa. Recall from our French revolutionary that the revolution was sublime just like Apollo. Hence, everyone praises divine and just diversity. Anything that stops this "justice" is viewed as evil. As the body was viewed as dangerous and needing control, now social controls themselves or norms of virtue are viewed as dangerous and needing to be escaped and subverted. As we wanted to subvert the body, now we want to subvert "society" the new or displaced demon in our lives.

Divine-right monarchy creates one cultural milieu, while a deified electorate creates another. John Stuart Mill recognized an intrinsic and rationalistic hierarchy when he wrote, "It is better to be a human being dissatisfied than a pig satisfied; better to be Socrates dissatisfied than a fool satisfied."[108] It is clear that the West is turning into self-satisfied egomaniacal pigs.

Cathartic Rock and Roll is the "Versailles" of our inverted culture and politics in that both are displays of power. The Disney channel had a show *Boy Meets World*. So as Louis XIV introduced himself to an impressed world, so now do boys, and "the people," our new rulers. During the American Revolution, a man who supported the King said, "I'd rather be devoured by a lion than a pack of dogs." While I don't believe this is the last word on the subject, I do believe it captures a certain amount of truth in the cultural and social realm. We've certainly seen his prediction come true.

The transformation, over the past two centuries, of the West's reaction to suffering is particularly important. The traditional view was that suffering was sent by God to test our perseverance and faith, and was an opportunity to achieve salvation.[109] Most

---

[108] *Utilitarianism* (1863), ch 2.

[109] Rolf Toman, *Baroque: Architecture, Sculpture, Painting* (H.F. Ullmann, 2007).

people had a positive emotional response to this. During the early nineteenth century Franz Schubert described how, "pain sharpens the understanding and strengthens the mind; whereas joy seldom troubles about the former and softens the latter or makes it frivolous."[110]

Shakespeare wrote, "Sweet are the uses of adversity, which like the toad, ugly and venomous, wears yet a precious jewel in his head."[111] Such thinking was common in the period, and was part of the mind-over-matter perspective. Confinement by suffering was a challenge to be overcome by the mind. But then by the time of Victor Hugo's *Les Miserables* and definitely by the Great Depression, suffering started to become an object of pity, as it was with Jesus.

In the Charlie Chaplin film *Modern Times* (1936) a thief is portrayed as motivated by suffering, like the main character in *Les Miserables*, and the audience is supposed to pity him instead of reviling him as a criminal as was normal during the nineteenth century. It is common today for sociologists to justify crime with narratives of suffering, such as poverty, child abuse, and ancestral slavery. We saw this with John Wayne Gacy. This is the thesis of Hugo's novel. Oh! How everyone is miserable today and pities one another! As is evident in the very title of the novel, almost all 1250 pages of *Les Miserables*, intend to evoke pity and arouse sympathy:

> Two children of unequal height,…one appearing to be seven years old, the other five, timidly turned the knob of the door and entered the shop, asking for something, charity, perhaps, in a plaintive manner which rather resembled a groan than a prayer. They both spoke at once and their words were unintelligible because sobs choked the voice of the younger, and the cold make the elder's teeth chatter. The barber turned with a furious face, and without leaving his razor, crowding back the elder with his left hand and the little one with his knee, pushed them into the street and shut the door saying: "Coming and freezing people for nothing!"[112]

---

[110] John Reed, *Schubert: The Final Years* (London: Faber and Faber, 1972), 268.
[111] *As You Like It*, Act 2, Scene 1.
[112] Victor Hugo, Charles E. Wilbour, trans., *Les Miserables* (New York: Modern Library, 1992), 818-19.

It is hard to imagine a scene more miserable or worthy of pity, reflecting the image of Jesus on the cross: The injustice! Hugo was ahead of his time. And recall Jeremy Bentham's belief that, regarding animals, the question is not whether they have reason, but whether they suffer.

Jackie Evancho is a Classical cross-over singer and she has a song called "To Believe" (on the DVD *Dream with Me*) and it basically portrays the poor as pitiable or as Christ-types. At one point she sings "The cries of the poor!" Instead of "Lord, why have you forsaken me!" now it is the cries of the poor as victims of the social body as we saw in Hugo. You certainly can't criticize this holy narrative today without risking being accused of being evil.

During 1994 Pope John Paul II said: "Christ continues his agony in so many of our brothers and sisters: in men, women and children, in the young and in the old, in so many Christians and Muslims, in believers and non-believers."[113] And he made an even stronger claim when he said, "In reality, the name for that deep amazement at man's worth and dignity is the Gospel, that is to say: the good news. It is also called Christianity."[114]

So he is essentially saying that man is the Gospel, and, by implication, can replace it with what ever he dreams up and feels good about. So again, we see the movement from the "sincere" individual to institutions, instead of the reverse, which had been the case for centuries and got us under control.

And this new perspective has increasingly dominated the culture in recent decades. Philosopher Paul Gottfried recently reported that liberal politics has largely replaced the Bible for the mainline Christian dominations.[115]

Pope St. Pius X saw this happening, and he said in 1903, "While, on the other hand, and this according to the same apostle is the distinguishing mark of anti-Christ, man has with infinite temerity put himself in the place of God."[116] I am not trying to

---

[113] *General Audience*, Jan. 12, 1994.
[114] *Redemptor Hominis* (#10), March 4, 1979.
[115] Paul Edward Gottfried. *Multiculturalism and the Politics of Guilt: Toward a Secular Theocracy* (Columbia & London: University of Missouri Press, 2002).
[116] *E Supremi Apostolatus*, Oct 4, 1903.

advocate religion here, but trying to show that this impulse is well understood within religious circles.

Needless to say visions of suffering inspire most today and this is holy writ today and not just to a Pope, but to most in "academia," and so it is hard to get people excited about the rationalist tradition and its creations, like the classical tradition in the arts. This is experienced as controlling and artificial: meretricious. As an early Christian theologian once asked, "What does Athens have to do with Jerusalem?" The tension has always been there, and we see with "St. Hugo" and others which side has been getting the upper hand during the last two centuries.

Similarly, regarding suffering, in an episode of *Friends*, Rachel is dating a man, and she encourages him to tell her about his childhood. At first he is reluctant, but she goads him, and eventually he starts gushing about the endless amount of suffering he had endured at the hands of hostile parents and peers. Eventually he is curled up on Rachel's lap, and in tears. Of course, this is too much and she dumps the "cry baby," though she acknowledged that it was "beautiful" that he bared his soul. As Jesus's suffering on the cross was depicted in art as having a kind of beauty, a tragic beauty, now common people's suffering is beautiful, righteous, and worthy of pity. Every modernist today wants to be the main character in *Les Miserables,* a Christ-type. At one point Hugo calls him "Jesus Christ."

The process of transference of divinity with power can be seen among the Hellenistic cities of Asia Minor. As Price noted:

> I wish to suggest that the cities established [ruler] cults as an attempt to come to terms with a new type of power. Unlike the earlier leaders and kings the Hellenistic rulers were both kings and Greek, and some solution had to be found to the problem this posed. There was no legal answer and the cities needed to represent this new power to themselves. The cults of the gods were the one model that was available to them for the representation of a power on whom the city was dependent which was external and yet still Greek. By borrowing and adapting

this pre-existing model of classification it proved to be possible to accommodate the new kings.[117]

We see a similar process in ancient Athens during the founding of the democracy. The newly formed democratic organizations adopted mythical heroic ancestors to create the aura of political legitimacy.

Similarly, in the modern world when power shifted during the eighteenth and nineteenth centuries, divinity and the other attributes of the upper class, like wisdom and uniqueness, were also transferred and used to make coherent and justify the new power relationships and justice between the divine lower class and the oppressive or evil upper class.

The will of newly deified mankind would now empower the lower orders and the appetites. Hence the will or anger now fights for the low against the high, and this is perceived to be righteous, even among most of the middle and upper-classes.

We will see this repeatedly in opera and film. Instead of fighting to perfect ourselves, now we fight to perfect "society" or the evil upper class and purge our lives of the evil or confining classical tradition. Hence the high arts are commonly viewed as illegitimate especially among the "educated" like the post-modernists. In the past century, the high arts, like opera, have almost evaporated from the cultural landscape.

The San Francisco Opera recently reported that if opera was as popular today as during the mid-nineteenth century in their city, we would have to have twenty opera houses working seven days a week. That is how popular opera was.

Today, San Francisco has one, part-time company. Opera, like the rest of the traditional high arts, is pretty much on life support, and that is precisely how most in the liberal arts want it.

The rebels in *Les Miserables* are mostly working class people, students, and vagabonds. Again, the suffrage was systematically expanded throughout the last two centuries. Traditional moral and artistic forms were broken as people rebelled against the traditional confining definition of social order and beauty. Instead of using the

---

[117] S.R.F. Price, *Rituals and Power: The Roman Imperial Cult in Asia Minor* (Cambridge UK: Cambridge University, 1984), 29-30.

mind to rebel against, or liberate them from, the natural confinement of the body and nature, as we saw in Reynolds, the West started to rebel against the confinements of the mind. Modernists looked to raw nature and the body as a way to attack the traditional definition of freedom and beauty.

Instead of imposing order, they started to oppose order. Instead of freedom through the mind, like with Schubert, now it was freedom from the mind through the body, and through everyone being unique and unlimited, like God, as we saw in the advertisements and other areas of pop culture. This was the fundamental objective of the inversion.

As it was once mind over matter, now it is matter over mind. We saw this in thinkers like Marx. "Express Yourself!" is the reigning dogma today. We should be sincere about our suffering, instead of thinking about the reality principle of difference. Today, the West has a growing problem of obesity and a self-satisfied population that is resistant to being told what to do. Most Westerners today believe in going with the flow, and letting it all hang out. Few today, even among Republicans, are cultural conservatives. There are indeed some good arguments for a moderate popular sovereignty, but few during the nineteenth century believed that freedom should be extended to moral and cultural areas. In fact, social and cultural conservativism, with its control, was viewed as the basis of political freedom. It was viewed as an object lesson in rationality, an essential tool in political freedom, just as it is in the practice and mastery of science.

Chapter Four: Opera — Myth Made Flesh

So if the common man is seen as reflecting Jesus, and thus is the rightful ruler, then who is the Satanic enemy? It is the upper class, their morality, aesthetics, and the governments they run. Two recent titles from a university press suggest this: *Moralism: A Study of a Vice* and *In Praise of Non-Sense: Aesthetics, Uncertainty and Postmodern Identity.* These attitudes, typical today, apparently are considered to reveal wisdom, insight and justice.

As the devil rebelled against God, and this defined his evil, the upper class during the nineteenth century were viewed as rebelling against the righteous and suffering lower class, and even for inflicting their suffering. Victor Hugo describes the soldiers of the government as "Demons" and portrays the upper class or their representatives as evil. This was a common tactic among French revolutionaries. Hence, today modernists believe that the upper class is evil while the lower are righteous, good, and victims to be pitied. Look how sincere they are, just like Jesus. We now look to them for "moralism" right along with many other low cultural references, like raw nature and the sublime. We will see this again in the film *Titanic.*

Suffering is an essential ingredient to this mix. The lower class could never rise in the divine hierarchy or be Christ-types unless they could show that they suffer at the confining hands of the upper class or society: groups, institutions, and norms.

In Mozart's opera, *The Marriage of Figaro*, the lowly servant Figaro is engaged to Susana, but his master, the evil Count, plots to seduce Figaro's fiancé. Figaro suffers oppression, but he's also a fighter, asserts his rights and ultimately triumphs, inspired as he is by the new, bottom-up, theory of justice. At one point, Figaro says, "Figaro says no." He was sincere about this. The Platonic will is now used to new ends or moving in a new direction, to get angry and crush a new evil up there. So the upper class, instead of viewed as imposing virtue, are now viewed as imposing evil. The lower class is now viewed as imposing virtue and righteousness.

When nineteenth-century composer Gustav Mahler was a child, he said that when he grew up, he wanted to be a martyr. And when opera composer Richard Wagner was a young man, he went into a church, saw a crucifix, and imagined himself being crucified.

In Wagner's *Ring* cycle of operas, the folk hero Siegfried is a Christ-type who suffers to redeem humanity, and battles against the evil power of the aristocracy, or the gods and the moneyed elite. Wagner recycles Christian and pagan imagery and ideas at the service of resurrecting the natural in human nature.[118] Siegfried is Wagner's "ideal man."

Gilroy Gardens, a nature theme park in California, advertises with the phrase, "Where children play on a higher ground." We see an inversion of Plato with nature as high. A contemporary philosopher believes that rocks have the highest or most real existence. This would certainly have appealed to Mozart and Wagner. In Verdi's opera *Il Trovatore*, Leonora says that she will sacrifice herself to save the life of her boyfriend Manrico. Manrico's mother is a lowly Gypsy, who at one point says, "Even the wretched have a God."

This is viewed as just and revealing insight. The Gypsy, Manrico, and Leonora are all oppressed by the evil Duke, or by upper-class societal dominance and rules. Gilda in *Rigoletto*, Cavaradossi in *Tosca*, Liu in *Turandot*, are all Christ-types as they suffer at the hands of cruel authority figures or for the sins of the social body or "society." In *Tosca*, after being tortured by the police, Cavaradose learns of Napoleon's victory at Marengo, and he cries "Victory, this the day of vengeance when the evil will tremble. Liberty stands proud and tyranny crumbles. You'll see me rejoice for the pain I have suffered. You're shaking with fear, you hangman." Of course,

---

[118] Joachim Kohler, Steward Spencer, trans., *Richard Wagner: The Last of the Titans* (New Haven: Yale University, 2004).

Jesus rejoiced in the pain he suffered. As we are indebted to Jesus we are now indebted to Puccini, another author of our salvation. In Verdi's opera *La Traviata*, a courtesan is forced to leave a man whom she loves because the man's father insists that she is too low or morally polluting for his son. She agrees to leave him out of a sense of self-sacrifice.

The father eventually realizes that he is oppressing her, or is confining, and encourages the couple to come back together. So we see the triumph of unconfined nature or emotion over society, as we saw in Hepburn's request to be simply loved in *The Philadelphia Story*. No savvy modernist wants to be an example of purity, like a statue or an angel.

In Puccini's opera *Tosca*, the singer Tosca and her painter boyfriend are oppressed and ultimately killed by the evil chief of police who is into sadomasochism and drunkenness. The injustice! The social body is simply perverted, and needs control, but people are innocent and don't need control.

They suffer for the sins of society, or are Christ-types. Instead of the law directing us upwards towards our better, ideal selves, now it is seen as simply evil. One German political thinker believes that we need to "assume guilt for political sins" which we can expiate by promoting revolution.[119]

We see how this impulse is driving opera plots, and much moralizing politics today. The culture of the last two centuries is one huge cry for freedom from evil. All that matters is where we place the evil demon. This is what largely divides the left and mainstream right and creates internal debate.

Regarding the rise of the middle classes and developments in opera plots during the eighteenth century, Weaver noted that:

> The conversion of the private performances of opera in private theaters into performances before a paying audience, even if the control of the theater remained in the hands of noblemen, made it a financial necessity to respond to the

---

[119] Dorothee Sölle, *Political Theology*, trans. John Shelly. (Philadelphia: Fortress Press, 1974), 92. Quoted in Paul Edward Gottfried, *Multiculturalism and the Politics of Guilt: Toward a Secular Theocracy* (Columbia & London: University of Missouri Press, 2002), 48.

tastes and demands of an ever-widening public.

The change accounts for the many protestations by opera librettists that they were obliged to satisfy the low taste of the audience. The effects of these sociopolitical changes upon opera, as the first of the major [musical] forms to become popular, is apparent and has been often noted.[120]

As politics became democratized, opera, like the plastic arts, became vulgarized. Low is now the ideal and influences the high, while the high is increasingly viewed as meretricious. This has killed the classical fine arts; for instance UC Berkeley changed the name of its fine arts department to "art practice." At least they are honest that they have given up on beauty all together.

Between 1890 and 1910 Richard Wagner was the most popular opera composer in Europe. But starting during the early 1930s and through the War and to today, Wagner was surpassed in popularity by the lower-level music of Verdi, Puccini, Mozart and Lortzing. This occurred throughout Europe and even in Germany.[121] Appeals to the people, even by the National Socialists, so eroded notions of the power of the mind that it lessened the popularity of Wagner's higher-level, more mental or grand music. A professional Wagner tenor recently said that Wagner's music is more mental. And a woman who attended the Metropolitan Opera for 40 years agreed that Wagner music is more cerebral.

A common complaint against Wagner is that his music is "heavy." Once when I heard it, the speaker's top lip went up showing disgust. As the body used to be disgusting, now the social body is disgusting. This is consistent with the conceptions of modernism that we have seen. If to boogie is the ideal, as we saw among the Vikings, than more physical music, like the Italians, would be preferred, while Wagner, whose music is more mental, or top heavy, is experienced as oppressive, heavy or unjust and to be thrown off. Another way of describing Wagner's more mental music is "sublime"

---

[120] Robert L Weaver, "The Consolidation of the Main Elements of the Orchestra: 1470-1768." *The Orchestra*, Joan Peyser, Ed. (Milwaukee: Hal Leonard, 2006), 33.

[121] Ulrick Muller and Peter Wapnewski, *Wagner Handbook* (Cambridge MA: Harvard University, 1992).

or even "light" as one singer recently put it, but one would only think of these terms if you liked that particular effect, aesthetic, priority or *ranking* effect of the music.

It should be said here that Wagner had a more symphonic conception of orchestral writing, as apposed to the more "um-pa-pa" of the Italians, and this creates the grander and the greater mental engagement or animation. It is like the difference between a Beethoven symphony and a Strauss waltz. No one would confuse the two; at least no one with any taste, discernment or moral neutrality. Interestingly, a person with a Ph.D. in music recently said that he could see that this style could be considered "pompous and overblown."

So again we see the metaphors of the formally maligned body applied now to malign high culture and the mind. It is simply, at best, meretricious. Similarly, it is common for people to say that some romantic music, like by Tchaikovsky is too emotional; of course, we don't like indulgences of the social body, but the body is fine. And this explains the trends in the last century toward more tight fisted performances or dry performances of Classical music. (Wagner once quipped that "the people" make a better concept than reality.

In general he thought that they were brutes, and they are the model for the crude characters of the giants in the *Ring*.) By the 1930s, the unconfined people collapsed into themselves and into the lower-level music of Verdi and Puccini (and, they eventually generated rock and roll); though certainly the lyrical writing of the Italians is wonderful and very worthwhile.

Though with our skewed values, it is clear that we need to return to a more functional definition of power or, in other words, return it to empowering the mind. If we do, as we did during the nineteenth century, then our aesthetic senses will probably improve accordingly.

With Italian opera, the politics and philosophy are more on the surface. *Tosca*, with its clear portrayal of the good democrats as oppressed by the evil tyrants is a particularly good example. With Wagner, the politics is more symbolized. I saw the *Ring* about 3 times without being really aware of how the characters symbolized

Wagner liberal philosophy and politics. You have to read books that explain all this. With *Tosca* it's crystal clear and requires no special knowledge.

Our recent aspirations to freedom are not new. I will try to show that it just became reconfigured, redistributed or re-expressed. Escape and freedom from threatening evil are big parts of both the Classical and Judeo-Christian culture. One of the best examples from Classical myth is in the story Orpheus and Eurydice. She is bitten by a snake, dies and goes to the underworld. Orpheus goes to the underworld to save her or bring her back, but while he is bringing her back up from Hades, he makes a mistake, and he loses her, and she descends back to Hades. So we see here the basic idea of the desire to escape from evil death elaborated into a story or narrative.

This basic idea is the driving force for much of Christian theology and ethics. Adam and Eve made a mistake and fall from grace and "descended" to the evil pains of the material world and death. For both Orpheus and Eurydice and Adam and Eve, all their problems start with a serpent, and this starts the journey to and from evil. Similarly, the devil made a mistake and was expelled from heaven, falls to earth and rules over sin, the decay of the mortal world and death. And Jesus successfully repels the Devil temptations, and most importantly, Jesus is successful in his Harrowing of Hell.

Ever since, the West has been trying to escape: first, the material world, and to seek shelter in visions of heaven, or the monastery, and second, with the inversion: the evils of imposed, "enslaving" society, our fallen, low state in class, gender and race. Today, this is what we are trying to escape by rising above or subverting. As we wanted to escape and rise above the body, now we want to escape and rise above the social body, like class, gender and race. As we maligned the body as "pompous and overblown," now we malign high society, like Wagner or Donald Trump. Class, gender and race are "too much" and offensive as the body once was.

In the early Christian period, one of the best examples of escape is Mary Magdalene. She started out as a prostitute, but converted and escaped, and ended her days in freedom in a cave. During the Middle Ages life was understood to be a journey from the fallen state or perdition to heaven, and a well known example of this is the journey that Dante makes himself in his poem the *Comedia* which describes his journey from hell through purgatory to heaven. This pretty much is the ideal for most of European history, with some variations for country, class and period. For instance, in an Oscar Wild play from about 1890, an upper class Victorian woman is looking out her window, and says wistfully, "I try to escape from the world." In general the West has been obsessed with control, both personal, social, political and scientific. This helped to give rise to beauty in art.

All that varies is where we place the evil spirit that needs to be controlled; either in the body, or in the public sphere, forming, at least for us and with our traditional metaphors, the social body. This was clear in the operas and their notions of who is evil and who represents justice and righteousness.

The traditional ascetic perspective started to change with the romantics, and it was gradually replaced by worldliness or sensuality with the inversion; in addition, we also started to malign the upper-class as the new evil and this became the norm by the 1960s. First we started to see the upper-class as evil and needing to be escaped from and purged, and then the notion of imposing evil was further extended to conceptions of gender, race and the high arts.

It was believed in the nineteenth century that individuals needed to adhere to the ideals of love, not hating or killing, and giving alms; similarly, now the left, with displacement, believe that "society" or the government needs to adhere to the Christian ideals of love, not killing (war) and giving alms or welfare. So again, as we saw with freedom, the left and right have the same moral vocabulary, they just see the demon in a different place: public or private.

Today, we want to escape the "hate" of class, gender and race, and so have urgent feelings about legislating against this and promoting this in popular culture. For instance, Virginia Slims, a brand of cigarettes marketed to women, ran a television ad that carried the phrase, "You've come a long way baby." And the pilot for *Friends* starts with Rachel urgently coming into the gang's favorite café wearing a wedding dress, and distressed as she is trying to escape her impending marriage. In a later episode, she meets some girl friends, and their tempting marriages and pregnancy are heavily stereotyped or portrayed as meretricious.

The basic plot of *Les Miserable* is about a criminal avoiding arrest by the evil police. The criminal is triumphant, while the stalking police officer "dies." And the novel *Anna Karenina* is about Anna's escape from an oppressive marriage to a bureaucrat who is sometimes portrayed as subhuman. In the early eighteenth century, rescue was a popular plot for opera libretti, like rescue from pirates or other threatening situations. By the late eighteenth century, rescue became an identifiable genre, and commonly portrayed was rescue from political oppression.

The most famous example of this type of opera is Beethoven's *Fidelio*. Benoit Groult is a feminist activist, and her recent autobiography is entitled *My Escape*. Ford has a SUV called *Escape*. And Eugene Delacroix's iconic painting of the French Revolution is entitled, *Liberty Leading the People*. Similarly, a recent study reported that the "pilgrim lover" was a popular theme with Rococo painter Antoine Watteau.[122]

Recall here Enya's song Pilgrim about the individual who is on a search for himself. And during the 1970s in the United State streaking became a fad with people running nude across a football field, for instance. As an inversion of Mary Magdalene, many people's hearts are warmed today by the thought of a wildlife *refuge*, and have visions of themselves communing with good nature, and escaping the evil city or society. Pop singer Katy Perry was engaged and married near the same lion sanctuary in India.

Dr. Hobson is an emeritus research psychiatrist at Harvard Medical School and he has devoted his life to putting dream analysis on a strong empirical and scientific basis. In his recent book published by Oxford, summarizing a lifetime of research, he describes how, "Dreams are indeed instigated by the release

---

[122] Colin B Bailey, "Genre Painting in Eighteenth Century France: The Huntington Collection." Shelley M. Bennett & Carolyn Sargentson, Ed. *French Art of the Eighteenth Century at the Huntington* (New Haven & London: Yale University Press, 2008).

in sleep of primitive drive mechanisms of the brain, and these primitive drive mechanisms do include the instinctive media of sex, aggression, and *escape* [emphasis added]. The feelings that go with approach behaviour (elation, joy, happiness, love), avoidance behaviour (fear, anxiety, panic) and confrontation show-down behaviour (fighting, assaulting, shooting) are also there."[123] We have seen how a particular schema of good and evil channels these basic emotions.

Further evidence comes from the life of Richard Wagner. He was a utopian socialist who was opposed to all forms of authority. This is how he described the existing institutions of his time, like marriage, industry and opera companies: "Let us treat the world with contempt; for it deserves no better; but let no hope be placed in it, that out hearts be not deluded! It is evil, *fundamentally evil…*it belongs to Alberich [an evil character in one of his operas]: no one else!! Away with it!"[124]

So we see the theme of escape and rebellion, but instead of the body, now the social body. Notice that he could have just as easily been talking about the body and "worldliness." As we saw in Hobson, these emotions of hostility always want to bubble up, and so need to be kept under control by institutions and authority figures.

This idea of cultural escape or freedom is simply a new expression of psychological and political rebellion that is the very basis of modern politics. For instance, during the American Revolution, Virginian Richard Bland wrote, "When subjects are deprived of their civil rights, or are dissatisfied with the place they hold in the community, they have a natural right to quit the society of which they are members, and to retire into another country.

Now when men exercise this right of *withdrawing* themselves from their country, they recover their natural freedom and independence [emphasis added]; the jurisdiction and sovereignty of the state they have quitted ceases; and if they unite, and by common consent take possession of a new country and form themselves into

---

[123] Dr. J. Allen Hobson, *Dreaming: An Introduction to the Science of Sleep* (Oxford & New York: Oxford University Press, 2004), 149.
[124] Bryan Magee, *Wagner and Philosophy* (London: Penguin Books, 2000), 40.

a political society, they become a sovereign state, independent of the state from which they separated."[125] Pagden reported that Jefferson used a version of this argument.[126]

So we see that this impulse toward freedom and escape was during the last century increasingly applied to social and cultural issues. The old saying was "freedom with responsibility" but this is now mostly gone. People traditional understood or recognized that cultural and social conservatism was the basis of political freedom. If you are out of control, then you certainly are not in much of a position to think rationally about the weaknesses of human nature, and politics.

Any sense of the reality principle is pretty much out of the college curricula in the liberal arts. We can't let anything get in the way of the sex, drugs and rock and roll. Recall John Adams' belief that the constitution is only for a moral population.

An exhibit at the Asian Art Museum in San Francisco was entitled "Out of Character: Decoding Chinese Calligraphy." Now, relative to the subject it would have been just as appropriate to name it *In Character*, after all this is where the meaning resides, but, in the spirit of escape the curators chose *Out*. This attitude and imagery is very common today and very much defines post-modern aesthetics, with their idea of "de-centeredness," and defines the evasive impulses behind modern identity politics.

For instance, women certainly don't want to be "in character," or consistent with their body images, as they were during the nineteenth century. And a pop song sung by a woman had the line, "I can't be defined." And post-modern psychologist Jacques Lacan once said, "I hope that my work can never be reduced to a thesis." It is easy to see how this attitude helps to inspire the trends of anti-intellectualism today. As the meaning for the Chinese characters is now "out" so it is for us in general today. This attitude helps to create the entire discipline of the social sciences with their moral

---

[125] Richard Bland, *The Colonel Dismounted: or The Rector Vindicated*, [Williamsberg], p. 12, in Bernard Bailyn (ed) *Pamphlets of the American Revolution. I 1750-1765*. Quoted in Anthony Pagden, *Lords Of All The World: Ideologies of Empire in Spain, Britain and France, c. 1500-c. 1800* (New Haven & London: Yale University Press, 1995), 128-129.

[126] Pagden, ibid.

resistance to bio-determinism. Recall that we're unlimited today in their eyes or ever going "out" or escaping and subverting.

In *Landscape and Memory*, Simon Schama says that in history, the only groups that idealize nature are urban populations or those who are protected from the brutality of nature. The music group Abba has a song called *The Tiger* and it is about how the city is a threatening and ominous place, and is described as full of stalking tigers. I have noticed several times writers and artists portray the city as evil. For instance, Diderot called cities "monsters of nature" which nature seeks always to destroy.[127]

Today the tendency is to experience urban areas and the new social class arrangement as a threatening environment, as we used to experience nature and our "wild" bodies. Because of the prevalence of death and violence people experienced the world as a threatening place, and religion responded to this. Mormando describes how in a seventeenth play, "...the Devil prepares for his assault on the dying Alessio: "Alexis is preparing his heart for death; in this last combat, then, let not my daring plan fall short in cunning or force, for a soul, up to is very last moment, remains exposed to danger."[128]

Similarly, today, "society" is out to get us; we are surrounded by the temptations or hell of class, gender and race and we muster all our strength to combat this evil. In contrast we now experience nature as idyllic, a refuge, or something to escape to. So again we see inversion. So for Orpheus and Eurydice and Adam and Eve, the serpent or nature is hell to be escaped, while for us it is heaven or a refuge, and the urban areas are hell.

Billy Joel was a very popular musician, and on his CD *The Stranger*, there are no less than four songs that pertain to the idea of escape from society and finding refuge in authenticity. The first song is titled *Movin' Out*, and the lyrics include, "Anthony works in the grocery store, savin' his pennies for someday. Mama Leone

---

[127] Guillaume-Thomas Raynal, abbe. 1781. *Histoire philosophique et politique des etablissemens et du commerce des Europeen dan les deux Indes,* 10 vols. Geneva, V, 10. Quoted in Pagden, Ibid, p. 161.

[128] Franco Mormando, *Bernini: His Life and His Rome.* (Chicago & London: University of Chicago Press, 2011), 342.

left a note on the door, she said, "Sonny, move out to the country." Workin' too hard can give me a heart attack. You ought to know by now who needs a house out in Hackensack? Is that what you get with your money? It seems such a waste of time, if that's all you get with your money? It seems such a waste of time if that's what it's all about. If that's movin' up, then I'm movin out."

The song continues with two more scenarios of similarly futile and harmful upward mobility. At one point all of this is described as "crazy." All three scenarios end with, "If that's movin' up, then I'm movin' out" the title of the song. Billy Joel put this song first on his recording so he must feel pretty strong about it. I can remember as a child growing up in radical Berkeley that this attitude and moral reasoning was very common. As the body was once viewed to be crazy, futile and dangerous, now "society," or the social body is crazy, futile, dangerous and needing to be escaped. This form of the old gloom and doom and visions of damnation to be escaped are clearly the moral impetus for much of the counter culture today.

The second song on the recording, *The Stranger*, is a personalized version of social delusion and alienation. Here, our "masks" or roles we play with others are fake, and we need to go "out" as we saw in the museum exhibit title. We are essentially "strangers" even to ourselves, and this of course is "dangerous," so we need to "go south" or escape. And much of the song describes the troubles it creates with us and others. So as we were alienated from our fake bodies, now we are alienated from our fake social bodies, and succumbing to this creates problems. Society! Temptation and damnation!

Of course, "alienation" is a very common theme in modern culture, and now we can see why; the object of fear and revulsion simply switched from the body to the public sphere or the old social ideals, characters in our minds and controls. So, for instance when we have impulses to relapse into the old value systems, or study history or see any of the relics of the past, suddenly we feel "alienated." So instead of viewing these as creating a just order, and concomitant beauty and greatness, they are viewed as creating unjust disorder, distortion and debasement. *This* is what we need to rebel against. This perspective created the popular phrase during the 1960's of "Tune in, Turn on, Drop out" or escape the alienation through solipsism. Similarly, we traditionally were tuned into Jesus, turned on by Jesus and we dropped out of the world. All of this is now applied to ourselves and the new movement of subjectivism as the quote shows. We need to escape society and find refuge in our authentic selves. People sincerely believe this today instead of thinking about the reality of difference and the universals of mind. We are all united by subjectivism and the low instead of the high.

A very common example of social body alienation in the United States is when white parents say, "I don't want to live in that neighborhood because they have bad schools." They can't say because those schools have too many blacks and Hispanics, because this would be expressing alienation from the body, so they express alienation from the social body which is comprehensible, legitimate and legal.

To express alienation from the body, in many contexts, creates cognitive dissonance, and starts one down the slippery slope to "discrimination" or enjoyment of the social body. We have to crucify the social body today and not the body. This is the source of many of whites' apparently suicidal impulses and ideas.

We can also see here how whites are able to practice self preservation at the level of self reporting, but less in terms of behavior, though they can sometimes, as avoiding "bad schools" clearly shows. In order to completely guarantee their well being whites would have to talk about each specific black as being a bad risk, but, with our general level of comprehension, this is not allowed, as it was in South Africa and the United States until recently.

The third song on Billy Joel's recording provides a much desired antidote to all of this fakeness. It is called, *Just the Way You Are*, and includes the following, "Don't go changing to try to please me. You never let me down before...I don't want clever conversion. I never want to work that hard. I just want someone I can talk to." So notice that there is no pressure to try to improve your self, or adhere to ideals, and, it is anti-intellectual, which is a similar impulse and which is also very common today. So we want to escape from the mind and into the body and have a good time. People sincerely believe this.

A song that uses much stronger imagery to forward this attack or inversion is *Only The Good Die Young*, and is a combination of lampoon and lament from a man's perspective on his love for a repressed Catholic woman; it describes essentially the "trapped" state of the woman that he is trying to court. Of course she is trapped by religion and its usual restrictions, and Joel uses these restrictions as a pivot to redirect the traditional hatred of the body onto the traditional controls or ideals.

So instead of hating the body, now we hate the restrictions, society or the social body. The song begins, "Come out Virginia, don't let me wait. You Catholic girls start much too late." So the very first two words refer to a confined state that needs to be escaped. But this is mild compared to other images. She is also, "locked away" in a temple. And she "pays a price." Joel characterizes himself as rescuing her, and "The stained-glass curtain you're hiding behind never lets in the sun. Only the good die young...They didn't give you quite enough information." She needs to wise up about the social body or she will continue to be in the stifling dark. He mockingly says about 3 times that sinners have more fun, and this kind of imagery and sentiment is very common today. At one point he says, about the sinful crowd that he's part of and that's supposed to rescue her, "We ain't too pretty..." This image is part of the wholesale rejection of beauty that we have seen because of, apparently, it's controlling aspect. By implication, ugly is good and a relief which is how he characterizes himself in general in the song.

There is salvation in the ugly and being out of control. So three times in the song he uses images of entrapment, and that she is suffering for it, and that it will ultimately kill her: "Only The Good Die Young." So instead of religion bringing salvation, it brings death, which of course is an inversion. Almost every line of the song uses traditional imagery, ideas and morals, but simply redirected to attack the old institutions of control. This song is mild in comparison to what we will see in film, like in *Alien*, which is about a dragon that devours people and that comes from "society." I agree that there were problems with the nineteenth century, but as will become clear by the end of this study, the cure killed the patient.

The film *Roman Holiday* (1953), as the very name makes clear is about escape. Audrey Hepburn plays a princess who is on a good will tour of Europe. After hearing a review of all her social duties, she becomes hysterical. Her assistant says to her, "Control yourself!" and Hepburn responds, "I don't want to!" Of course, this is what people were screaming during the solipsistic '60s. The scene takes place in her very ornately decorated bedroom, and at one point the camera focuses on some gilding to make clear how oppressive the whole situation is for Hepburn and worthy of rebellion. At one point she looks out her window and sees some real people dancing on a barge; this is the vision "heaven" and her climatic destination in the film.

After her staff put her to bed, she escapes the palace, and becomes a "regular girl" out to have a good time. She meets Gregory Peck, and they both go dancing on the barge, and even have a run in with the law, as part of the general mayhem and good times on her "holiday." She cuts her hair very short as part of her liberation.

So the movie is about her escape from stifling civilization as symbolized by the palace and her lifestyle, to the gritty streets of Rome and fights with the law and even a fight with the secret service on the barge who try to "enslave" her by bring her back forcefully to sinful civilization. Her obligation to her family and nation gets the better of her native and wise instincts, and she goes back to the palace to resume her life.

Of course by the next decade many people dropped out completely, and were never heard from again so liberated were they. They were liberated all the way to the drug-induced grave. At one point Hepburn and Peck have champagne, but they don't take the reasoning to the point of sex. We certainly wised up on that issue.

There is a little known film called *Holiday* (1938) staring Cary Grant and Katherine Hepburn, and it is basically about how Grant wants to drop out of a good job and take a holiday. As part of the care free atmosphere in the film, much of the story is about how Grant is initially attracted to an uptight society girl, but he has the conversion experience, as did Audrey Hepburn, and dumps her and starts to pursue the girl's care free sister, Katherine Hepburn. Much of the plot to another Cary Grant film, *Bringing Up Baby* (1938) is about the same contrast in female personality types, with, again, Katherine Hepburn representing Miss Wild and Crazy as she literally *drives* the plot of wild pursuit of a leopard. The genre that this film is part is called "screwball comedy" and it clearly gets its energy from a redirection of our hysterical concerns about self-mastery and salvation as we saw in the discussion of Christianity in the chapter on the state of nature. In light of what happened in later decades, it is clear we took a good idea a bit too far.

While writing this film description I saw an internet ad for a credit card that had the phrase, "Keep Your Cool" accompanied by the picture of very relaxed looking black man with sun glasses. This association is very common today because of its positive, or shall I say contemporary resonances.

There is another Audrey Hepburn film about getting cool or taking a vacation. *Sabrina* (1954) contrasts uptight business man Humphrey Bogart with playboy William Holden. Just in case you miss the characterization, Bogart at one time is described as having "ice water" running through his veins. Bogart eventually gives up his stifling business career and sales away to Paris with Hepburn on the ocean liner *Liberty*. And recall Eugene Delacroix's iconic painting *Liberty Leading the People*. So as we wanted the liberty from our sinful bodies and sought to enslave ourselves to virtuous society, now we want liberty from enslaving society and freedom in the body. Of course, we thought that by enslaving ourselves to society we were gaining salvation or a higher freedom. Today of course we want the lower freedom. We want to be cool, like the blacks and Vikings, the *real* men. A Christian song described the situation well when it said, "You want freedom, but you don't know how to choose." Obviously, evolutionary science is the only source of sure knowledge about human nature. Story time needs to come to an end. As we used to tell ourselves stories about nature, now we tell ourselves stories about human nature.

Here is how a theater in San Francisco describes a film by Godard, *Pierrot Le Fou*(1965). "Fleeing a bourgeois existence, Jean-Paul Belmondo and his babysitter/ex-lover Anna Karina go on the lam to the south of France, battling gunrunners, gas station attendants, and American tourists. A profound turning point in Jean-Luc Godard's career, this landmark film recalls the gangster cool of *Breathless* and *Band of Outsiders* while also pointing towards the increasingly essayistic, apocalyptic visions of *Two or Three Things I Know About Her* and *Weekend*." This film is portrayed as "relevant" or modern, and notice that to underscore the point of the narrative of escape, that the female character shares the name Anna Karina with Tolstoy's famous heroin.

Recall that modernism has simply inverted the path to salvation. Instead of from hell to heaven, now from heaven to hell. Nature and our relaxed bodies, and all the hellish conflict that can come with this, are now the vision of salvation. For instance, a Berkeley English professor reported that students prefer Dante's portrayal of the Inferno to his portrayal of Heaven. If the West does not actively define or consolidate itself in constructive terms, as we did during the nineteenth century, then, given the power of the emotions, we will naturally be assimilated to the rest of the world. Women's new empowerment is factor here. The nineteenth century understood this about our relations to the non-whites, that we could be assimilated or "succumb."[129]

Before the 1960s there were two types of people; the ascetic, virtuous, church going type, and the hedonistic body orientated group. The blacks fell into the latter, and good people wanted to avoid them and the rest of their type. So we see the pattern of escape and freedom. Of course, today we have inverted this and now are suspect of the "uptight," as in "white and uptight," and what to move in the direction of the body and all of its cultural, social and political expressions. Instead of being "church going" now we are "black going." So we are still divided into two groups; we have just inverted good and evil, what we want to move away from and toward. Instead of moving toward church, or this salvation, now it is toward the blacks and everything they represent. This is just divine today: "beam me up," said the white woman about her black boyfriend. So modernism is just Christianity turned into a primitive

---

[129] James Morone, *Hellfire Nation: The Politics of Sin in American History*, (New Haven & London: Yale University Press, 2004).

fertility religion. Whites think that blacks are their leaders. This is big part of the appeal of Obama.

On the night of a US electoral race between Republican Mitt Romney and black Democrat Barrack Obama, a young woman said, "If Romney wins I'm moving to Canada." And after Republican George W. Bush won an election, the Canadian consulate was flooded with visa requests from Americans. Certainly the image of society getting the upper hand, or all those unrepentant, "hateful" whites, is distressful for many people. Bridget Bardot, an animal rights activist, recently threatened to leave France if two sick circus elephants were killed.

Twice during the 2012 campaign I heard Romney referred to as "an old white guy." In general "old" is a way to pass negative value judgment. And old people are sometimes described as being "heavy with years." So, in other words the social body, "white people," is certainly decaying, heavy, entrapping or deserves a wholesale negative value judgment just as the body and non-whites once did.

So whites have gone from condemning non-whites in general, to condemning themselves, and this is very common, and in fact is considered a sign of "enlightenment" because of its compensatory aspect.

These savvy individuals "make the leap" of consciousness and so show moral insight. Of course we always believed we needed Jesus to compensate for our sins, so now we have simply added the non-whites to the pantheon. Both are visions, vision to rejoice in, at least from one perspective. We will see this logic again in the last chapter, *Modernism's Theology of Race*.

We've gone from being medieval flagellants, to being modernist or social flagellants. As "It should be you up on that cross," now it is "It should be society up on that cross" or class, gender and race. If a white does not believe this today he is damned. It is indeed dangerous for a white to reject white guilt in public. Millions of people are robbed, killed and injured every year because of that distorted logic. We indeed have come a long way, babies.

When Poland rose up in rebellion against their Russian rulers during the mid nineteenth century, Polish patriots called Poland the "Christ of Nations."

In a movie version of *Les Miserables* (1998), a poor, working class woman is fired from her job because she has a child out of wedlock. Because of her poverty and abuse, she succumbs to tuberculosis and dies. She suffers for the sins of society or the narrow-minded values of the manager who fired her. He ultimately feels guilty over her death, repents, adopts the woman's child, and raises it as his own.

In all of these examples from opera and film, there is an adversarial relationship with the lower class being righteous, victimized, aggressive and using their will to seek dominance and to realize divine "justice" that is unconfined or unlimited. As Louis the 14th conceived of his tyranny to be righteous, now the "people" consider their tyranny to be righteous. Needless to say, the cultural effects of these two forms of tyranny are very different, as the last two centuries make vividly clear.

A history professor recently observed the profound influence of political correctness in academia:

> No history textbook can today pass muster unless it highlights the insignificant, reduces absolutes to local accident, and eliminates grand narratives in favor of a collection of tales, full of sound and fury, whose chief goal is to elicit pity, sympathy or guilt.[130]

Only unique, diverse and unconfined details and emotion count today. As the Catholics have books of martyrology, academic works today are books of victimology. Opera singer Eileen Farrell released a recording called "I've Got a *Right* to Sing the Blues" [emphasis added]. In this title, we see the union of natural rights, suffering emotion of the individual, and cathartic aesthetics. Modernists have reduced the West to a collection of blubbering idiots. And the savvy enjoy this.

Around 1915, expressionist artist Egon Schiele was convicted of creating child pornography. After release from prison, he made a drawing of himself as St. Sebastian. In most Old Master

---

[130] Allen Guelzo, "Hero, Standing." *Imprimis*, May/June, 2009. Volume 38, Number 5/6, page 4. Reprinted by permission from *Imprimis*, a publication of Hillsdale College.

paintings of this subject, the Saint is standing firm as arrows pierce his body. We saw this strength in the traditional idea of mind over matter and enduring or drawing strength from pain. In Schiele's version, his body is convulsing with pain as he takes the arrows. In other words, he had a right to sing the blues. He suffers for the sins of society. As Christian martyrs were Christ-types, so is Schiele and everyone else today.

The history of the word "society" needs a closer examination at this point. It has changed meaning significantly during the last two centuries. At the beginning of the nineteenth century, as seen in the novels of Jane Austin, it meant the upper class and their social life, as in the best society or *beau monde*. When Greta Garbo was starting her career, a friend introduced her into "smart society."[131] This image of the upper class as smart or superior is the traditional Platonic conception. In contrast, Durgnat described one of Garbo's co-stars, John Gilbert, as "scatterbrained." This is how Plato would have described the lower class. It should be said here that psychologists can determine someone's IQ by their writing,[132] so you can tell the dummies by how they talk and if they have thick, unintelligent looks on their faces.

2/   This body based perception, with the rationalist bias, was an important basis of class elitism and racial hierarchies in earlier history. It should be said here that, relative to the distribution for white Americans, 90% of blacks have an average to below average IQ, and only a third of one percent have an IQ above 125.[133] So if you combine this fact with the kind of behavior you tend to see on the street, it is easy to see the kind of perceptions that tend to get formed. Traditionally, whites pursued a strong survival instinct, and it still has some force, though only at the level of behavior, not at the level of self reporting and politics.

By the 1960s the term *society* had morphed into a negative and evil force that infects and corrupts people, in social conditioning

---

[131] Raymond Durgnat and John Kobal, *Greta Garbo* (New York: E. P. Dutton., 1967).

[132] Frank Sulloway, professor of psychology, UC Berkeley, personal communication, 2012.

[133] Richard Herrnstein & Charles Murray, *The Bell Curve: Intelligence and Class Structure in American Society*, (New York: Free Press, 1994).

from groups, institutions and norms. This displacement of evil was easy to do because of the connection in the mind between self and body imagery or the collective.

If the unrestrained, pompous individual was no longer evil, then society was the next best candidate because of the fluid connection. For instance, in a California high school, if a student misbehaves, it is the teacher's fault. Administrators presume that the students are good kids and the teacher is responsible for maintaining class order. In this situation, society is bad. This is what is culpable and what we try to escape. So it is common for kids to romanticize cutting class.

Rousseau described this new concept in the eighteenth century. He argued that people are born good but are corrupted by society. We saw this with John Wayne Gacy. As we have seen in the operas, the nineteenth century was a transitional age when the upper class was viewed as evil and hostile but not responsible for creating the personalities of the public at large. This moral perspective is also an inversion of Plato, because for him the upper class were good and wise, and a source of confining control on the evil of the lower class, who were traditionally viewed as the criminal class. (Sociologist James Henslin reported that today in the United States, 90% of homicide offenders are lower class.[134] As we saw in the state of nature, everyone was "lower class.")

Early nineteenth century conservative Joseph de Maistre believed that religious observance and social hierarchy were necessary to control evil or crime. Today modernists believe the opposite: that the lower class and its representatives in government must control the upper class or the evils of big business. This creates the evil image of the nineteenth century robber baron and money bags. Instead of the lower class being "robbers" and murderers now it is the upper class. The word *villain* derives from the French word for the lower classes.

Gradually over the past two centuries, evil was displaced from the body, from sexuality, and from the lower class, to the upper class, their art and proper morals or etiquette. In England during the early eighteenth century, people started to view individuals who

---

[134] James Henslin, *Social Problems* (Englewood Cliffs NJ: Prentice-Hall, 1990).

were paid enforces of sexual control as corrupt or, in other words, evil. So we see the beginning of displacement. And at about this time, the public policing of sex stopped as individual rights started to play a larger role in people's value system.

This rebellious attitude toward sexual expression stayed mostly underground among the middle classes, but broke out and became the norm by the 1960s. By the late eighteenth century, it started to become a common tactic of the left to accuse the upper classes of sexual perversion.[135] So instead of seeing the aristocrats as high and an ideal, we started to see them as low and contemptible. So we see displacement. We saw this with the perverted and drunken chief of police in the opera *Tosca*. And in Donizetti's opera *Lucrazia Borgia*, based on a play by Victor Hugo, a man walks up to a sign with Borgia's name and removes the B revealing "Orgia."

In the opera this is portrayed as moral insight. And someone said during the French Revolution, "A king capable of dominating by the ascendancy of his genius, like Louis the XIV, who did everything out of vanity, and who always put himself before his people."[136]

He was just a fool. It was common for abolitionists to call slaveholders "robbers and murderers." A recent news headline read, "Generals Behaving Badly". Of course you would never see a slogan that read, "Blacks Behaving Badly" as you did, metaphorically speaking, before the 1960s. Also, during this time the traditional positive qualities of the upper class, such as being smart, worthy and beautiful were moved down to the lower classes. During the mid-nineteenth century, a movement called "The Young Germans" arose, and one of their beliefs was sexual liberation. Wagner belonged to this group. Moreover, by 1900 there started to be more sexual imagery in public.

It is easy to see how the traditional perception of the discrepancy between ideals and behavior, that drove anti-clericalism for centuries, could turn into social body fear and hatred. It just

---

[135] Faramerz Dabhoiwala, *The Origins of Sex: A History of the First Sexual Revolution*, (New York: Oxford University Press, 2012).

[136] Abbe Henri Gregoire, "Opinion…on the Royal Veto." *The French Revolution: A Document Collection*, Laura Mason & Tracey Rizzo, Ed, (Boston & New York: Houghton Mifflin Company, 1999), 77.

needed amplification and legitimation that resulted from displaced evil and political empowerment of the people. Now the traditional authorities are evil and people are good.

By the 1920s and '30s in Hollywood film, sensuality was more accepted than it would have been fifty years earlier. A colleague of Greta Garbo said that Garbo didn't think that sex was evil.[137] Garbo came from the lower class. In the film *Love* (1927) based on the novel *Anna Karenina*, actors John Gilbert and Greta Garbo play a couple in an adulterous affair. The woman proposes that they keep it a secret. The man responds by saying, "We can't go around acting as if our love is scandalous." So their love is righteous. The body is righteous. Off the set, John Gilbert used to brag, even to studio executives, that his mother was a prostitute. Attitudes were definitely changing.

The displacement of evil, via the connection in the mind between self and group, collected the notions and metaphors previously linked to the body, to the lower class, and to nature. It shifted them upwards through Platonic hierarchy to the form-creating faculty of the mind—to the upper class, and their art. Suddenly the traditional forms, instead of being viewed as liberating, were viewed as confining and oppressive. The elements of nature and the body that were formerly low, confining, cluttered, claustrophobic and evil became high and good. Sex and the body became beautiful and the lower class became smart or worthy, as upper-class society had once been viewed.

Conversely, sexual repression became evil and something itself to be repressed, as an outside alien force, as we can see in the male character's comment about his affair in the movie *Love*. This rebellious attitude of course created the extreme sexual liberation of the last 50 years, like streaking, as people rebelled against the very idea of control or repression. This is what we get angry about and want to escape from, as we saw. This impulse defines the energy of screwball comedy. I can remember as a child growing up in Berkeley that the very word *repression* had deep and ominous resonances. Instead of the heroic inspiring self control, as in the past, it now

---

[137] Mark A Vieira, *Irving Thalberg: Boy Wonder to Producer Prince* (Berkeley CA: University of California, 2010).

started to inspire extreme expression, like among primitive people as we saw in the state of nature.

Social controls on behavior and their upper-class and religious proponents came to be seen as claustrophobic pollution, instead of the body and emotion themselves. Virtue became mere dark-age clutter or confinements to be swept away, and escaped. Again, the transference was eased by the connection between felt emotion of the individual and the emotions of the large vocabulary of body images in the unconscious or dreams. So social forms of repression became evil, and the individual became good or beautiful instead of the reverse, which had been the case for centuries.

As divinity once came down from the king to the people, so did all the good or ideal characteristics of the upper class. The lower class became, as we have seen, smart or wise, dominant, and thus worthy to be listened to, as the lower classes used to listen to the upper in earlier centuries. So, not only did perception of evil move upwards, but perception of good moved downwards. In the *Commedia dell'Arte* or Italian street theater of the eighteenth century, aristocrats and professionals were portrayed as fools, while the lower class were portrayed as wise. This is evident in Mozart's opera *Don Giovanni*, which portrays the Don as ruthless and without conscience, while his servant is portrayed as conscientious. This is another example of the upper class portrayed as perverts. One historian said that the Enlightenment had an idealized everyman, and this was in part the basis for the French Revolution. A painting by Edward Manet of a beggar, from about 1870, hangs in the Norton Simon Museum in California. The commentary to the painting says that at that time people believed that the poor had special wisdom. Of course, this is often implied in *Les Miserables*. This helps to explain the hyperbole cited earlier when fast food chains and television advertisements describe average people.

That the upper class is viewed as evil and mindless today is clear in films such as *Titanic*. The upper class is explicitly described as mindless while a lower-class character is portrayed as full of wisdom. This is common in popular culture and film. Over the last thousand years the theocracy of the Middle Ages was replaced by divine-right monarchy, which in turn was replaced by divine-right individualism. With the decline of the church and aristocracy came a rise by the nineteenth century in secular heroes such as Beethoven, Goethe, Liszt, and the industrialists and inventors. The Romantic artists believed in a cult of individual emotional expression and style.

Cambridge historian Tim Blanning, in his recent study *The Romantic Revolution: A History,* shows how with the secularization of society in the eighteenth century, there was a corresponding sacralization of the arts, and a rise in the creative genius, to compensate. To illustrate, he quotes Goethe's impression of an art gallery: "This sanctuary…imparted a unique feeling of solemnity which much resembled the sensation with which one enters a church, as the adornments of so many temples, the objects of so much adoration, seemed to be displayed here only for art's sacred ends."[138] And Grillparezer, in his funeral oration for Beethoven, said of the composer, "The thorns of life had wounded him deeply, and as the cast away clings to the shore, so did he seek refuge in thine arms, O thou glorious sister and peer of the Good and the True, thou balm of wounded hearts, heaven-born Art!"[139]

And Liszt claimed that for *all* musicians "Beethoven's work is like the pillar of cloud and fire which guided the Israelites through the desert—a pillar of cloud to guide us by day, as pillar of fire to guide us by night, 'so that we may progress both day and night.'"[140] (If Liszt had only taken his own advice.) So we see again the idea of escape, this time with the guidance of art instead of Jesus. And by the early nineteenth century it started to become common to describe composers as high priests. Haydn described himself in this way. All of this is consistent with the deification of man that we have seen, and will continue to see. Instead of "The Works of God," now it is "The Works of Man." And it is common for institutions to brag that they promote "diversity" as an escape from the "old law."

One important way that we connect with other people is through the mind and its images and concepts of other people. This

---

[138] Tim Blanning, *The Romantic Revolution: A History* (New York: Modern Library, 2011), 31-32.

[139] Ibid, p.33.

[140] Ibid, p.34

is evident in anthropomorphism. We not only move from self to others through the connection, but also from group to self through resonance, as we saw in the discussion of homosexuals in the first chapter and the pressure they feel and often adapt to. If the individual was not to be seen as evil, then the group and its norms was the next best candidate. It is an easy transition. The individual's vision of heterosexuality and its image in the mind, as we saw in dreams, are examples of confining, evil society that must be overthrown for modernism. The curse of modernism is not mere liberalism. Not just the left believes in it. It is something to which even many Republicans are sympathetic. What motivates modernists of every ideology is the vision of triumphant individualism. This is particularly the case among libertarians and objectivists, or the followers of Ayn Rand.

All of the notions of sin today are simply the socialization or externalization of individual sins via the connection in the mind. That this transformation has occurred is clear if we survey the change in the nature of the seven deadly sins or their socialization.

The seven deadly sins were: pride, covetousness, lust, anger, gluttony, envy, and sloth. "Pride" has been turned into or socialized as class elitism and rule, snobbery, as we saw in Hugo, and White supremacy or any other form of group or traditional race based insubordination or uppitiness from whites; though only for whites, but not for other groups.

This insubordination from whites defines the social sin of Prideful racism, and it countered by diversity. Traditionally, people believed that pride was the root of all evil. It is easy to see a certain amount of this in popular culture today. "Racism" is often seen as the source of many maladies today. For instance, there is a popular bumper sticker that reads, "If you want peace, fight for justice." Of course what this means is eradicating whites or at least any sense of their needs and interests.

"Covetousness" and "gluttony" have been turned into, "consumer fetishism" which is intrusive or confining for people. Hence many people today eat to their hearts content because there is no sense of individual responsibility or self control. After all, who can do anything about "consumer fetishism;" it exists "out there" in "society." What should we do, lynch television executives for running commercials on cars, and bacon and eggs? Just give the modernists time and they'll see it, and of course those angry, accusing impulses are common. After all, they're *so* righteous!

"Lust" has turned into "sexism" and "gender" which exists "out there" and is viewed as evil and hence infects and corrupts people with their oppressive confinements. We want to be *out* or escape from "sexism" as we wanted to escape from bestial sex. For instance, when normal sexuality is expressed in certain public contexts, like the work place, it is suddenly transformed by the savvy into "sexual harassment" or a confining, cluttering and claustrophobic imposition: a form of cognitive dissonance, as the body caused cognitive dissonance. "Vanity" has been turned into "media images of beauty" which are oppressive and confining and bears a clear resemblance to "consumer fetishism." "Anger" is often related among the left to pride and creates the image of the sin of war which is always group based and very confining to its victims or for most in the West today. The left are upset today about war, but not crime or individual anger.

My favorite socialized expression of anger is "gun violence." It's the responsibility of Smith and Wesson. Another socialization of anger and pride can be seen in the traditional sin of crime. This is now the fault of "poverty" or some other social inducement. There is a book called *Savage Inequalities*. What insight! The reason the Vikings liked to kill each other was because they had swords.

Envy of course is the sin of social or national expansionism, the Nazis' irredentist impulses being the best, most notorious and high profile example. The sin of Sloth is the lack of social action: "Are you fighting for diversity?"

With this displacement we see why it is easy for people to sing the praises of the impulse to "Just hang out." It is hard to be any freer of confinements then when one is just hanging out. And notice that this is similar to the virtue of "letting it all hang out." If one is just hanging out, then this is the just the first step to letting it *all* hang out. Freedom at last! Escape!

The externalization of evil expresses itself in notions of social space. For instance during the course of the twentieth century, "bad neighborhoods" replaced bad people, "bad schools" replaced bad kids, and "social inequality" replaced body inequality. I recently heard woman mention "bad cities." And this is similar to "gun violence."

The theological virtues—faith, hope and charity, have also been socialized. A motto for Obama's first election campaign was "Hope." It is a great moral imperative on the left for the state and "society" to have these virtues. But the individual is free.

So the popular conception is that society is sinful and is the source of sin. Fighting this is what defines justice and right action, as in "social justice." As we had our bodies thrust upon us in Genesis, and we rebelled by controlling ourselves, now we have our social bodies thrust upon us, and we rebel by controlling "society," the social body. This is what we want to escape from. Of course this contrasts with the traditional, subject centered perspective that created unnatural, though peaceful social order and beauty in art. So the basic issue is that we either want to escape our sinful biological nature, or we want to escape all the social controls that were traditionally in place to suppress it. It is easy to see which one is natural, as we saw with the Vikings. We will return to the power of story later.

One Christian writer stated that "sin is self".[141] There is not much left of human nature outside of the deadly sins. Now most believe that "sin is society." What insight! Those Savage Inequalities! Traditionally, "consciousness" referred to awareness of the evil desires of the body and the importance to keep them in check. During the 1960s, "consciousness" started to refer to awareness of the evils of the social body and the importance of crushing them. And the traditional definition of heresy was treason against God. So you certainly can't support "society" today without creating an uproar like during the Vietnam War.

Those paragons of humility were truly inspirational. And Bach wrote a Cantata called "A Mighty Fortress is our God." Hence treason against the social self, like racism, and staying inside the fort of the unconfined body and diversity are the highest virtues. You certainly can't tell people what to do today. At least not in certain

[141] John R. W. Stott, *Basic Christianity*, p. 77

contexts, like about individual freedom, but you can in other areas like where "social" issues are involved. In this area, people snap to attention or are easily controlled.

In order to compare the old and new manner of control, let's examine an eighteenth century English woman and her effort to reform her ways of sinful prostitution. She became an indentured servant in America, and here is how she describes her new life to her mother: "Your once darling daughter, for whom you thought nothing good enough, is now a slave. Think not I tell you this to grieve you; no, my Mother, rejoice, for it is this that must draw my soul out of the horrible pit; it was not in voluptuous pleasure I was to find my God, it was in adversity. I hope that my fate may be a warning to them to whom the beginning of my life has been a parable. Yet, Oh! For God's sake forgive my crimes, and let your prayers be night and morning offered up to the throne of mercy for me."[142]

First of all, like for Schubert, she gains strength through adversity. And her life is a parable, like Mary Madeleine. So we see, again, how people found salvation through enslaving the flesh to a higher power, both in heaven and on earth. This saves her from "the pit." So we see images of high and low.

Of course we have inverted this today, and now "society" takes us into the pit that we need to escape, and we find our God in pleasure and diversity or, in other words, in ourselves. We want to be slaves to our selves, to our solipsistic passions, or to put ourselves first instead of God or an external standard as it was traditionally defined. This is how we define justice today and the appropriate objects to attack—those that get in the way of the solipsism. Instead of the body, now society or that which limits. Recall **Roger** Bacon's belief that the most difficult thing is to subordinate your will to that of another.

We now see how this basic impulse is clearly a factor in creating the inversion or rebellion. We naturally want to use the self as the standard and this can be seen in any nursery. There was an early Christian group that believed, "The only rule is there's no

[142] Faramerz Dabhoiwala, *The Origins of Sex: A History of the First Sexual Revolution* (New York: Oxford University Press, 2012), p. 270.

rules." This may be the same impulse that is expressed today against the social body. Self against the group instead of self against self, as we saw in the reformed prostitute. Though as the woman fought against herself through God, now whites fight against their social selves through the non-whites or an external group. Through the non-whites, each individual white finds liberation from the social body or the old controls and identity, as the woman finds liberty from her body. In both scenarios, dependent rank is the structuring psychology. Whites are now dependent on non-whites instead of God and the old identities.

This explains the new definitions of love and generosity— as being out group directed instead of being in group directed. I would agree with most today that we took good ideas too far traditionally, but I think it is equally clear that we have gone too far in the opposite direction in the name of righteous, redeeming rebellion. We need moderation and rational understanding, which was the Greek motto.

The old system got us in order relatively fast because they took human problems, like selfishness, and projected them onto a universal battle between angels and devils, which was something we were already very familiar with as pagans. So they intensely socialized morality in such a way to break the ego.

We today need to take a more quantitative approach. It may not be quit as effective, but it will probably have less negative side effects, like turning into its opposite, as it has recently. In antiquity, ethics was largely separate from religion, and they had great and orderly societies. We don't need perfection from people, just excellence, which antiquity shows is attainable without fanaticism.

Art can play a role in that people who are sensitized to aesthetic beauty will respond negatively to moral ugliness. The Greeks had the same term for both evil and ugly. If we start to make the same equation, then this can play a role in our moral reform, as long as it is accompanied with moral instruction in both public and private as it was traditionally. We need to surround ourselves with both moral and aesthetic beauty, like during earlier centuries.

"Tax the Rich!" is a rebellious impulse today. As Christians had the confining evil and suffering of our bodies thrust upon them during the expulsion from the Garden, they now have the confining evil and suffering of society, social conditioning, the upper class, Classical art, and government thrust upon them. This is the source of the abuse excuse common today, an external source, and why in the high school described earlier, administrators assume that kids are good, but teachers are bad. "Society" is bad, not people. There is no longer original sin or equivalent. Again, this transference sprang from the fluid connection between self and others or group.

In an episode of *Friends*, a character says, "Monogamy is too cruel a rule" which of course comes from "society" or "out there" or a confinement "from them." This is simply unjust!

Most modernists of the nineteenth and twentieth century were raised as Christians, so we can see how the traditional notion of Christian freedom morphed into the modernist idea of freedom. For Christians, "freedom" was freedom from the confining or sinful body or evil. We can see how this inspired the aesthetic priorities of Reynolds in viewing nature as confining.

For modernists, freedom is freedom from the oppression or evil of the upper class and the state against the heroic and virtuous lower class. Freedom also became freedom from upper-class art forms that became experienced as confining, cluttering and as thrust upon us. Recall that the classical statues were destroyed during the Middle Ages because they were "possessed by demons."

As an art critic said about the *Salon* of 1824, "The cry for freedom has been heard by the artists." Within a few decades of this, the classical tradition was almost completely dead or "purged" as evil. With a new concept of good and evil came a new definition of freedom, new forces to be fought for and against, to get angry about, just like during the first dark ages. Modernism has simply recast the battle between good and evil. To be unconfined is good while to be confined is evil, as we have seen. This logic generates much politics on both the left and right.

For instance, Social Democrat theorist Leif Lewin said: "State authorities ought so to change society as to make it possible for the many to experience the feeling of freedom." "With the coercive powers of the state," Lewin looked forward to "so altering social conditions that all enjoy equal prospects of experiencing the feeling of freedom and of developing their potentialities."[143] The Republicans have their own formulations of "freedom" but they both borrow a concept, and its strong emotional appeal, from a religious perspective that dominated for a millennia. Again what we see here is simply the difference of opinion in where the evil demon is believed to reside.

Confinement, captivity and claustrophobia, things to be criticized and rebelled against today, are common themes in traditional Christian literature. As theologian John R. W. Stott observed:

> Sin does not only estrange; it enslaves. If it alienates us from God, it also bring us into captivity.... A university professor describes in his autobiography how he was traveling one day on the top of a bus when "without words and (I think) almost without images, a fact about myself was somehow presented to me. I became aware that I was holding something at bay, or shutting something out or, if you like, that I was wearing some stiff clothing, like corsets, or even a suit of armor, as if I were a lobster."[144]

Twice I've heard Christians refer to sin as "chains" and being "imprisoning." This is not a new development, but has a long tradition going back through Christian theology and to the Old Testament. Gary A. Anderson, in his historical study *Sin*, describes how: "Crucial to this discussion is the notion that sin in biblical thought possesses a certain "thingness." Sin is not just a guilty conscience; it presumes, rather, that some "thing" is manufactured on the spot and imposed on the sinner.

In the early strata of the Bible it is either a burden that is lowered upon the shoulders of the guilty or a stain that discolors

---

[143] Leif Lewin, *Planhusallningsdebatten* (Stockholm: Almquist & Wiksell), 1970, p. 77. Lewin quoted in Bo Rothstein, *Just Institutions Matter: The Moral and Political Logic of the Universal Welfare State* (Cambridge: Cambridge University Press, 1998), 48-49.

[144] John R. W. Stott, *Basic Christianity* (London: Inter-Varsity Press, 1971), 75, 128.

one's hands; in the later strata the image of a stain remains, but the image of the burden is replaced by the idea that a dept has been recorded in the heavenly account books."[145] The corollary of this is that the stain of sin has to be cleansed, burden needs to be lifted, and the debt paid.

This kind of dynamic fleshes out many popular tales in history of sin, compensation and redemption. When evil was displaced to the public sphere, suddenly it became a "thing" a "society" that needs to be lifted from our shoulders, a dept to be paid and something to be escaped.

For instance, twice I have heard American slavery described as a "dept" that needs to compensated for, and this logic generates the reparations movement. So instead of individuals feeling the social pressure to not sin, now this has been socialized, and people militantly look outward to purge the evils of society, like the "thingness" of external or "objectifying" racism, sexism and elitism or these alienating "masks."

For instance, Ford's vice president for product development, Richard Parry-Jones, pointed out that "we are trapped in a mono-cultural environment that is dominated by old white males." Similarly, Ford CEO Jacques Nassaser complained to managerial subordinates in 2000 about "not liking the sea of white faces in the audience."[146] And the premier of Canada's first multiracial sit-com was described by a Canadian journalist as a "relief"[147] from the heavy weight of sin. And during the 1970s "healthy tan" was a popular phrase and image. Whites are just lamentable sickness to be escaped. We now have feelings of guilt, disgust and avoidance of oppressive "society," which we want relief from through the non-whites. These impulses and perspectives are very common, especially among the "educated" and define much private and public

---

[145] Gary A. Anderson *Sin: A History* (New Haven & London: Yale University Press, 2009), p. x.

[146] Mark Truby, "Diversity Gives Ford a New Look." *Detroit News*, August 20, 2000, A11. Quoted in Gottfried, p. 35. Paul Edward Gottfried, *Multiculturalism and the Politics of Guilt: Toward a Secular Theocracy* (Columbia & London: University of Missouri Press, 2002).

[147] Brian Gorman, "New Vision TV Sitcom Offers Extremely Diverse Characters," *The Western Star* (Canada), 53, no. 33 (February 8, 2003), p. 3.

policy. We need to purge society because it makes us imperfect or turns us into an object. So society is imperfect, the object, while people are perfect. Society is to be hated, "white people," while "the people" like non-whites, are to be loved as innocent Christ-types who suffer for the objectifying sins of society. We saw this in the operas.

In history, calamities, like plague and the Jews captivity in Babylon were commonly attributed to sins. Similarly today; when something bad happens, people commonly don't think about human flaws, but political, social or historical ones, like "racism." The "thingness" is external, not internal. Put another way, whites feel alienated from themselves in a different, external way than previously when it was more subject centered. So instead of the individual feeling obligated because of his sins or sinful nature, now "society" or the thingness of evil "white people" are obligated. This helps to create the entitlement mentality that plays a large role in politics and academic thought about redemption.

Traditional Christians had impulses to rebel against and control their bodies' enslaving, confining evil. They aspired to the unlimited in God, so they looked up for relief. As Tarnas describes the situation during antiquity: "The mystery religions expressed a similar understanding [to astrology] of the planets' dominion over human life, but perceived in addition a promise of liberation: beyond the last planet, Saturn (the deity of fate, limitation, and death), presided the all-encompassing sphere of a greater Deity whose divine omnipotence could lift human soul out of the bound determinism of mortal existence and into eternal freedom. This highest God ruled all the planetary deities, and could thus suspend the laws of fate and liberate the devout individual from the web of determinism."[148] As one Christian recently put it, "If my vertical relationship is good, then my horizontal ones work themselves out." In the first scene of the opera *Faust*, the titular character says, "I languish alone, powerless to break the bonds that keep me in this world...cursed are human passions! Cursed are the chains that hold me here."

---

[148] Richard Tarnas, *The Passion of the Western Mind: Understanding the Ideas That Have Shaped our World View* (New York: Ballantine Books, 1991), 84.

In similar fashion, but applied to the social realm, during the nineteenth century the lower classes, liberal intellectuals, and avant-garde artists had impulses to rebel against the social control of the evil upper classes and their art and government. The finer elements were now experienced as thrust upon them, confining and enslaving. People started to aspire to the unlimited in themselves. This became the righteous and pure battle for freedom. People were tired of feeling confined and of all the impure clutter. Richard Wagner was opposed to laws, contracts and marriage, and instead believed that free love could unite people.

If everyone is Jesus, then certainly universal love is the obvious conclusion or moral insight. And universal love, as a way of achieving redemption, is a big part of the motivation for popular and political culture today. This results in the stigma against "hate." We now apply it to group based relations and ideas to the point of academic censorship. Whites hating each other are of little significance compared to their attitude to non-whites. This of course is an inversion of the nineteenth century view of love and redemption.

As traditional Christians felt "hemmed in" or enslaved by the fallen body, and wanted elevation and freedom, now modernism felt hemmed in and enslaved by confining social hierarchy and beauty in art, and want elevation, purification, destruction or revolution. During the late nineteenth century, in the Henry James novel *The American*, a character describes the experience of attending a ball in Paris in these terms: "I felt as if I were walking up and down in the armoury, in the Tower of London!"[149] He felt trapped like a lobster. Similarly, Plato described the ethereal soul as trapped in the prison-like body, and this inspired the Christian interpretation of "the fall" from grace and transcendence in Genesis. Instead of the body oppressing the spirit, today we have the "spirit" or social pressure, as it was traditionally defined, oppressing the body.

On an episode of *Friends*, Phoebe, Ms New Age, is dating a geeky scientist. They are alone together in his lab, and at one point he says that he want to kiss her in a really romantic fashion, and then he points to his desk which is covered with papers, and says that he

---

[149] Henry James, *The American* (New York: Signet Classics, 1872/1965), 339.

wants to kiss her right now on the desk, and that he wants to swish all the papers off the desk and through her down and kiss her. She then says, "You're a swisher trapped in the body of a scientist." So instead of the low swisher trapping the higher spirit of the scientist, now the scientists is trapping or lowering the swisher. So instead of mind over body, now it is body over mind.

In *Les Miserables*, a convicted, lower class criminal is described in a trapped state:

> Through the diseased perceptions of an incomplete nature and a smothered intelligence, he vaguely felt that a monstrous *weight* was over him [emphasis added]. In that pallid and sullen shadow which he crawled, wherever he turned his head and endeavored to raise his eyes, he saw, with mingled rage and terror, forming, massing, and mounting up out of view above him with horrid escarpments, a kind of frightful accumulation of *things*, of laws, of prejudices, of men, and of acts, the outlines of which escaped him, the weight of which appalled him, and which was no other than that prodigious pyramid that we call civilization [emphasis added]. Here and there in that shapeless and crawling mass, sometimes near at hand, sometimes afar off, and upon inaccessible heights, he distinguished some group, some detail vividly clear, here the jailer with his staff, here the gendarme [police officer] with his sword, yonder the mitered archbishop; and on high, is a sort of blaze of glory, the emperor crowned and resplendent. It seemed to him that these distant splendors, far from dissipating his night, made it blacker and more deathly. All this, laws, prejudices, acts, men, things, went and came above him, according to the complicated and mysterious movement that God impresses upon civilization marching over him and crushing him with an indescribably tranquil cruelty and inexorable indifference. Souls sunk to the bottom of possible misfortune, and unfortunate men lost in the lowest depths, where they are no longer seen, the rejected of

the laws, feel upon their heads the whole weight of that human society, so formidable to him who is without it, so terrible to him who is beneath it.[150]

So we see that evil is an alien, external weight, and not internal. And someone said during the French Revolution that the people "attempt finally to throw off a yoke that has weighed on them for so many centuries."[151]

And historian Simon Schama, in his *A History of Britain*, quoted a nineteenth century, striking laborer who used the same image to describe his group's perceived predicament. A music historian said that Arnold Schoenberg developed his atonal system of music to "get rid of the underbrush of tonal harmony."[152]

Similarly, a dance historian wrote that the nineteenth century choreographer Marius Petipa "was over seventy two; he had great experience, but was weighed down by cliques and stereotyped methods of production."[153] Dance was purified by subsequent attacks from the modernists. Recall here how everyone feels social pressure or weight because of the connection in the mind.

In the opera *Andrea Chenier* (1895) which takes place in Paris during the Revolution, Maddalena says, "Suffering, dying in a bodice, heavy as armor, a man would not want to wear, or in a corset they promised would not harm her, ridiculous convention!" (act one).

As the body was dangerous, now society is dangerous or harmful. In an episode of *Sex and the City*, Carrie Bradshaw is trying on a wedding dress, and she suddenly sits on the floor, and cries, "I'm suffocating! I'm suffocating!" and in desperation removes the dress.

---

[150] Victor Hugo, Charles E. Wilbour, trans., *Les Miserables* (New York: Modern Library, 1992), 80.

[151] Duc d'Aiguillon, M. "Motion Concerning Individual Privileges and Feudal and Seigneurial Rights," *The French Revolution: A Document Collection.* Ed. Laura Mason & Tracey Rizzo. (Boston & New York: Houghton Mifflin Company, 1999), 74.

[152] Robert Greenberg, *How to Listen to and Understand Great Music*, 3rd Edition, DVD lecture series (Chantilly VA: The Teaching Company, 2006).

[153] Natalia Roslavleva, *Era of the Russian Ballet* (London: Victor Gollancz, 1966), 134.

We have all heard repeatedly from feminists how oppressive marriage is for women and worthy of attack or purification. It is simply confining clutter to be brushed aside or purified. We should all simply love one another. A recent movie is called *No Strings Attached,* and the ad for the film showed a man and women sitting near a bed in night clothes. This title shows that the producers and viewers see themselves as being knowledgeable or savvy about the sin of entrapping marriage, just as people during the nineteenth century viewed themselves as being savvy about the trap of sin.

As this savvy insight about subversive sex is common today, the similar insight about deplorable racism, sexism and elitism is just obvious and the savvy never tire of showing and sharing their subversive wisdom. This is a particular point of pride with "professors."

Not only does this insight drive entire careers in "academia" but even entire departments. In fact we can go further and say that about 80% of the liberal arts are devoted to the ritual demonstration of their wisdom and savvy insights about "society" and bowing and scraping before the Victim. Notice that there a competition to determine who can be the most subversive, and so earn the right to be the savviest. These are the people who win the big awards and grants.

What to do about the looming evil? We should all simply love one another, as Wagner and the hippies think. What could be savvier, simpler and even simple minded. As one Christian recently said, "Teach me to love the unlovable." There is purity and redemption in love, though it does not require much thinking, just blind obedience to the new tyranny. This is viewed as savvy today. In another episode, Bradshaw put it succinctly: "marriage plus baby equals death."

The savvy insights today! As sin equaled entrapment and death, so now does marriage and class, society, social pressure, or confinement. The problem today is not seen as pressure from base nature and the body, but social pressure felt in the mind. Or at least we now experience it as evil instead of as good, as a "relief" from our sinful nature, as a source of instruction as we saw with the reformed prostitute.

One way that dominant male chimpanzees express their rank is by jumping, leapfrog fashion, over lower ranking apes.[154] Dominant apes often express their rank by being literally higher than the others. Such strategy or confining oppression is evident in human behavior. Royalty are sometimes referred to as "Highness" and they "ascend" to the throne. And school boys like to play King of the Hill. In the ancient Greek religion, the gods hold court on the top of mount Olympus, and the ancient Celts worshiped mountains. This perspective can be seen in today's political culture.

In an episode of *Friends*, Phoebe, Ms New Age, contests the idea of evolution. Another character compares the certainty of evolution with gravity, and Phoebe responds by saying, "I feel less pulled than pushed" and then she bent her body at the hip. As the dominant chimp presses down to show his dominance, now science and the upper classes are seen as pressing down or oppressing as we saw with Hugo and his pyramid of civilization or group pressure instead of seeing it as liberating, as we did traditionally. People need to criticize this confinement, throw it off and be purified to be liberated, real, whole and unlimited. To legally enforce limiting heterosexuality as in the nineteenth century would be a confining and oppressive sin. We want to ascend to heaven today to be with the other righteous gods.

This perspective is reflected in a recent set design for a production of the ballet *Swan Lake*. In the first act set, a large wall represents the oppression that prince Siegfried feels; "he's trapped," according to designer Jonathan Fensom. Similarly, after looking at a piece of ornate eighteenth century French furniture, a woman commented that it "makes me feel claustrophobic" or confined. And an art historian said that a similar piece of furniture suffered from "suffocating luxury", and another piece he described as "vulgar,"[155] as nature was vulgar for Winckelmann, as quoted earlier. And this is how an art historian describes the art collections of Florence: "'Stendhal syndrome'...is the sense of unease, oppression, and

---

[154] Frans De Waal, *Chimpanzee Politics*, 25th Anniversary Edition (Baltimore: Johns Hopkins University, 2007).

[155] Richard Bretell, *Museum Masterpieces: The Metropolitan Museum of Art*, DVD lecture series (Chantilly VA: The Teaching Company, 2007).

anxiety that attacks visitors to Florence, exposed to such a glut of beauty…"[156] I once was in a gallery of French eighteenth century art, and praised it to a young woman, and she simply said, with a disgusted look on her face, "It's so ornate." As the body was evil, disgusting and viewed as oppressive, so now is limiting society. During the eighteenth century, people believed that the body was disgusting but ornate galleries were beautiful, while today the body is beautiful but ornate galleries are disgusting. Recall that during the middle-ages the Classical statues were destroyed because they were "possessed by demons."

A music journalist recently attended a concert in an ornate European parlor, and this is how he described the experience: "A chamber concert in the exquisite mirrored salon…could be a daunting affair for a sensitive musician. Row upon row of gilded stag heads stare down accusingly from the painted walls, trophies bagged by the castle's one-time owner, Augustus the Strong, Elector of Saxony.

But the sublime strains of a Beethoven string trio played in this intimate acoustic instantly banishes thoughts of the barbarous acts that took place centuries ago."[157] Something tells me that if he saw some animal heads in the local pub, he wouldn't have given it a second thought. The accusing, evil oppression of beauty! Ornament, as a product of imposing society, is viewed as needing to be purified or purged, is sinful, and thus it is viewed as a confining "crime" according to architect Adolph Loos.

Again we see displacement. It is pollution and clutter to be purged, as the lower aspects of the body used to be viewed as pollution to be purged. And recall here that abolitionists referred to slaveholders as "robbers and murderers."

Mission furniture is box-like and very popular with humility loving leftists in the San Francisco area. I once was in a store that sold it, and I heard the salesman pitch it to someone by pointing to a chair and saying that it had "clean lines." Pierre Boulez, a modern

---

[156] Alexandra Bonfante-Warren, *The Pitti Palace Collections* (Westport, CT: Beaux Arts Editions, 2006), 11.

[157] "Musical Journeys: Moritzberg Festival." Staff Writer. *Gramophone* Awards Issue, 2012. Volume 90, no. 1089, p. 131.

composer, said that, after listening to Beethoven, he "cleans out" his ears by listening to Stravinsky. The iconoclastic impulse is indeed driving the culture, and not just in art, but pretty much strait across the board in all areas of our social lives. This is why we have purged or cleaned up class, gender and race.

It is common knowledge around the universities today that it is a great sin to succumb to beautiful society, and not live for the low. A medieval saint, who worked in a leper colony, once drank a bowl of pus to demonstrate humility. One can see this impulse at work in today's social and political culture. One certainly doesn't want to be uptight about the distinction between nature and culture. It is a great moral imperative today to be relaxed in our bodies and to feel one with the world.

The film *Guess Who's Coming to Dinner* (1967) is about the reaction of a pair of Black parents, and a pair of White parents to the proposed marriage of a Black man and a White woman. The White father objects to the marriage, and a priest tries to discourage this reaction by saying, "You're not going to make heavy weather of this?" The Black father also opposes the marriage, and his son attacks him by calling him and his beliefs "dead weight." Traditional views on "race" and miscegenation have become oppressive and confining weight or pollution.

It offers no vision of the unlimited. Since traditional notions of "race" resulted from attitudes and laws promoted and instituted by Westerners, so Western culture is now seen as pressing down. It is pollution, according to the new perspective or new definition of confinement. From modernist perspective, we must purge ourselves of impure, limiting Western Culture. The chains! And people love to hear stories of slave revolts. The victory over evil! Modernists can just imagine themselves ascending to heaven or being led out of Egypt. You certainly can't impose the thingness of racism on people today: they revolt.

Marriage between a white and black is redeeming and so more real or authentic, while marriage between a white man and woman is meretricious. A black man once said that we should pass a law requiring all people to marry someone of a different race. This is a clear demonstration of how enlightened, insightful and real he is, and an exemplar for all humanity. These kinds of moral flourishes were popular during the nineteenth century, and they're popular today.

The feelings of imposition that we see among Christians and modernism result from the input or pressure from sinful or confining "group body" imagery. People feel stimulation or pressure from bodies and body imagery, as we saw in the first chapter, and this is evident in the idea of having our bodies thrust upon us by God in Genesis. Traditionally this stimulation was seen as impure "temptation." That word is largely gone from the culture, but it was powerful before about 1960. Now of course there are the endless temptations from society, like race and gender.

The professor quoted above was keeping something at bay, or felt enslaved or hemmed in like a lobster because he was rebelling against the stimulation of his impure body, the sinful stimulation or temptation coming in from impure body imagery, this, traditional thingness. This would result in stimulation or confining and impure debasement.

Obviously, he got the idea and feelings from Genesis and Plato. We also see this with modernism; Hugo's character felt enslaved or hemmed in by confining, impure civilization because of the pressure of perceived class hierarchy or impure, artificial society that comes in his senses through other bodies and especially the upper class.

We also saw this in the "accusing" animal heads and the disgusting art gallery. As the professor revolted against the sinful feelings of impure stimulation, Hugo's character rebelled against the confining and impure feelings of being at the bottom of the class hierarchy, or of having this thrust upon him resulting in his "smothered intelligence." He wants to escape. His crushing debasement clearly resulted from society and not his own nature.

Today, not just the lower classes, but almost everyone, on both the left and right, rebel against confining, cluttering and impure society. Only the most conservative support confining nationalism. As the professor felt "oppressed" and enslaved by the impure, and desired to keep something out, so does Hugo and so do most people today. Whites want to keep themselves *out*, as we saw from the Ford administrators. It is a great moral imperative for whites to be out of character.

I believe that it will be helpful for understanding the psychology of oppressive evil and power to stop and examine a recent scientific study on the psychology of the dragon. In his excellent book *An Instinct for Dragons*, anthropologist David E. Jones presents his discovery that humans are hardwired to conceive of dragons, and the evidence is very strong. First of all, almost all groups of people, including Eskimos have a notion of a dragon. In addition, dragons often play a large and important role in culture and religion, and often in similar ways around the world and across the ages.

Jones first discovered that the dragon is a composite image—reptile, raptor and cat—of the predators that often prayed on Primates and humans over millions of years. He presents evidence that many primates and humans show innate fear of snakes even in infancy, at eleven months,[158] before there is any significant exposure. Jones describes how "The dragon is a composite of shapes, smells, and images that trigger defensive behavior, fear, or *avoidance* in primates [emphasis added]. The various signals—like the diving shrill and shriek of the raptor attack and the vision of two sets of separated toes with talons attached—would select for those ancient primates that could perceive the true nature of these signals quickly."[159]

So what is clear from the evolutionary context is that humans have an innate sense of claustrophobia when it comes to threatening situations. People are even easily threatened by being stared at, let alone seeing a snake or predatory cat coming at them. We are strongly prone to feel *bared down* upon, as we have seen repeatedly, from a perceived evil. Recall the music journalist describing the ornate concert hall, and his frightened response to the animal heads, and how they stared down "accusingly," and that evil white people are now a burden to be lifted. We shall return

---

[158] David Buss, *Evolutionary Psychology: The New Science of the Mind* (New York: Allyn & Bacon, 2012).

[159] David E Jones, *An Instinct for Dragons*. (New York & London: Routledge, 2002), 94.

to the dragon when we examine the film *Alien*, which is about a modern day dragon, the dragon of evil society that is out to get us and is always barring down, like gender and race. This is what we want to escape from today as we saw in *Guess Who's Coming to Dinner*. We want our wills to be unlimited, and not bared down upon, as Roger Bacon pointed out.

To return to political psychology, perception and differentiation between self and group or body imagery are essential steps. Bodies and class markers, like clothing, stimulate everyone. The fundamental factor is, "Do we have feelings of acceptance or rebellion against the confining and the 'impure'?" Before the eighteenth century most people accepted hierarchy, but then they started to have feelings of rebellion, as modern homosexuals rebel against the confining and impure norms of their official body imagery, instead of fitting in as they do in most parts of the world and in most of history.

As homosexuals once fit in, people once fit into their place in the great chain of being. Today of course we have strong feelings of rebellion, and this is frequently romanticized in the educational system and media. We want to be out of character.

One female college administrator said, "Chaos is good" as a strategy to attack a norm, like race. And recall female sexuality here and that it always wants to work its way into the public and be instantiated in popular culture and politics. As we shall see this impulse towards chaos is so powerful for both men and women that it has developed an aesthetic expression. Victor Hugo describes the importance of the irregular:

> Until now all that [police officer Javert] had above him had been in his sight a smooth, simple, limpid surface; nothing there unknown, nothing obscure; nothing which was not definite, co-ordinated, concatenated, precise, exact, circumscribed, limited, shut in, all foreseen; authority was a plane; no fall in it, no dizziness before it. Javert had never seen the unknown except below. The irregular, the unexpected, the disorderly opening of chaos, the possible slipping into an abyss; that belonged to inferior regions, to the rebellious,

the wicked, the miserable. Now Javert was thrown over backward, and he was abruptly startled by this monstrous apparition; a gulf on high.[160]

Like the dragon and the accusing animal heads, Hugo's "gulf on high" is a "monstrous apparition." This is very strong imagery from both writers. What we see is that instead of finding salvation in the escape from nature and into civilization, now we want to escape civilization into nature.

In addition, both of the terms, the *irregular* and the *unexpected*, figure large in our assessment of modernism. We hear them regularly from the mouths of modernists themselves as this aesthetic is an idiomatic strategy of resistance. If you don't like an imposed definition of order, than something like the irregular would be most beautiful. One psychologist said that fantasies can be more powerful than reality. The terms of our social relations are largely determined by psychology and philosophy.

As traditional Christians had feelings or fantasies of rebellion against the enslaving stimulation from confining and impure body imagery, temptation, and sought the regularities of Godly virtue, now people have fantasies of rebelling with Godly, perfect irregularities against impure social hierarchy, the norm or society. There is nothing worse today then being a dupe of society, of class, gender etc., as there once was nothing worse than being a dupe of the body or the devil.

Both resulted in impure false consciousness and moral collapse. As the ideal once was to rise above or transcend the impure body by adhering to the group, now the ideal is to break or rise above impure society, the impurities of confining class, gender and "race" through the assertion of subversive irregularities. One woman said, "I became a lesbian for political reasons."

And another woman went out of her way to say to me, "My last boyfriend was Jamaican." These righteous, savvy impulses are the norm today in the left leaning parts of the country. And recall the sense of righteousness surrounding the "rebellion" of interracial marriage. This is what is perceived to represent moral

---

[160] Victor Hugo, Charles E. Wilbour, trans., *Les Miserables* (New York: Modern Library, 1992), 1144.

insight or justice among the savvy as it promotes diversity and the destruction of evil white people. This impulse gives the savvy their aloof righteousness and the desire to attack the advocates of impure society. A woman threw a cup of water in the face of biologist Edward O. Wilson during a lecture because in his books he reveals bio-determinism.

A Columbia professor proposed that all research into human variation should be outlawed. The aloof and disdainful attitude today is "You're not going to tempt me with confining notions of class, gender or race," as Christians were not to be tempted by the sinful body. As Western culture was once above the body, now modernists are above the social body. As Westerners once made jokes and laughed at the body, now they make jokes and are dismissive of society.

A Steven Sondheim song, *The Ladies Who Lunch*, on Barbra Streisand's CD *Broadway* is a parody of femininity and women's traditional role: "Here's to the girls who play wife, aren't they too much! Keeping house but clutching a copy of '*Life*." They're in character! How disgusting and ridiculous. So we see the image that, for the savvy, the social body is fake, a mask that women wear, as we saw with Billy Joel, and an encroachment, like an oppressive predator, which is how we used to experience our overbearing bodies. Recall that someone thought that Wagner is "pompous and overblown." Only a dark-age religion such as modernism could inspire such dark-age attitudes and behavior as attacking science and beauty.

This explains the popularity of relativism and particularism among the savvy young. It is a strategy to suppress the evil social body—pressure from the stratified group, parents and the mind. That an individual's nature comes from out there makes perfect sense given the connection that exists in the mind; but also because the confining and stratified group is evil or alien, it also makes sense to attack and suppress it as something outside, a thingness, as we once did the body. As the body was contagious, now the social body is.

"Everything is relative" for the savvy, and if not, then you are damned. You certainly don't want to succumb to the temptations of the social body. It is true that human behavior can be changed, but not human nature nor its hierarchical aspect and dynamics of body imagery. We have more limited options than is generally believed.

The new use of the word "vulgar" as we saw above in the discussion of art is an example of the displacement of our traditional ideas about the body and nature onto confining, imposing, excessive and impure high art. Similarly, regarding French Neoclassicism, Bordes notes:

> During the Consulate and Empire, the number of publications reproducing vases attests to a novel *vulgarization* of antiquarian knowledge and a new appreciation for the naiveté of these models [emphasis added].[161]

As it was once naïve and vulgar to fall for the body, now it is said by the savvy to be naïve and vulgar to fall for society. Similarly, Regis Michel notes: "Here Greece is just an empty form. A pure formalism—or rather: a fetishism."[162]

As the body was once illusion or empty form, so now is classicism. The savvy believe that the social body is mere imposition, vulgar, impure, and fetishistic, as the savvy understood that the body was once impure and fetishistic. The social body is seen today as the confining and disgusting condition of injustice to be criticized, overthrown or purified. "All art forms are equal!" is a common piece of wisdom today from the savvy as part of a strategy to suppress the social body.

Again, we see the resulting transference of metaphors from the body and nature to the government, upper-class norms, and the Classical tradition. During the 1920s, the avant-garde referred to the nineteenth century as "The bad nineteenth century," or unjust. Clothing fashion by this time started to show the natural contours of the body as people threw off the offensive, enslaving, polluting, and impure oppression of finely patterned and formed clothing styles.

---

[161] Philippe Bordes, *Jacques-Louis David: Empire to Exile* (New Haven: Yale University, 2005).

[162] Regis Michel, *Le beau ideal ou l'art du concept* (Paris, 1989), 127 translated in Bordes (2005), 275.

The inversion of Platonism appears in other areas of life. Arthur Lovejoy was a philosophy professor at Johns Hopkins University for about 20 years, and he is the founder of the discipline of intellectual history.

In *The Great Chain of Being*, he describes how by the early nineteenth century, developments in science and theology were motivated by an inversion of Platonism. Harvard published this book in 1936. It has been in print ever since and is considered a classic.

Jeffery Russell, a history professor at the University of California, reported that during the middle ages it was common in morality plays to portray heaven and hell as inversions of each other. So as heaven represented eternal bliss, hell represented eternal pain. As a blessing from God was a good, so a curse from Satan was a blight, and so on.[163]

So there was a tight unity in people's thought about the two realms. So all we had to do was something like shift political power and righteousness, in the context of Platonist psychology, and good and evil and their respective realms instantly switched places in people's minds. Now for the savvy, the defacto hell of nature, and our appetites, are conceived is a good, paradise, as popular culture and films like *Dances With Wolves* clearly illustrate.

And culture and civilization are often experienced as meretricious, if not down right evil as is the popular opinion in academia and is shown in many films like *Terminator*. Because of a desire for security or salvation, people naturally move in the direction of power. This is an example of dependant rank, which is common in animal behavior.

During the nineteenth century, the triumph of good over evil resulted in redemption. The battle today is transformed by modernism. People achieve redemption by attacking the evil or impure white race, the upper classes and the Classical tradition. Several times I have read leftist leaders, including a white, say that the world won't be made right until the white race is exterminated. Adolf Loos, an early modernist architect, sought redemption from

---

[163] Jeffrey Russell, *Lucifer: The Devil in the Middle Ages* (Ithaca & London: Cornell University Press, 1984).

historical styles.[164] Seeking redemption through art was a common idea during the nineteenth century, and was adhered to by Chopin and Wagner. We saw this idea with the sacralization of art.

Academic departments today brook no contradictions, disrespect, or lack of love from students when it comes to modern art theory or aesthetics. As looking at a Byzantine icon should inspire love from its savvy votaries, looking at modern art should inspire love from its savvy votaries because of its subversive and sacred status. So if you love modern art, then you are redeemed or good—savvy—while if you do not love it, then you are unredeemed, a heretic, or evil.

Recall here how the romantics sacralized art, and this was viewed as savvy, and that art provided an escape, replacing Jesus. Modern art provides an escape from entrapping and stifling beauty. It is streaking in paint. If loving modern art is necessary to graduate, then who would want to commit the crime of loving ornament and real beauty? It would resemble worshiping the devil, the very vision of the regular as we saw in Hugo's description. Society!

The temptations of Beauty! In Act One of the opera *Andrea Chenier* (1895), which takes place during the French Revolution, Gerard says:

> Gilded palace, I loathe you! The image of a *vain* world besotted with *corruption* [emphasis added]! Dainty gallants in silks, bedecked with treasures, dance your dances, and enjoy your minuets. Your graceful gavottes and useless measures! Your fate is sealed, I warn you! Frivolous race, and *vile!* [emphasis added]

It was staring down accusingly at him, so he wants freedom from the evil vanity and pollution. His moral perspective on beauty and its proponents is that of most of the savvy: It is nothing but frivolous or impure clutter to be swept away. As the body was perceived to be vain, so now is society, or the upper class and their meretricious lives and homes.

Recall the French revolutionary who accused Louis the 14th of being vain, and that Wagner's music is "pompous and

---

[164] Carl E. Schorske, *Fin-De-Siecle Vienna: Politics and Culture* (New York: Vintage Books, 1981).

overblown." Modern art is seen and experienced as "saving" us from all of this—is ritual subversion, and so is nothing more than a vision of salvation, like medieval art. An orthodox priest said that Byzantine icons are deified flesh; similarly, modern art is deified flesh. We are ritually being saved from the social body, like with streaking, not the body which of course is now seen as the source of salvation. Simon Schama says in his *A History of Britain,* that Gothic architecture is particularistic.

This helps to explain its increasing popularity since the nineteenth century. This has been the fundamental trend in art since the early eighteenth century. The rococo painting of Watteau is sensuous, colorful and with loose brush strokes, all in the service of rejecting the high seriousness, grandeur and polish of the academic art of the seventeenth century.

This perspective helps to explain trends in understanding traditional classical music. For instance, Alexander Barantschik, concert master of the San Francisco Symphony, said that "Music is smell." It is hard to find an image lower and more purged of "society" than this. These kinds of cultural references have to be included today for of fear of succumbing to the social body. And recall the earlier quote from the author of a book on Beethoven who observed that we need to look in garbage cans to understand Beethoven. This was put at the beginning of his book as a kind of disclaimer. He wanted to make it clear that he was a virtues man and not an advocate of the social body. It was common in the early modern period to begin books with the reassuring fact that it had been approved by the church. So as we used to look to the church, or an elite, for validation, now we look in garbage cans or take a good sniff, and this is viewed as savvy.

So we see modern art simply results from the application of the idea of political freedom to culture. Similarly, Socrates often makes mistakes with his argument from analogy: in other words, a pattern of logic or argument that applies to one area of life may not work in another because of their different natures. We need to be very careful what we call evil, and of blanket perceptions.

One modern art critic sensed the connection between modern art, or at least Picasso and religion:

Picasso's great painting [*Demoiselles d'Avignon*] is a kind of vital revolt against a Classical tradition of which Ingres was the leading symbol and which fascinated Picasso: a tradition he had at once to smash to pieces and reinvent. This is what his *Demoiselles* do, chopping up the old classicism with an axe and parading over the ruins in all their barbarous sexual power. Picasso's painting—a brothel scene—shattered the canon at the heart of Classical since ancient times and "savagely" desacralizes the human figure. Yet at the same time, in drenching that figure in the vitality of non-European traditions—as if in the blood of some pagan sacrifice— he gives it a new sacred dimension. No question: it was at the cost of this destruction that Picasso was regularly able to revive the great Mediterranean tradition and provide humanity with radiant myths.[165]

We saw earlier how important sexual liberation and the redemption of the body were for the formation of modernist ethics. Now we see again, how those ethics are expressed aesthetically. His irregular style allows for complete individual and unlimited expression or freedom, freedom from the predator, both his own and that of the figures.

Recall that in the state of nature men swagger, and have loose and relaxed body language or are not "uptight" like a work of art or Audrey Hepburn. Although Picasso does not use explicit religious images, it was still clear to the writer that Picasso was working within a mythic context for the creation of his "sacred" modern art which smashes to destroy, redeem, and be reborn. It is a vision of salvation from a predator.

As it was viewed as righteous to subvert a predator, now it is viewed as righteous to subvert threatening beauty. Instead of the heroic being employed for self-control, and for maintaining art that inspired self-control, the heroic is now used to attack the norm of self-control. We now look to the "perfection" of irregular tribal and modern art instead of the picture perfect art of the classical style.

---

[165] Manuel Jover, *Ingres* (Paris: Terrail/Edigroup, 2005), 247.

In response to the feelings of infringement from classicism, the savvy have developed several ways of redeeming and purifying rebellion. They consist of expressing and romanticizing the emotions, and doing anything stylistically and ideologically to attack the Classical tradition and elevated social controls in general. As we wanted to purify the body, now the savvy want to purify society of the dirt and pollution of Western beauty. Contrasting modern art with the Rococo painting of Boucher, Hyde and Ledbury observed the place of ethics and purity:

> The persuasive power of the modern (ist) aesthetic—of a *self-critical*, *pure*, anti-theatrical, autonomous, and, above all, "deep" and serious minded painting that operates in a realm far remote from that of decoration, or even representation, and must exist in a certain antagonism with patronage—may be too great for Boucher's painting to withstand [emphasis added].[166]

Notice the first things the authors reported were "self-critical" and "purity." We certainly have high moral standards today; anything to avoid the predator of beauty. The drive toward the particularisms of modern art, and not the universalism of the mind, is what now defines *high* and *pure*.

Notice that this is similar to the "clean lines" of Mission furniture. The classical tradition also resulted from self-criticality and purity, but because the political and moral context were different, inverted, so the aesthetic is inverted: controlled instead of out of control.

And recall that Billy Joel wanted to purify us of the vice of religious restrictions and fake society. One Marxist during the 1920s was explicit:

> "In the name of our To-morrow we will burn Rafael, destroy museums, crush the flowers of art. Maidens in the radiant kingdom of the Future will be more beautiful than Venus de Milo.[167]

---

[166] Melissa Hyde and Mark Ledbury, *Rethinking Boucher* (Los Angeles: Getty, 2006), 2.

[167] Lothrop Stoddard, *The Revolt Against Civilization* (New York: Charles Scribner's Sons, 1923), 202.

No predators will every get the better of him. A few years ago French conductor and composer Pierre Boulez wrote that the opera houses should be burned down or purified. People once burned witches to purify or save them, and we saw this in the tirade against the "vile" beauty of the gilded palace.

The objective of one savvy modern artist is to provoke moral outrage.[168] This is what is perceived to be insightful, high-minded and savvy. So we see the redemptive value of the irregular or particular. As we saw in chapter one, moderation or control is the basis of classicism, with a balance between the body and control or form. For modernism, it is extremism and the unlimited that is loved, allowing as it does the heroic body and irregularities to be fully expressed.

Moderation is viewed as boring or an impure imposition as we see with the stigma against sexual repression. So in San Francisco there is a restaurant chain called "Extreme Pizza", and in Edmonton, Alberta, there is a restaurant called "Extreme Pita," and a San Francisco bank had as its slogan "Extreme Banking." As God was unlimited, so now are people and they resist impure limitations or confinements.

Who would ever want to be trapped under a predator, or have their will limited? Certainly not the savvy. Nineteenth-century writer E.T.A. Hoffman said that Beethoven's Fifth Symphony was "unlimited."

Today, "no limits" is a popular phrase with advertisers. For instance, a recent billboard carried the phrase, "No Dentures; No limits." Recall here that a social scientist recently said that he objected to bio-determinism because it implied that people were limited.[169]

As we wanted to transcend the predatory body by imposing social and mental control, now we want to transcend the predatory social body, or the old controls, through individual extremism and

---

[168] Ulrick Muller and Peter Wapnewski, *Wagner Handbook* (Cambridge MA: Harvard University, 1992).

[169] Carl N. Degler, *In Search of Human Nature: The Decline and Revival of Darwinism in American Social Thought* (New York: Oxford University Press, 1991).

the unlimited. And people band together to promote these values. At root, the mania over freedom and the unlimited is inspired by the desire to not be under a predator and to have free, empowered wills. Conflict is nothing new; all that varies is where we place the evil demon. Outside or inside.

And recall here Roger Bacon's observation that the most difficult thing to do is subordinate your will to that of another. It is obviously much easier to see evil in the other than in yourself. Classicists emphasize natural limits on behavior and intelligence, and the need for social control on native inclinations to evil, hostility, or crime. The savvy, in contrast, experience limits as claustrophobic imposition from the group.

So they rebel against anything limiting, such as conceptions of class, sex, "race" and native intelligence that press down on people, pollute with impurities and thus should be attacked with irregularities. "Be Yourself!" people yell today. Hugo goes so far as to say that limitations create criminal impulses. At a leftist demonstration a person had a sign that read, "**Everything for Everyone!**"

No limits there. If you tell people to figure things out on their own, this is the kind of wisdom you get. These people elect our representatives. Of course the social scientists, and the rest of the liberal arts, are no better, and they also reject bio-determinism.

The only way we can correct the situation is to assimilate the liberal arts to evolutionary psychology and create a real, authentic scientific elite as we have done in our study and understanding of nature. Most of the work has already been done and is easy to understand. One doesn't have to understand calculus to understand the evolutionary science of human nature.

This fear of an imposed standard, like those from the nineteenth century, is the source of today's fear of any suggestion of biological determinism. It is equated to the Nazis (the poster boys for imposing evil). Modernist dogma is that human nature's imperfections come from society, not from within.

The social body's impulses toward predatory differentiation and discrimination are evil. Modernists strive to purge the social body, not the physical body, and this is viewed as savvy. A recent study has found that eugenics is popular among professionals in Israel, but out of fashion in Germany.[170]

Gottfried characterizes the new perspective well when he reported about one German thinker: "Assessing recent German assaults on historical, genetic, and anthropological research, Claus Nordbruch concludes that facticity is a matter of little concern for his countryman. Far more crucial to the custodians of political correctness is the maintenance of a contrite mood that serves social reform."[171]

As we had to have a contrite heart in response to our sinful body, now we must be contrite about our sinful social body, work for "reform" and combat "discrimination" or succumbing to the predatory social body, the past.

This is why most horror stories today begin with the phrase, "During the nineteenth century..." We certainly want to be out of character today.

Wieland Wagner is the grandson of Richard Wagner, and was director of the Bayreuth opera festival during the 1950s. He said that his productions were "an adventure in the quest for an unknown goal."[172]

Whatever results would be unexpected or irregular, and this is the rebellious point. This is a vision of subversive salvation. Kevin McKenzie, Artistic Director of American Ballet Theater, said in print:

> In a world where you can preorder entertainment—comedy, romance, adventure—an evening at the ballet takes you someplace that's *unpredictable*. Even if you've seen that particular ballet before, it will be different each time, because of the *human* element. You may be impressed with the dancers' *athleticism* or with the work's theatrical energy, but in any case your

[170] Yael Hashiloni-Dolev, *A Life (Un) Worthy of Living: Reproductive Genetics in Israel and Germany* (Dordrecht, The Netherlands: Springer, 2010).

[171] Paul Edward Gottfried, *Multiculturalism and the Politics of Guilt: Toward a Secular Theocracy* (Columbia & London: University of Missouri Press, 2002), 48.

[172] Fredrick Spotts, *Bayreuth: A History of the Wagner Festival* (New Haven: Yale University, 1994), 228.

assumption will be *challenged.* That's why we go to live performances [emphases added].[173]

Notice that he not once mentioned beauty in order to avoid the predator. The motto of Idaho Dance Theater is "Experience the Unexpected." Anything to undermine the predatory norm. They featured on a dance program a piece called "Body Works." Not to be outdone, the motto of Opera Long Beach is "Expect the Unexpected."

The liner notes to a recent recording of Chopin's piano music has the title, "Lord of misrule: Chopin the rebel" and starts with the following sentence, "The whole of Chopin's piano output might well be published under Roald Dahl's title, *Tales of the Unexpected.*"[174] Similarly, an art magazine is called *Juxtapose.* Matthew Guerrieri started his history of Beethoven's Fifth Symphony with the story of how a Dadaist "artist," Stephan Wolpe, in 1920 took 8 record players and played the Fifth at the same time, but each player played at a different speed.

Commenting on this performance, or "provocation" Wolpe describes how: "One of the early Dada obsessions, or interests, namely the concept of the unforeseeability. That means that every moment events are so freshly invented, so newly born, that it has almost no history in the piece itself but its own actual presence."[175] So there is no narrative barring down on it. We want Beethoven's Fifth to be out of character. Obviously this event has no aesthetic value, but it clearly has some appeal, and as we have seen, it is moral, or is ritual subversion of beauty and greatness.

One of the mottos of the San Francisco Ballet is: "Worlds Collide. Bodies Fly. Hearts Move." This appeal to the low is how the high arts are often pitched today. Professional wrestling, which

---

[173] Kevin McKenzie, "Bringing Magic to Center Stage: The Art of American Ballet Theater," in Nancy Ellison, ed., *Classic Style: The Splendor of American Ballet Theater* (New York: Rizzoli International, 2008), 7.

[174] Roger Nichols, "Lord of misrule: Chopin the rebel," Liner notes for CD entitled, *Chopin,* pianist Simon Trpceski (European Union: EMI Records, 2007), 3.

[175] Matthew Guerrieri, *The First Four Notes: Beethoven's Fifth and the Human Imagination* (New York: Knopf, 2012), 4

is about colliding bodies, and popular culture are the ideal that the high now follow. Promoting these values only hastens the day when the arts will die completely. At this point they are dead as a living tradition or ideal, and only exist for the morally suspect antiquarians who seek them out. During a recent year, only 2% of Americans attended an opera. And this occurs in the context of the fact that 25% of whites have college degrees.

Musicologist Joseph Kerman said that it was a desire for freedom that was driving stylistic change during the nineteenth century.[176] An example of this is that after Richard Wagner heard Brahms perform his retro *Handle Variations*, Wagner said something like, "It is surprising what can be done with the old forms with some talent."

We see the same attitude with the Dada performance of the Beethoven, and this is ubiquitous today. Becker, in his *TheHeavenly City of the Eighteenth Century Philosophers*, makes the point about the enlightenment that they were more interested in destroying than understanding, so it was not a great era of history writing. This destructive impulse is particularly clear with Rousseau. What mattered was that you were pointed in the direction of heaven at the end of history.

So, similarly in art today, it doesn't make any difference what you do, as long as you don't do *that*. So all "art" is ritualized freedom or subversion; like the freedom that comes from dancing around a golden calf or avoiding a predator.

This idea has penetrated pop culture. For instance the motto of a restaurant chain is "No rules, just right." Of course, multi-culturalism is based on no rules, but you then you "get it right." You are then out of character. And about the best thing you can say about an artist today is that they "break barriers." Any idea of objective standards is long gone.

All that matters is subverting the social body, or the very idea of standards. Similarly, a student said that what defines quality in art is a work's ability to be different. In other words, art as streaking or predator avoidance.

---

[176] Joseph Kerman & Gary Tomlinson. *Listen*, Sixth Edition (Boston & New York: Bedford/St. Martin's, 2008).

This is venerable for the savvy. A recent newspaper article, in the "Life" section, on a TV documentary about the body, had a picture of several children wearing White T-shirts, and on each shirt was written in a large font one word such as, "VOMIT," "EAR WAX," "SWEAT," "MUCUS," "PUS," and "TEARS."[177] Modernists see this as purity incarnate. Just the body, and no rules of containment, like among the wild Vikings and their free "performances."

An announcer for a show distributed by Public Radio International read a published poem that included the phrase "beautiful vulgarity." There are two music groups called *The Beatles* and *The Monkeys*.

There is a recent film entitled *The Elegance of the Hedge Hog*. The subtitle to a recent book is *A Conversation with Grass Hoppers*. An artist recently sold a work of art to a museum comprised of a can of his shit, entitled *Artist's Shit*. The best part is that it will eventually explode.

At that point it will be completely out of character. Another artist put a crucifix in a jar of urine, apparently to help create "relevance" for modern viewers or the savvy. This is a transitional device from the old to the new images of predator avoidance or purity and sublimity.

Matthew Guerrieri is the music critic for *The Boston Globe*, and he recently published a book on the history of Beethoven's Fifth Symphony, and the book was published by Knopf. His music blog is named *Soho the Dog*.

There is an internet search device called Dog Pile. So we see that as beauty was a vision of purity, now, for the savvy, vulgarity is a vision of purity and elegance or at least predator avoidance. Similarly, Stoddard noted:

> [Regarding] Tolstoy's instinctive aversion to civilization and love of the primitive, "if a stone lies on top of another in a desert, that is excellent. If the stone has been placed upon the other by the hand of man, that is not so good. But if stones have been placed upon each other and fixed there with mortar or iron, that is evil; that

---

[177] Staff Writer, *Idaho Statesmen*, February 15, 2010, C1.

means construction, whether it be a castle, a barracks, a prison, a customs-house, a hospital, a slaughter-house, a church, a public building, or a school. All that is built is bad, or at least suspect." The first wild impulse which Tolstoy felt when he saw a building, or any complex whole, created by the hand of man, was to simplify, to level, to crush, to destroy, so that no stone might be left upon the other and the place might again become wild and simple and purified from the work of man's hand. Nature is to him the pure and simple; civilization and culture represent complication and impurity. To return to nature means to expel impurity, to simplify what is complex, to destroy culture.[178]

Tolstoy, in *Anna Karenina*, uses an image of entrapment to describe Anna: "At once thoughts of her home, her husband, her son, and the cares of the coming day and those to follow *surrounded her* [emphasis added]."[179] Tolstoy and Anna felt trapped. Certainly rules are to be avoided or escaped as bearing down.

On a Christian radio station a woman described how the Lord loves a young mother who, though she has babies hanging on to her, and though this is "heavy," still makes time for Bible study.

What Tolstoy is expressing in the extreme is the reverse of the Classical view of the relationship between nature and civilization or urban constructs. During antiquity, the city was seen as a haven, or escape, from the barbarism and violence of nature. This is clearly seen in that the Polis or city-state was the preferred mode of life. In the Greek view, the worst condition for a man was to be heartless and stateless.

The wanderings of Odysseus are the best example of this in myth from the period. Aristotle goes so far as to define Man as the "political animal." And Roman myth is very focused on Aeneas and his heroic efforts to found the city of Rome. This is how a sixteenth century Italian historian describes the state of life: "When I consider

---

[178] Lothrop Stoddard, *The Revolt Against Civilization* (New York: Charles Scribner's Sons, 1923), 132.
[179] Leo Tolstoy, *Anna Karenina*, Richard Pevear and Larissa Volokhonsky, trans. (New York: Penguin, 1877/2000), 103.

to how many accidents and dangers of infirmities, chance, and violence the life of man is subject, and in what infinite ways; and how many things must concur in a year so that the harvest will be good, there is nothing that amazes me more than to see a man that is old, a year that is fertile."[180]

In the 72 years between 1276 and 1348, for instance, there were sixteen famines. Before the nineteenth century, most people lived life on the edge, and were duly cautious.

The traditional reactions are based on the need in a state of nature to create and celebrate control or culture; to escape the predator both animal and human, as we saw among the predatory Vikings and Africans. Recall that Plato said that the northern tribes were spirited. The hero who slays the dragon, a common story in many societies, is generally interpreted as representing the victory of culture over nature.[181]

And Homer in the *Odyssey* uses the term *nostos*, which means *returnings* or, in context, escape from danger. We get *nostalgia*, which means to go back in time, but in the context of Greek culture *nostos* meant a spatial return, to return home or a journey to a safe place.

Travel at the time was very dangerous, so they longed to escape danger and get to a safe place. So here we see the old fashioned idea of escape from evil or sin, though more in terms of evil in others than in ones self, but the idea was not entirely separate at the time. We saw similar imagery in the Liszt praise for Beethoven as describing him as providing light and cloud.

This perspective or dichotomy between nature and culture dominated until the eighteenth century, when it started to become inverted. Suddenly cities were seen as corrupting and to be escaped, and nature as pure and innocent and conducive to virtue: a haven. There was an inversion of good and evil.

This is clear in the writings of Rousseau and Jefferson, and came to define Romantic ideology, and now dominates the West.

---

[180] Quoted in Alexandra Bonfante-Warren, *The Pitti Palace Collections* (Westport, CT: Beaux Arts Editions, 2006), 14.

[181] David E. Jones, *An Instinct for Dragons*, (New York & London: Routledge, 2002).

(After Voltaire read Rousseau, he said something like, "I don't think I can support this, after all I have not been down on all fours since I was a baby.") As we have seen, with natural rights came an empowering of the lower orders, and by association in the Platonic psychology the appetites, and so nature more generally. During the seventeenth century, people were awed by the aristocracy and high clergy, but no longer, and instead became more self-centered as they lowered their sights.

People are now awed by themselves. Because of the connection in the mind, the force of evil that was to be fought against was displaced from the body to the public sphere and was, naturally, to be "purged" as we saw with Tolstoy. (A very clear and popular example of this is the film *Ghost in the Machine*, which will be analyzed in chapter 5.) Confining or oppressive evil also went up to the "vile" aristocracy resulting in their gradual, and sometimes rapid, purgation by the savvy. So no longer was nature viewed as barbaric and something to be escaped, but class, and eventually gender and race.

About 1900, a man said that the ideal of modesty for women was "barbaric." No longer the evil body, but the evils of class, gender and race were to be fought against and purged or "domesticated", brought "under control" or legislated against and escaped. People today that strongly support notions of class, gender and race are viewed as evil and a "wild" predator and in need of being broken, reformed or tamed. The scientist James D. Watson was fired from his research position for saying that genetics played a role in low African IQs and income.

Commenting on this, a colleague said "When he's off script, Watson can be a wild man." So blacks aren't wild, but Watson is. So instead of notions of race and class being viewed as a taming and liberating influence on people, which was popular before the twentieth century, it is itself now viewed as deviant by the savvy. We now see by the Enlightenment and the Romantics a redemption of nature and thus of its exuberant, subversive and fun irregularities.

Writing during the eighteenth century, William Robertson described mining as a kind of disease: "For it is observed that if any person once enter this seducing path, it is almost impossible to return; his ideas alter, he seems to be possessed with another spirit; vision of imaginary wealth are continually before his eyes, and he thinks and speaks and dreams of nothing else."[182]

And, similarly, regarding the growing Spanish empire in the New World, Vazquez described it as "Inconvenient, pernicious and noxious."[183] It is easy to see that with the displacement of evil and when social life started to get more complicated by the early modern period people, that parts of it people disliked would be maligned in ways that were familiar with from traditional understanding of the body.

To modernists, the irregularities of nature are the ideal that influences modern art and design. The weight of the irregularities of nature, once viewed as confining and claustrophobic, as we saw in Reynolds, are now viewed as liberating against the limitations of the mind, which once was viewed as facilitating transcendence, liberation, or the unlimited. Aesthetics have been inverted. Norms in the mind and form are now considered claustrophobic, so people enjoy the sublime and staring off into outer space to get closer to heaven to be with the rest of the gods.

Righteous-feeling subversion against form and beauty is the dominant morality and aesthetic today as we saw with Picasso. "Subvert the dominant paradigm!" glares the bumper sticker. As we wanted to subvert the imperfect body and nature, now the social body and this is viewed as savvy. Another expression of this is the anti-intellectualism common today especially among the young and the "educated" like the postmodernists. We saw this in the academic books about the "vice" of moralism, and the praise of non-sense.

In the Classical tradition, nature is imperfect and requires arrangement or perfection by the mind, as we saw with Plato and Reynolds, while in Romanticism and today, nature and its unexpected irregularities are pure, purifying, and perfect. Those rebellious and purifying irregularities are the model for much

---

[182] Quoted in Anthony Pagden, *Lords Of All The World: Ideologies of Empire in Spain, Britain and France, c. 1500-c. 1800.* (New Haven & London: Yale University Press, 1995), 73.
[183] Quoted in Pagden, p. 58.

modern art and the drive toward particularism, diversity and the savvy escape from classicism.

In an episode of *Friends*, uptight and controlling Monica is excited to have a Victorian style dollhouse. In response, Phoebe, Ms New Age, builds her own dollhouse, but it is flimsy, crude, irregular, and colored with bright and strident colors. After savvy Phoebe shows off her new doll house to everyone, who are huddled around it, Monica tries to get attention and support by saying, "Look at my china cabinet!" and her friends give a faint "ya", don't really look at it, and then go back to adoring Phoebe's house. Modernists know who is morally and aesthetically righteous here. They know who represents entrapment and who represents savvy freedom. Monica's uptightness is consistently portrayed as weird and a little scary, while Phoebe's flakiness is portrayed as real and healthy.

It is common in the series for Phoebe to romanticize the irregular, or the subversion of normal narratives of life like marriage and family. This is viewed as savvy, as we saw in the Sondheim song. Many times she describes how her mother committed suicide and her step father was a pimp. She agrees to be a surrogate mother for her brother, and she has triplets. In an early episode she said, "I pulled out four eye lashes; that can't be good." And these kinds of irregular statements are common from her.

They come out of nowhere, just like meteorites from space, dance at the American Ballet Theater or opera at Bayreuth. She doesn't get married until the tenth season, and the marriage ceremony takes place with steal drum music, and on a snowed in street in Manhattan. All of this is highly stereotyped and has redemptive value for the culture, as people during the middle ages achieved redemption by romanticizing the stereotyped or ideal behavior of monks. With monks what is being promoted is the control of the irregular, while with Phoebe it is the expression of the irregular and subverting narratives of normalcy and control. This is viewed as savvy. This explains why you're not normal today unless you're a pervert, or even better, unless you adopt a black baby. Diversity! Predator avoidance! Redemption! Relief!

There is an even more extreme example of this stereotype of redemption. The recent film *Rock of Ages* is about the heavy metal subculture of sex, drugs and rock and roll. The story focuses on a girls coming of age into this brave new world, but an important subplot is the attempt of a conservative Christian group to close down a heavy metal club. The real point of the film is simply to celebrate as savvy the near constant sex and drugs and to portray the Christian group as benighted and hypocritical. So we see inversion. The film could be categorized as "monastic modernism" because of its extreme stereotyping, as we saw with Phoebe. This film exemplifies that expression is good, but repression is evil as we saw among the Vikings. Again we see inversion of the nineteenth century.

So we have simply gone from one extreme to the other, instead of trying to achieve the Greek ideal of moderation, and a rational and quantified understanding of what's good for our health and social life. It is clear that the heroic or extremist Viking in us has yet to die. This heroism is what is perceived to be the savvy insight. We certainly don't want to live deflated and mundane lives, like a scientist. It is predictable that there would be negative side effects from recently emerging from a state of nature. Looking historically and cross socially, fantasy land is the natural condition for people while science is only an invention of the last 500 years and has yet to penetrate many areas of our social lives.

An example of the displacement of evil to the public sphere and even the family, as we saw in *Anna Karenina*, can be found in Roman Polanski's film *Rosemary's Baby* (1968). A young couple—struggling actor husband, submissive housewife—decide to have a baby. In order to guarantee a successful acting career (succumbing to his social body, greed, or staying in character), the husband makes a pact with Satan. The Devil can have intercourse with his wife, impregnate her, and keep the child after it is born.

After making the agreement, the father becomes "absent" as he is preoccupied with his growing career, the evil materialistic carrot that the social body, or this particular character, tempts men to pursue. He has become a "thing" that the wife is alienated from and wants to escape, and the savvy recognize this. The latent message is the leftist belief that men aspire to power because they're evil, not because they want to satisfy desire. Aspiring to power in a middle class or sedate fashion is false consciousness and meretricious. He is not a "*real*" man." The actor's wife feels oppressed by her husband and complains to him. In this family, the White male father is the active agent for the Devil, the social body, and evil emanates from him. "White men are evil," says the feminist. This is the dominant perspective on those who stay in character.

Another agent for the social body is the White male doctor. He is also a friend of the Devil and works with the father to make sure the mother has the proper care to bring the little Devil into the world. The mother could have avoided evil if she had gone to someone beautiful, beyond the reach of the Devil, such as a female doctor or, better still, a midwife and the savvy recognize this evasion of character.

In the film, parents, especially fathers, bring evil into the world. Evil is not innate to the body. If the father had not made his agreement with the Devil, if he had not succumbed to his social body, the child would have been born sin-free and pure of body. But because the family is evil and conditions people into a state of sin, the baby is born possessed by the Devil, with piercing eyes and little claws for hands and feet. The father then gives the baby to the Devil.

The wife has been very resistant up to this point, rebellious against the evil White male husband and doctor, being their victim. She tries to escape her character. But at the end, she, too, succumbs to the temptation of motherhood, to the innate evil of her position, and begins to take the role of nurturer to the baby. She is a victim, subjugated by the claustrophobic "social institution" of motherhood.

As a mother, she offers her services to the Devil to help raise his child. She is the evil social body, the creator of evil. She too has become a thing. The state and family create monsters, and this is the savvy insight. We will see many examples of this in the chapter on film history. As Whites were once prone to paranoid fantasies about the body—such as Dracula, witches, and goblins, all bodies of pure evil—they are now prone to fantasies of evil in the family, the social body of pure evil.

White men are the "head of the family" and in general are the aggressive agents for the social body, so naturally "White men are evil," the embodiment of the polluting social body. His evil is primary, while hers is secondary.

Example of inversion is that during the nineteenth century, sex was stigmatized but the family, a social institution, was romanticized, while today this has been reversed. The family is now often seen as evil; for instance there was a TV show and the advertisement for it said that it was a "send up" of the family. This is common today.

Regarding the pollution of evil, the nineteenth century was less monolithic than we are today; they vacillated between viewing the body as evil, on the one had, and viewing public sphere as evil, on the other. For instance, in the opening scene of Wagner's opera *Das Rheingold*, the dwarf Alberich is in sexual pursuit of the Rhine maidens, and, in disgust they say that he is a "Dirty old devil" and that he should "stop fouling the air with his curses." In the opera *Tosca*, a priest inspired in part by Jesus says:

> [Certain women] compete with the Madonna and have the stench of the devil.

During a recent production of this opera in San Francisco, they cut this line from the super titles.

And Jesus said:

> It is what comes out of a person that makes him unclean. For from the inside, from a person's heart, come the evil ideas which lead him to do immoral things, to rob, kill, commit adultery, be greedy and do all sorts of evil things; deceit, indecency, jealousy, slander, pride and folly—all these evil things come from inside a person, and they *defile* a man.[184] [emphasis added]

These quotations show that during the nineteenth century they were still prone to the old view that the body was the source of impure pollution, and for that matter temptation, and the savvy understood this. This was mostly the case with the middle-classes. Similarly, a film historian describes peoples' reaction during the Depression to the polluting egotism from film stars:

---

[184] Mark, 7:21-23.

during this period, Americans required their stars to be modest, self-effacing and without pretensions...If the public smelled even a whiff of egotism, snobbery or arrogance in a performer's demeanor, he or she was likely to fall quickly out of favor.[185]

This of course, as we have seen, has been transformed or displaced during the last century. Now we are disgusted by Donald Trump and "racists, homophobes, sexists and colonialists" like China in its colonial relation with Tibet.

In an episode of *Friends*, Monica, commenting on the smell of a friend of Phoebe, simply says, "The odor" and with a tone of slight disgust. Phoebe responds with a righteous tone by saying that her friend "Will shower when Tibet is free."

As the body was once seen as the source of confining pollution or impurity, now the savvy see society as confining, impure and the source of pollution. China, for pressing down on Tibet, should be attacked as an impure character. Tibet needs to escape.

Only spontaneous movement from below is righteous and pure, breaking the norm in the mind by the efforts of an individual or revolutionary group, as we saw with Tolstoy and his attacks against civilization. This is the new purity, redemption and savvy escape from the predator.

In a Berkeley café I saw an Asian woman with a sweat shirt that had the word *Tibet* in a large font style typically used by college sports teams. And on the other side of the shirt were Asian alphabetic symbols. This is meant as a savvy statement of wisdom, moral insight and elevation. This subversion is certainly redeeming as it represents escape from the character of the West. It is of great moral urgency that we replace Western civilization and its evil agents as soon as possible.

This is what we need to escape from so we present *Tibet* or the blacks, etc. or *other* people and institutions that represent appropriate ideals of purgation or destruction. As we wanted to assimilate the body to heaven, now the savvy perspective is to

---

[185] Richard Jewell, *The Golden Age of Cinema: Hollywood 1929-1945* (Malden MA: Blackwell, 2007), 271.

assimilate the evil social body, the West, to the redeeming third world, a more natural and diverse place. It is common, when in a discussion on the third world, for whites to refer to themselves with a disgusted and dismissive look on their faces. The social body humility!

Nietzsche once said, "I feel like washing my hands after reading the Bible." We see inversion here with the view that Christianity is polluting instead of purging. The character of the West is just disgusting!

I think the best example of the relationship between purification, salvation and the deification of humans comes from ancient Greece. A recent study describes how "[a priestess] told him he was blessed, happy, a god. He was pure now. 'Vile impulses' and 'loathsome thoughts' had been cleansed from his mind. His soul had been passed through the winnowing sieve, blown by new, by brutal, then tender, gusts of wind."[186]

Like in ancient Greece, we today by purging society become gods or are predator free and ascend to heaven to be with the other gods. In addition, recall here that during the nineteenth century people achieved redemption by the triumph of good over evil.

As we understood history as a story of us coming to terms with our sins, now we understand history as us coming to terms with the sins of our social body. Put another way, education used to be done in the context of us understanding our sinful passions, while now it is done in the context of our original sins of our social body and this is the savvy insight. For instance people are now acutely aware of our original sins of social Pride. This sears our consciousness today.

So people convulse with pain when they hear stories of killing of any of the approved victims, like the blacks and Indians. In contrast we like to hear stories of slave revolts, or Indians killing whites. About 4 times I have seen a bumper sticker that read "Custard committed Siouxicide."

As the weight of our sins took us down to hell, now the weight of the sins of our social bodies take us down to hell. This is

---

[186] Ann Wroe, *Orpheus: The Song of Life* (New York: The Overlook Press, 2012), 193.

certainly a heavy character. The savvy now see that whites are just pollution to be purged. This is not a new development.

In *Les Miserables* Victor Hugo made a remark similar to Tolstoy's but, in addition, made the connection between revolution and the attack against pollution:

> This danger, imminent perhaps in Europe towards the end of the eighteenth century, was cut short by the French Revolution, that immense act of probity. The French Revolution, which is nothing more nor less than the ideal armed with the sword, started to its feet, and by the very movement, closed the door of evil and opened the door of good. It cleared up the question, promulgated truth, drove away *miasma*, purified the century, crowned the people [emphasis added].[187]

As the French Kings wore crowns and were pure, so now do the "the people" and drive away the impurities or confinement of hierarchy. This is certainly the image of the dragon or stinking devil. So again we see the battle between good and evil, and how this defines a new definition of goodness, purity, right action, savvy justice and escape.

This is also reflected in the rise of expressionist art by about 1890, and in the fragmentation of art styles occurring in the 1920s. Expressionist art is irregular and its practitioners and proponents are the first to admit it because of its expressive and assaulting nature.

Making art became an expression of pure, liberating subjectivity, like writing a letter or declaring an ideology such as Dadaism, Futurism, or Surrealism. Picasso was explicit about the political nature of his art. He said, "Painting is not done to decorate apartments; it is an instrument of war against brutality and darkness."[188]

An odd claim, given that he painted deliberate distortion, in a style that drove toward the irregular and particular, like during

[187] Victor Hugo, Charles E. Wilbour, trans, *Les Miserables* (New York: Modern Library, 1992), 864.
[188] Ian Chilvers, *The Oxford Dictionary of Art* (New York: Oxford University, 2004), 541.

the middle ages and their battles against dragons. If we were to go back in time, and ask a Byzantine icon painter why he painted in his style, he would say, "to combat brutality and darkness." It looks like the best things in life don't change.

So again we see the transference of traditional Christian moral ideas of good and evil onto the leftist or populist perspective, with the irregular and the left of course being "good" and in a war against the brutality of society and its characters that forever bares down. We saw this when Louis the XIV was described as vain. Of course that is mild by today's standards, so I'm sure that it is common for professors today to say that he represented "brutality and darkness."

At the beginning of his book on the gardens of Versailles, Prof. Ian Thompson about three times refers to Louis VIX and his aspirations in very negative terms before admitting that Louis imposed an autocracy to stop further civil wars among the nobles.[189] I'm sure that at least one modern painter has considered putting him in the pit of hell, as Dante would have done. This is the savvy conclusion. This is pretty much implied by most modern art with its prevalent ideas of freedom.

As we saw in the first chapter, there is a moderate, even necessary, role for morality in art, but if it dominates in the way that it does today, and did during the dark ages, then it simply destroys art and turns it into pure ideology or a moral lesson. This helps to explain why both medieval and modern painting tends to be flat and particularistic, and that visual interest or beauty is not the point. They are more to be "read" from a moral and intellectual perspective, than enjoyed, as least from a sensuous perspective as it was traditionally defined.

One female artist who read the first edition of this book agreed that old master art has "content," as opposed to the simple catharsis or subversive nothingness or minimalism of most modern art. Though there is enjoyment in redemption and the unlimited, like a roller-coaster ride, or being free from the serpent, and this is evident in Abstract Expressionism.

---

[189] Ian Thompson, *The Sun King's Garden: Louis XIV, Andre Le Notre and the Creation of the Garden's of Versailles* (New York: Bloomsbury, 2006).

This helps to explain the popularity of conceptual art. Most art today is fantasy, like looking at a picture of outer space, and there is no real sensitivity to discernments in the visual world. Of course, this implies a standard but this option has been rejected. During the mid eighteenth century, Jean-Baptiste Chardin was admitted to the French Academy as a still life painter, and one day a colleague whispered to him, "The figure is more difficult." Needless to say, today this kind of subtly is lost on most people. No one wants to consider any of the normal, mundane characters, like the human form. Art is just a vehicle for catharsis, "spiritual" meditation, like with Picasso, and intellectual edification, all within the context of a style of particularism, contrast and subjectivity.

Except for secular catharsis and subjectivity, all of this applies to medieval art. Minimalism in art is just an act of modesty which signifies the wise acknowledgment of the artist and viewer that succumbing to the idea of objective standards, content or character is evil.

Though, regarding catharsis, notice that during the middle ages they liked the crucified Jesus. I suspect that at some level, the catharsis of expressionist art is the catharsis of the suffering individual, who suffers for the sins of the social body, or for the sins of those who recognize that modern art is just rebellious noise. We saw this with Egon Schiele and his self-portrait as St Sebastian which represented his persecuting prison time.

The savvy recognize this. (It is a bit off the subject, but if one applies the theory of history painting contained in the book *French Painting in the Golden Age* by Christopher Allen to modern art and its suffering individual, it works perfectly.)

Thomas Ades is a modern composer, and the title to a recent book on him is *Thomas Ades: Full of Noises*. While this is meant to be tongue in cheek it is clear that at some level modernists are aware what's going on.

In about 1985 a gallery in San Francisco exhibited paintings of standard Christian stories, like the Deposition, but the artist added a pornographic element. So for instance, in this scene, Jesus is being held by two men, and Jesus has an erection, and on the ground with her dress up to her waist is a nun on all fours and smiling. And Jesus has a delirious look on his face, but he is still looking at her.

Several other paintings used the same device. So this is a good example of how modernists associate the use of Christianity with the expression of modern values of expression, in this case, sexuality; this is a good example of being out of character. And we saw this new use with the expression of suffering with Egon Schiele and the other expressionists. And recall that we saw another example of this transitional device when an artist put a Crucifix in a jar of urine.

So we see again both the heroic and Christian traditions used for expression instead of self-control. We see use of Christianity in the image of the singer Madonna. She combines her name with a raunchy sex appeal. It is common for entertainers to change their name, but she used her birth name because it worked well in the current milieu combined with her style and objectives. Her whole life is devoted to being out of character.

Blending like this is common in history. For instance, during the conversion process of the Germans, missionaries created crucifixes with Christ on one side and Thor on the other to help create familiarity, high status and relevance. We see the same device used by Schiele and the artist of the pornographic treatment of the Deposition.

In terms of values, they are inversions of each other, but to create the aura of historical familiarity, status and relevance modern artists use traditional imagery. So instead of promoting repression, now the modified imagery is used as a pivot for expression.

We see that this is an inversion of the Missionaries' device of using Thor/Jesus to promote suppression instead of expression. The Vikings were indeed very expressive as we saw. So we are leaving our nineteenth century character and getting down and dirty.

An important influence on art was technological development around 1900. Telephones, cars, and motorcycles sped up the pace of life. This increased the sense of freedom. For instance, a man who rode one of the first bicycles said, "The freedom is exhilarating." The heady atmosphere that this created helped promote a sense of rebellion against all the old social and moral restrictions that had existed for centuries. Here we see in the form of exhilaration the sensation of escape and freedom. But it is clear that there is a direct line from this to the pornographic Deposition.

Resistance to form is apparent in television advertisements today. Phantasmagoria is common. To get the viewers attention, objects change from one form to another, or they crash against one another. The wild play of imagination is emphasized, rather than the solidity of objects or their form, as they were during the 1950s. A recent *You Tube* video showed babies skating in an acrobatic fashion, and a woman thought it was hilarious. A music video showed people flying in midair with sparks coming from their feet. With powerful graphics programs, these kinds of ideas for design and drama are easy and common.

The emphasis on imagination is common today in popular and academic culture, while form and beauty are largely ignored if not outright stigmatized as encroaching impurities that need to be attacked. An example of the traditional perspective on form can be seen in the discovery of dance as political art. Ivor Guest noted that:

> The glorification of the prince was the raison d'etre of the Renaissance court festivity, of which the French Ballet de Cour became a supreme example.

Regarding dance at the court of Louis the fourteenth, Guest continues that:

> The focal figure, however, remained the king, who moved with superb elegance and, by personifying some allegorical character such as Apollo or the Sun King, conveyed the political message of his absolute authority.[190]

We see a parallel today with the absolute authority of the bestial aspects of the individual expressed in movement.

On an episode of *Friends*, Rachel decides to go running with Phoebe. When they run, Rachel is embarrassed because Phoebe runs with her arms and legs flailing around.

---

[190] Ivor Guest, *The Paris Opera Ballet* (Alton, UK: Dance Books, 2006), 5-6.

Rachel tries to make excuses to not run with Phoebe, but Phoebe eventually figures out that Rachel is embarrassed and reprimands her for being concerned about what other people think instead of being focused on their friendship.

Eventually Rachel is convinced and starts to share and enjoy Phoebe's hysterical running style. As she is running with her arms and legs flailing around, she yells, "Look how free and graceful I am!" Distortion and hysteria are seen as the new grace or movement of the sovereign and unlimited individual, as we saw in the YouTube videos.

It is clear that Rachel has a sense of joy in the release or escape from being normal and limited, and the savvy enjoy this. This is a morality tale about the importance of the triumph of virtue and justice. Eruption of the irregular and unexpected also develops in dance today.

One historian of dance said that it is easier to define what modern dance is not, than what it is. Any disjointed and cathartic distortion of the body is seen as dance today. This is done in the name of self-expression, which is seen as good, righteous, pure and of course, subversive, and this is the point. Can you blame anyone for not wanting to be under the tiger?

It is common to think today that art is simply a matter of convention, but according to one former ballerina, ballet is a science:

> Ballet [was] a system of movement as rigorous and complex as any language. Like Latin or ancient Greek, it had rules, conjugations, declensions. Its laws, moreover, were not arbitrary; they corresponded to the laws of nature. Getting it "right" was not a matter of opinion or taste: ballet was a hard science with demonstrable physical facts. It was also, and just as appealingly, full of emotions and the feeling that came with music and movement. It was blissfully mute, like reading. Above all, perhaps, there was the exhilarating sense of liberation that came when everything worked. If the coordination and musicality, muscular impulse and timing were exactly right, the body would take

over. I could let go. But with dancing, letting go meant everything; mind, body, soul. This is why, I think, so many dancers describe ballet, for all its rules and limits, as an escape from the self. Being free.[191]

So we see here, again, the Classical idea of freedom, escape, and real fulfillment through rules, control or limits; here we give form to our bodies and energy to create something higher and more meaningful than simple catharsis, nonsense or the adrenaline driven thrill of escape.

It is the same difference between a hysterical cry and articulate language. Yes, we can act like animals, as we saw with Rachel, but this simply results in becoming slaves to our passions, and our dehumanization. Ballet, with its geometric control, while popular with audiences, is taboo and derided by modernist critics of ballet, who also state that it dehumanizes the dancers.[192] Presumably they will eventually believe that it dehumanizes the viewers and that it is "barbaric" like Louis XIV.

The differences in style between modern dance and ballet imply different definitions of human nature, regularity, and purity. With ballet, consistent with Plato, humans reach their highest potential by disciplining or literally elevating and purifying the body with the mind. Female dancers sometimes go on point to appear as if they are floating and in flight like angels.

As with Renaissance art, a blending of geometry and movement is beautiful, in the Classical sense. Here we have the triumph of the mind over the vulgar body. With modern dance, what matters is coming up with some floppy, cathartic and painful-looking series of irregular movements that attacks, overthrows, or purifies dehumanizing ballet or the mind. Beauty does not matter; what matters is ideology and embodying the modernist revolt and escape, as we saw with Rachel. Professional wrestlers are now the cultural ideal, instead of angels. To modernists, the triumph of this revolt represents the triumph of justice or of the pure, irregular

---

[191] Jennifer Homans, *Apollo's Angels: A History of Ballet* (New York: Random House, 2010).

[192] Janice Ross, *San Francisco Ballet at Seventy-Five* (San Francisco: Chronicle, 2007).

body over the mind and the savvy understand this. Regarding a performance of early modern dancer Isadora Duncan:

> one witness recalled an entire dance built simply on rising from the floor; it seemed as if the repressed of the world had shed their chains and triumphed over all tyranny.[193]

Hugo, or a hominid being bared down upon, could not have put it better. And recall that it is common for Christians to describe sin as chains. And this is a favorite image for the various race liberation movements. Again we see the idea of escape made into a narrative.

Ballet is Woman
—George Balanchine

Another sign of degeneration is the rise in status of the male dancer. Traditionally they were only on stage to accompany the female dancer, and they were not a normal part of the corps de ballet. Basically men can only really jump, and that is about it. Balanchine, a choreographer, makes this point. They are too muscle bound, while women are capable of great flexibility and grace.

But in the last 50 years, though, we have seen a rise in the status of the male dancer. The reason is obvious in that it is consistent with the "meat" nature of the direction of the culture in general. There are music groups called *Iron Butterfly, Led Zeppelin, Dead Kennedy's, Sidewalk Prophets* and of course, *The Rolling Stones*, and this kind of imagery in advertising and the visual arts are common.

There is a television show called, *Third Rock from the Sun*. Physical heaviness is more popular, instead of the lightness of the angel, so we see the rise in the status of male dancer, as we see that professional wrestling is now the "guiding light" for the whole culture.

A sign that modernists are driven by religious righteousness is that it is common for them to call classicists "evil" while classicists

---

[193] Selma Jeanne Cohen, ed. *Dance as a Theater Art* (Hightstown NJ: Princeton Book Company, 1992), 119.

simply consider modernists misguided, due to modernists' alleged good intentions.

So at this point we see that modern art is not simply a different definition of art, but actually is just anti-art; it does not make any difference what you do, as long as you don't do *that,* and the savvy recognize this. There is a book on modern art called *The Anti-Aesthetic.* I think we should take them at their word. Modern art is nothing but ritual, like medieval art, ritual subversion. As we wanted to subvert the body and predator, now we want to subvert the social body, or beauty.

As the body was the threatening, oppressive evil to be subverted, so now is beauty with the rest of the Western tradition. "Western Civ. Has Got to Go!" as the students like to chant, as if in church. Of course, young people look to the body and to non-Western, or more natural people, as an alternative.

I once heard third world people referred to as "mud people." He meant it as a put down, but it is clear that modernists like the heavy quality. Recall here the female journalist who asked rhetorically, "Why is dark skin so attractive?'"

In Hollywood film during the first half of the twentieth century the romanticizing of realism and emotion became holy writ. A film critic described Eric von Stroheim's film *Greed* (1925):

> If a contest were to be held to determine which has been the filthiest, vilest, most putrid picture in the history of the motion picture business, I am sure that *Greed* would walk away with the honors. In my seven-year career as a reviewer and in my five-year one as an exhibitor, I do not remember ever having seen a picture in which an attempt was made to pass as entertainment dead rats, sewers, filth, rotten meat, persons with frightful looking teeth, characters picking their noses, people holding bones in their hands and eating like street dogs or gorging on other food like pigs, a hero murdering his wife and then shown with hands dripping with blood.[194]

---

[194] Mark A. Vieira, *Irving Thalberg: Boy Wonder to Producer Prince* (Berkeley: University of California, 2010), 47.

What a vision of Tolstoy's irregular purity, just like the picture of the children in the White T-shirts mentioned earlier. Regarding the screening of this film, a film critic described how Stroheim:

> Sitting motionless in a straight chair, cane in hand and staring right ahead, as if boring through the screen, worships realism like an abstract ideal; worships it more, and suffers more in its achievement, than other men do for wealth or fame.[195]

Modernist ideals, bolstered by the old patterns of veneration, were creeping into popular culture. This is how people stood before and venerated medieval icons. And today this is how many venerate modern art which has basically the same low content as *Greed*. Stroheim could just has easily have been watching a film about the Jews crossing the Red Sea. After all, they are both about freedom.

In the film *Daddy Long Legs* (1919) a young girl misbehaves, and an adult excuses her by saying that she is just expressing her individuality. In the film *Anna Karenina* (1935), Greta Garbo's character says, "To not think; only to live and feel." There is a similar film called *Theodora Goes Wild* (1936). And the film *Bringing Up Baby* (1938) comprises two people chasing a leopard for over an hour. The *The Philadelphia Story* (1940) romanticizes drunkenness, as we have seen. The 1957 remake of *The Philadelphia Story* is called *High Society*, and the Bacchic figure here is not a drunk, but a man who loves jazz and is sponsoring a jazz festival.

The film opens with Louis Armstrong playing his trumpet. The high spirits and strength of Blacks as fantasized by modernists function today as a Bacchic ideal. Modernists experience Blacks today as they experience Niagara Falls, as just a delight. Many Hispanics and Blacks have a preoccupation with their bodies and emotions that we also saw among African tribes and the Vikings. (This is what you tend to see on the streets, at least in the United States.) Though, this orientation toward the body was purged from the Western ethical vocabulary during the intervening centuries, until recently, at least.

---

[195] Ibid., 46.

A recent book describes how "In typical romantic fashion Mailer idealized the backward and underdeveloped as spiritually exalted. In particular, African Americans, because they were poor and uneducated, were to be envied for the freedom from stifling middle class repression.

Knowing in the cells of his existence that life was 'war, nothing but war, Mailer wrote, 'the negro (All exceptions admitted) could rarely afford the sophisticated inhibitions of civilization, and so he kept for his survival the art of the primitive, he lived in the enormous present, he subsisted for his Saturday night kicks, relinquishing the pleasure of the mind for the obligatory pleasure of the body." (When in a similar vain, Kerouac wrote in *On the Road*, of 'Wishing to be a Negro...")."[196]

This is right from the horse's or modernists' mouth. Notice that the first thing he mentioned was the romantics. And someone once said that the 1960s was the triumph of the romantics. Notice that like the Dada performance of the Beethoven Symphony and its "presentness" the blacks live in the "enormous present." Neither the Dadaists or blacks want any controlling narratives.

It can be noted that when something like this is just posturing, it is one thing, but when it starts turning into reality, as we saw in the state of nature, that is another. Ideals do tend to have that effect. What comes to mind here is nineteenth century censorship. The pleasures of the mind are more than abstract, as modern technology, low infant mortality, and Renaissance art prove. This is somewhat on a different subject, but some populations, on average, don't have much of an alternative to the body, regardless of aspirations. Twice I've heard whites defend integration by saying that blacks are sexy.

Around 1930, film star Norma Shearer described her general approach to characters:

> I can't do the Garbo or Dietrich thing. I admire them
> both greatly and wish that I could play such characters
> as they interpret, but I have to go through a transition
> to become worldly. I begin by being very nice, and then,

---

[196] Brink Lindsey, *The Age of Abundance: How Prosperity Transformed American Politics and Culture* (New York: HarperBusiness, 2008), 136-137.

about the middle of the picture, I go *haywire* [emphasis added]. That's when things really grow interesting. But if I just stayed sweet and appealing, the roles I played would be very dull.[197]

Notice the aversion to being merely "sweet and appealing." The savvy certainly don't want to be like Audrey Hepburn today. She wouldn't last 5 seconds against a lion. Recall here the transformation of the West's vocabulary of images as moving from ethnocentric to diverse, as part of an escape, as described at the beginning of chapter one. This apparently is relevant today, as we saw with Mailer. In many films from the period, like *The Awful Truth* (1937), women are tempted by rich men, but they ultimately choose men whom they love, the *real* men. So again we have the triumph of emotion over impure society. Filthy lucre!

Though, it is clear today that money is no longer an indicator of moral and social virtue, as it was in the past. I believe that the best indicator for men, and women, is being what was called, "high minded" as in having high moral and aesthetic standards. Though, that will be a harder sell than heroically going haywire, swaggering, drinking pus and poverty.

In recent decades, the trend for expressing the emotions has gone beyond mere energy and high spirits and has started to be regularly vulgar in an extreme way as we saw with *Greed*. In *The Sweetest Thing* (2002) the female lead walks into a men's bathroom that is covered with graffiti, lifts up her dress, backs up to a men's urinal and does her thing. For the savvy, this is the new sweet or pure.

As should be clear, the word *pure* has changed meaning with the displacement of values that we have outlined. What was low has now become high, refined, or sweet. The raw body is now pure, and culture is pollution. In *My Best Friend's Wedding* (1997), a woman's tongue becomes stuck to the penis of an ice statue, and the two lead female characters, compete to make the most noise while snorting. In *There is Something About Mary* (1998), the male lead masturbates in a bathroom and the female lead applies his

---

[197] Mark A. Vieira, *Irving Thalberg: Boy Wonder to Producer Prince* (Berkeley: University of California, 2010), 186.

semen to her hair. These exemplify the modern notion of fun and humor. While redemption is often serious business, it can also be, apparently, very fun, a *Divine Comedy*. Today, of course, instead of going up for purgation and salvation, now we go down.

The inversion of Platonism is the driving force of the plot to the blockbuster film *Titanic* (1997), which takes place on an ocean liner in the year 1912. In overview, Rose is a young woman who is engaged to Cal, a wealthy, overbearing or oppressive man dressed in a tuxedo. She claims to love him, but expresses throughout the film nothing but contempt and fear of him, of his upper-class friends, and of their confining and impure milieu.

In contrast to Cal, fun-loving and down-to-earth Jack is a poorly dressed, penniless artist. He sees Rose in public and falls in love with her. He approaches her, they speak, and she grows to feel the same way. Her growing feelings for him are punctuated with innuendo and declarations that he and his low lifestyle are better than the overly delicate, refined, and polluting lifestyle of her wealthy fiancé. You definitely get the impression that Cal presses down on people for a living. Jack represents pure nature, while Cal represents evil and polluting culture. Control! How meretricious! Cal is definitely in character.

An early scene in the film shows Rose to be a modern woman. She has purchased a Picasso, the painting "Demoiselles d' Avignon," which portrays flat and distorted figures of prostitutes, and comments that "It has truth but no logic." Of course, it is precisely the absence of logic, or being out of character, that is the truth of modernism. Notice that they never let illogic get in the way, especially in politics. (Logic would get in the way of the blind veneration of goodness and purity.) In response, Cal shows his true colors by saying, with an arrogant tone, "Picasso, he'll never amount to a thing!" It is clear that he wants to press down on Picasso, and for that matter Rose, and she senses it. As the body was dumb and short sighted, without consciousness, now Cal is dumb and short sighted.

In a later scene, Rose, in disgust, runs away or escapes from a party of her rich fiancé's friends, and says to herself, as she is running, that she is sick of their "mindless chatter." It is common for the impurities of the regular and confined to create sickness and so should be attacked and purged. The plot makes clear that the upper class, not the lower, is impure and mindless, like a predator. She runs to the end of the ship in an attempt at escape, and is about to commit suicide by jumping off, when Jack sees her and convinces her to not jump.

This is the beginning of their bonding. A little later, she shows him her engagement ring, and it is so large that he says, "That would have taken you right to the bottom." Marriage certainly is "heavy" or oppressive, as we saw in *Sex and the City*; it makes one feel bowed over by something dominant and polluting. It makes you feel bared down upon, and puts you in a limited character.

Cal and his rich friends learn that Jack saved Rose's life and in appreciation invite Jack to an elegant dinner complete with parlor music. After the meal, Jack invites Rose to a real party comprised of lower-class people having a good time getting drunk and dancing to folk music.

For Plato, mind and its capacity for intelligible control were real while the material world and emotion were incoherent flux. For Jack, and now Rose, the lower classes and their jovial entertainment are real, a haven for escape, while the fine manners and art of the upper classes are unreal, fake or impure false consciousness: meretricious.[198] The best thing you can do in this situation is escape, if you can't destroy it.

As part of Rose's new and improved reality, Jack teaches her how to spit. Her first attempt is timid, but he gives her more robust examples of the fine art of spitting, and she improves. As part of her moral reform, Jack tells Rose that "she is trapped by her rich fiancé and lifestyle, and that it is up to her to save herself or else the fire that he loves in her will go out." Notice the word "trapped" as in "confined." She needs to save herself or escape her character. By "fire," he is referring to the wild emotion that animates most young people. Both Jack and Rose would have fit in well with the Vikings.

---

[198] Editor's note: The publishers are friends with one of the musicians in the Irish session scene. According to him, the film's portrayal of earthy folk as more authentic than the elite was precisely director James Cameron's intent, and the crew worked hard to convey that impression.

As part of their escape from the rich people, Rose and Jack go to the bottom of the ship and have sex in a car. After the sex, she says, "When we dock, I'm getting off with you." He responds, "This is crazy." She says, "It doesn't make any sense: that's why I trust it." Notice the similarity here to her to comment about the Picasso [on page 87]. Except that now she has extended it to include the element of trust. Naturally, one would only trust what has greatest reality; in this case escape or salvation from the meretricious world that is full of oppressive characters.

And it is common in the Christian tradition to romanticize ignorance. St. Paul once said that the foolishness of God is better than the wisdom of man. Considering that wise Jack "pushes up" with irregularities he is pure and real, while dumb Cal "pushes down" and so is impure and fake—overbearing. He is one predatory rock cemented on top of another, and he wants to cement you into place, into your place down on the hierarchy.

Modernists see such a confining vision as repulsive or impure, like a hominid under a lion or the Jews trapped by Pharaoh. As the Jews need to escape, so do Jack and Rose. Russell in his history of the Devil in popular culture reported that during the nineteenth century, the devil became a dapper gentlemen, just like Cal.[199] Probably the most well know example of this is the character of Mephistopheles in the opera *Faust*.

It becomes clear to Cal and his rich friends that Rose and Jack are in love. Cal becomes angry and confronts Rose. She becomes even angrier and yells, "I'd rather be his whore than your wife!" then spits in his face. We see clearly the influence of both Toulouse-Lautrec and Picasso during her visit to Paris. This represents the victory of nature over culture, and of salvation over damnation. This can also be seen in Dante's journey in the *Divine Comedy*, but inverted.

At the end of the film, Rose is portrayed as an old woman. Thinking back on the affair, she says, "He saved me in every way a woman could be saved." Again we have the theme of escape from an entrapping character. As traditionally the lower classes looked to

---

[199] Jeffrey Russell, *The Prince of Darkness: Radical Evil and the Power of Good in History* (Ithaca & London: Cornell University Press, 1988).

improve themselves by imitating the upper classes, now the upper classes are saved or purified by the irregularities of the lower. Hugo would agree with this.

Notice the use of the powerful word *saved* as in "Jesus saved me." He saved her from drowning in both the ocean and the abyss of an upper-class marriage, as Moses saved the Jews during the crossing of the Red Sea. We see the triumph of the low by the end of the film to the point that it even appropriates Christian images of salvation and escape to this end.

As people had impulses to ascend the divine hierarchy of culture, and be purified and redeemed, now they have impulses to go down to be purified and redeemed. The ballet *La Corsair* is about a girl who is sold into slavery but is rescued by a pirate who becomes her lover. Notice the theme of salvation from enslavement to a character, as in to the traditional idea of sin or a bad state or living condition. Instead of loving Jesus for her escape and salvation, she now loves a pirate.

As in *Titanic*, the girl is saved by a low character from enslavement to sin or a bad state. Instead of people looking up for salvation, they now look down.

Similarly, in *Giselle*, a "Fantastic Ballet in two Acts" a peasant girl dies because of the "base" nature of a Count, but when he worships at her grave, and his life is threatened, she is resurrected, and she dances to save him. So again the high needs the low for escape and salvation, animating a relation of dependent rank. We saw this in the first chapter where the feeble whites are excited and energized by the big, strong, exciting blacks, and as the Vikings were stimulated and saved by the trees. This is the level of the culture today. We've come a long way baby.

It is clear that the West is approaching cultural stagnation. A cartoon in *New York* magazine had a picture of a man dressed as a cave man and holding a club. Two women in modern dress are standing next to him and one says to the other, "Joe certainly has become more interesting since he read Camille Paglia."

He certainly is a real, stimulating, or beautiful vision just like Viking men. He would make a good modern dancer. He is a prime candidate for attacking impure culture considering that he only has one direction to go in, and that is up against the confining and regular. Recall here the nature of women's rape fantasies. The radio station KFAT realized that their image was too elitist, so they changed their name to KPIG.

Regarding the attacks on high culture, Camille Paglia, a respected humanities professor, said during a recent interview in *Opera News* that general cultural awareness among her students is radically diminished.

And that we are in a "major crisis" of cultural literacy. Any mention that high culture is just that, somehow superior, is met with a skeptical sneer, as most have heard from their "professors" that high culture, as the social body, is oppressive, illegitimate, deceptive and so meretricious. As the body was a trap, so now the social body.

I once asked a woman if she liked classical music, and she responded with the standard formula, "I like all kinds of music," (an example of diversity) but then she said something you don't often hear, "But I don't understand it." Classical music, being more complicated, more mental or higher, does often take more time and effort to understand.

There are psychological depths and dynamics in classical music that are missing from simple, cathartic popular music. But with today's value system or sense of alienation, there is no incentive for the uneducated to improve themselves. After all, who wants to search out their own oppression and be stifled? Wouldn't you rather just boogie and rap at the bottom of *Titanic* like Jack and Rose? This is real, righteous rebellion against the fake social body.

In an episode of *Friends*, Chandler says to Joey, "You even cry after Titanic" and Joey responds, almost in tears, "Those two only had each other!"

As people during the nineteenth century only had Jesus, now the wretched upper class needs the righteous lower class. Upper-class people smile today when they see lower-class people, instead of finding them disgusting, or entrapping, as they did during the nineteenth century. For instance, in the nineteenth century:

> Theatergoers at the upper end of the socioeconomic
> scale became less and less tolerant of what they saw as

the demonstrative and "uncivilized" behavior of the working-class occupants of the gallery seats.[200]

The model so far outlined for modernism and its notion of pollution helps to explain a peculiar early scene in *Titanic*. Jack, a young Italian man, and two Norwegians are playing poker. The Italian and Norwegians have personalities typical of those nations; the Italian has a big, glowing smile, while the Norwegians are tight-lipped and rigid. But one of the Norwegians is inclined to hostility, and at one point becomes so angry that he punches the other Norwegian in the face.

The scene makes no sense relative to the violent crimes rates in Europe during the early twentieth century. At that time, and through the early 1970s, Italy had high homicide rates, while Scandinavia had extremely low rates (though reputation has it that most of the crime in Italy is in the South). It is clear from the data that the more emotionally unrestrained a population, the higher the violent crime rates, while the less emotional populations consistently have lower rates.

To put it another way, the more that a population has a generous perspective on the emotions, the more prone to crime they are, or to emotional outbursts. The more constricted a population is, the lower the crime. The fight scene in Titanic goes against type. In reality, the Italian more likely would have punched the Norwegian.

Nevertheless, the scene fits the pattern of logic that we have seen in modernism. If social controls are evil and polluting, and create problems like hostility, as we saw with Hugo, then it makes sense that the tight-lipped Norwegian would be hostile. The body is innocent and good, and social controls on the body are evil.

Hence, the Norwegian is portrayed as evil, while the Italian is nice and jovial. His body is innocent or untouched.

This logic gives rise to the popular idea that social controls, like punishment, "don't work," as the body traditionally "didn't work." Twice I've heard people say, "Can you ever win a war?" This was said as if it represented insight. Recall here that the fanatical

---

[200] Robert C. Allen, "The Movies in Vaudeville: Historical Context of the Movies as Popular Entertainment," *The American Film Industry*. Tino Balio, ed. (Madison: University of Wisconsin, 1985), 87.

and rigid Nazis are the poster boys for evil. Films and folklore about escape from Nazis are popular, and are experienced as if they are "relevant," as stories of the horrors of the body, like Dante's *Inferno*, were experienced as relevant. As Hell was a chamber of torture and death, Nazi Germany is commonly portrayed as a chamber of torture and death.

As people traditionally liked to hear stories of Jesus' Harrowing of Hell, today people like to hear stories of heroic individuals defying and subverting the evil Nazis, the Harrowing of Hell. Today it is obvious that "Nazi Germany" is what you get if you succumb to the social body, and I've heard this logic of the slippery slope many times. (It should be mentioned here that a history professor recently described how because the German communists were creating havoc by rioting and so on, the electorate believed that they needed to take strong measures, and so voted in the National Socialists.[201])

Marsilio Ficino was a fifteenth century Italian philosopher and theologian who tried to reconcile Platonism and Christianity, and he was patronized by the Medici. He did the first translation of Plato into Latin, and his summaries of the Platonic dialogues were considered so authoritative most scholars did not read the originals, at least until about the seventeenth century. He was very influential; for instance he coined the phrase "Platonic love." His major work of theology is *Platonic Theology*.

To help understand the contrasting symbolism of nature and culture or movement and stasis in *Titanic*, it helps to quote Ficino: "After God, an unmoving unity, it is correct then to place angel next, an unmoving plurality; and then after angel, soul, which is more distant from God still, since it is plurality subject to movement. It is plurality because nothing after God can be absolutely simple unity. And it is in some respect subject to movement because the further it recedes from God, the closer it comes to corporeal qualities which are totally subject to movement."[202] The first thing to notice is its <u>similarity to the</u> contrast between Parmenides' *One* and Heraclites'

---

[201] Kenneth Bartlett, *Development of European Civilization*, Audio-lecture course, (Chantilly, VA: The Teaching Company, 2011).

[202] Marsilio Ficino, *Platonic Theology*: Volume I—Books I-IV. Michael J.B Allen, Trans. (Cambridge, Mass: Harvard University Press, 2001), 221.

flux discussed earlier. For Parmenides, all flux was illusion, as it is in some sense for Ficino or at least "less" or part of the corrupt world. For Ficino, "reality" was with static and unified God, what we all aspired to.

This quote is a Christian interpretation of a hierarchy of the world. This description reflects in part the belief at the time that the heavens were less mobile and corrupt than earth. And, to interpret a bit, as the King sits immobile on his thrown, so does God. The angels are an intermediary level with plurality, but with no motion. And of course soul is lowest, and so subject to movement and decay.

This is a nice way of reconciling Parmenides and Heraclites, and this was a goal for Plato. From Ficino we see the philosophical basis of diversity. All we had to do was redeem the world through empowerment and divinity, and suddenly diversity and movement became a good instead of an evil.

So for Ficino, stasis is good, while movement is bad. And this is a fancy, theological expression of the whole drive toward control of self and nature that has characterized most of Western history. So of course this is an inversion of the scene in *Titanic* where the rigid Norwegian is evil, while the mobile Italian is good, or of course vice versa, the scene in *Titanic* is an inversion of Ficino's scheme. Though there is a clearer example of this dichotomy in another film.

In the *Invasion of the Body Snatchers* (1978) evil aliens invade the Earth, and they take over by transforming human personalities. A person who has been taken over becomes completely emotionless or static, like the Scandinavians. By the end of the film the aliens have taken over most people, and the few remaining normal people have to be careful to not show emotion in public or they will be detected and caught. They commonly are shown trying to escape the evil aliens, as it is popular to hear stories about escape from the rigid and evil Nazis, and Rose from Cal.

So we see again, like in *Titanic*, stasis is pathological, while movement and expressiveness represents goodness. The perceived goodness results from the feeling that it represents power and allows for escape. We saw this logic or value system among the Vikings.

All of this reflects the priorities that grow out of the inversion of Platonist psychology and politics: the dynamic emotions in charge of static reason. We saw this in Tolstoy's perception that civilization, as a product of complicated or imposing reason, is evil, and we also saw this in the belief that cathartic pop culture is good, but high culture is evil. We will see this change in our views to nature many times, but in particular in the film *Dances With Wolves*, which portrays civilization as evil, and the natural Indians as good.

An even more common example of this contrast is that nerds and computer geeks are normally portrayed as inhibited, while *real* men, the kind that women prefer, are normally portrayed as more relaxed, expressive and more causally dressed, like Jack. So we know who's more "real" today, with our inverted and so more natural, culture. Recall female sexuality in the state of nature and that it creates its own ethic or fashions higher level thought if given an opportunity. We should mention that blacks have been killed for "acting white." Ghetto blacks killing middle class blacks does not result from blind ethnocentric rage, but from these individuals aspiring to fulfill the highest ideals of modernism; it should be said here that we see the origins of these aspirations or ideals with the romantics and their celebration of the low and diverse. And a black man once said to me, "white and uptight."

I was too much like the old definition of God, and not enough like the new definition. So the apparent self-centeredness from this black man, is in reality an exalted moral vision, as we saw with Ficino. After all the man thought he was exhibiting moral insight. And the whole point of the revolt of the 1960s was to forward a more natural and diverse culture, and so blacks and women were viewed as key to all of this. Recall here that a recurring theme in this study will be that the mind naturally wants to justify the body, as we saw among the Vikings.

An English woman said about her move from uptight or evil England to more relaxed France, "I'm out of there." Here we see the theme of escape in the context of the move from the controlled or evil to the less controlled or good. So we see that we also naturally want to move or escape from the evil unity of the white race, the former Godlike and static entity, to the goodness of diversity, the new Godlike dynamic entity.

A good example of all of this is the plot to the film *Room With a View* (1985) which is about a turn of the century, young woman who dumps her uptight fiancé because he refuses to play tennis, and instead pursues a more relaxed man. Similarly, I once heard two blacks talking and one said "White people!" and the other said, with a stern tone, "*They're changing.*" This inverted impulse is a large part of popular culture and politics, just as we saw in the state of nature.

A white man said during the 1950s that integration was unnatural. In the preceding discussion of hierarchy and movement we have significantly narrowed the possible definitions of "natural" or the good. I believe in this context it is easier to begin to talk about functional considerations, like crime reduction and censorship, both of the media and in the social sphere. Recall in the discussion of the state of nature I observed that one factor was the kind of men we are exposed to, or the extreme looseness and criminal impulses you tend to see on the streets. This may be less of a factor in Europe but it is conspicuous in much of the United States and South Africa.

Placing our new ethical priorities in historical context it is clear that we are as conformity orientated today as in the past, we just have an expressive ethic instead of ascetic one. In the past people believed that a primary goal of social life was the taming and education into virtue of the young. We still have this sense of civic obligation and virtue, we just have inverted the ethic from ascetic to expressive, and so diversity instead of unity is seen as the appropriate strategy given the nature of much of the rest of human population. Another factor is that the tradition is viewed as evil, so this creates an extra sense of urgency about abandoning it and promoting diversity as an antidote.

So instead, as we did traditionally, of viewing our education as existing in the context of an innately evil body, which had segregationist implications, now we view education in the context of an innately evil social body, which has integrationist implications. Put generally, salvation is now seen to be obtained outside the West and the white race as opposed to inside.

This is why you're not normal or ideal today unless you're perverted, like with body modifications—tattoos and piercings. It's our, expressive, version of being a monk or flagellant. Hence it is fashionable to adopt ethnic babies and so on. This explains why it is fashionable to celebrate bizarre "firsts." Like a recent news headline read "First gay marriage proposal at White House." As we used to celebrate exemplar individuals for their greatness, we now do for their weirdness and this is viewed as savvy. Instead of heroically subverting the base body with greatness, now the social body, as we've seen.

Another scene in *Titanic* shows Jack as a Christ-type. Cal frames Jack for a crime and Jack is put in custody by being handcuffed to a pole. Cal oppresses him, and Jack needs to escape. One of Cal's henchmen punches Jack in the stomach while he is handcuffed, because of his affair with Rose. This scene is modeled on the flagellation of Christ who was also tied to a pole and flogged.

We analyze this film in detail partly because it is a particularly good example. It is so systematic that it could be described as a modernist Platonic Dialogue or passion play. But also because of the film's popularity. Within a year of its release, in 1997, it was the highest grossing film in history, 1.8 billion, and was not surpassed until Avatar in 2010. It held that title for 13 years. Newspaper articles on the film during its run described how it reduced even men to tears, and how people were so obsessed with this 3 hour film that they saw it repeatedly. It won eleven Academy Awards, including Best Picture.

Its appeal is to the deepest roots of modernism. To place nature or the body and emotion above restraint is probably the easiest thing that people can do, and is probably the norm among primitive tribes, as we saw in the chapter on the state of nature, and certainly among apes.

During the middle ages, the knights considered the merchants to be retentive, and there is a picture of one defecating coins. This is similar to the common image of the nerd and computer geek. It is counterintuitive to be rationalistic and cultured or refined, and to be stratified accordingly, as we were from the Renaissance to about 1900, which is when the film *Room With a View* takes place. Dualism, the belief that there is a basic difference between the mind and body, may be out of fashion in science and philosophy, but it is alive and thriving in popular modernist culture. It clearly behooves us to reexamine this concept in light of recent cultural developments and changes in values and increased crime. Pinker makes this kind of point in his discussion of the manners revolution during the sixteenth century.[203]

It is worth noting that during the nineteenth century, entertainers were considered low class or disreputable. They were viewed as mere imitators, morally loose and hence low in Plato's hierarchy as they would be for Ficino. Society leveled the criticism of moral looseness on early Hollywood actors, though the studios tried to keep them under control with morality clauses in their contracts. As part of today's inverted culture, they are now the new glamorous aristocracy, replacing the industrialists and inventers of the nineteenth century as objects of fascination and envy.

Consider the concept of *poverty*. Before 10,000 years ago everyone on earth lived as hunter-gathers, and had almost nothing or were poor. Then people discovered the mind, as expressed by the domestication of plants and animals. During the last 3,000 years we have discovered reason and this has allowed us to conquer nature. Some individuals play a larger and more constructive role in this process and so accumulate more money and so rise above poverty. The question is not, "Why is there poverty?" but why have certain groups and subgroups risen above it?

Constructing a life style or standard of living above poverty is what requires an explanation—like because of higher intelligence and social organization. While in contrast, poverty is natural (as is violence, as we saw in the state of nature; so as you have to explain the construction of affluence, you have to explain the construction of peace).

Chopin describes the political mood in early nineteenth century Paris:

> You meet with crowds of beggars with menacing looks
> on their faces, and you often hear threatening remarks
> about that imbecile [King] Louis-Philippe…. The lower
> classes are completely exasperated and ready at any

---

[203] Steven Pinker, *The Better Angels of Our Nature: Why Violence Has Declined* (New York: Viking, 2011).

time to break out of their poverty-stricken situation, but unfortunately for them the government is extremely severe on such movements and the slightest gathering in the streets is dispersed by mounted police.[204]

The poor are seen as oppressed, as Anna Karenina was surrounded by her polluting family, and as the Jews were by Pharaoh. The regular pressing down on the irregular is to be lamented as we saw with Hugo. We certainly don't want to be uptight when it comes to the distinction between nature and culture, and instead want to be humble, drink pus and escape beauty.

In Chopin's description, as in Hugo's description of the prisoner, the lower class responds to natural poverty as if it were an artificial, imposed, social condition, are "menacing" with their newly empowered wills, and that King Louis-Philippe is an "imbecile," as Cal and his friends were "mindless." The lower classes now have a will more like that of the heroic Vikings, and many today enjoy this, as we saw in female sexual selection.

I once heard a Berkeley student refer to "blatant poverty." So again we see the metaphors of the formally maligned body now used to malign or demonize the public sphere, like the "blatant" or evil family and the upper-class. These are forces that want to put us into character.

Historian Simon Schama in his *History of Britain* makes it clear that it was a sense of rebellion against a perceived, evil poverty that was driving the labor movement during the nineteenth century. As part of our inversion of values, the lower classes are now seen as righteous or wise, have power, and are justified to be hostile, while the upper classes are fools, "mindless," who do not deserve to have power, and if they do, they are viewed as hubristic, as we saw with Cal in *Titanic*. This is what the savvy know today.

It is certainly illegitimate and hubristic for the devil to rebel against God and his stories. It is meretricious, and this is how the whites appear, to themselves and others, compared to the blacks, who in turn appear to be more "real," natural or authentic. This is the same ethical contrast in *Titanic*, and has clear implications for our

---

[204] As quoted in Jeremy Siepman, *Chopin: The Reluctant Romantic* (Boston: Northeastern University, 1995), 83.

moral perception and experience of the psychology of conflict that we saw in the state of nature. This is why many today romanticize the state of nature and natural people and behavior.

Chapter Five: Chained at the Bottom of the Cave, or the Power of Hierarchy

During the nineteenth century, people very much supported peace and love, but they just distributed these emotions differently then we do today. For them these emotions were to be cultivated between individuals within the group, nation or race, and especially within a church congregation. These emotions were not seen to be directed to out group members, who, after all, tended to be rather hostile, even among themselves, like the Indians and blacks, as we saw in the state of nature.

They were also viewed as being over-sexed, uncouth and vulgar, and this was further off-putting. So characteristics that Mailer found attractive in the blacks, were, during the nineteenth century, found to be disgusting. A recent study has found that whites during this time believed that you needed to minimize exposure to people like the blacks, or you yourself might ultimately succumb to hostility and sex.[205]

Whites at that time recoiled in response to bad people, or who had that image or set of associations. Recall the strong notion of the temptations of the flesh, and escape from the body, that reigned at the time. So again we see a distinction between control or culture and nature. In this case the nature of sex and violence that needed control. So the intense emphasis on peace produced what we today would call "racial discrimination" or succumbing to the social body. Today, with our critique of the evil social body, and valorizing

---

[205] James Morone, *Hellfire Nation: The Politics of Sin in American History*. (New Haven & London: Yale University Press, 2004).

unlimited emotional expression, at least in many contexts, the past is just at the very least incomprehensible or opaque, but mostly horrible. There is a recent book called *The Killing of History*, just like, in some sense the Old Testament or the law, was dead.

Of course we today define peace, love and humility as being out-group directed, as it allows us to beat, escape and transcend the social body with diversity. So we see, again, the displacement of metaphors about the body to the public sphere.

We think of this new peace and love movement as being a recent invention, from the 1960s, but it had supporters in England during the first decades of the twentieth century. (In general the Europeans anticipated things that only developed later in America.)

The battle at that time was between Winston Churchill, who represented the conservatives, and, representing the peaceniks, what is known as the Bloomsbury group, the most famous members being E.M. Forster, Virginia Wolf and Maynard Keynes. Valiunas, in a recent article, contrasting Churchill and the Bloomsbury group, said:

> If Churchill was for it—ardent patriotism, empire building as moral duty and ordeal, the primacy of public life over private, war as an eternal feature of human existence—Bloomsbury was sure to be against it. Bold iconoclasts and antagonists, the Bloomsberries, as they called themselves with a giggle, promoted peaceable cosmopolitanism and the incomparable sweetness of the private life well lived, the worldly salvation to be found in art and love, comfort and abandon. In Lytton Strachey's words, "a great deal of a great many kinds of love" was the desired apex of civilized living.[206]

Notice the image of "worldly salvation" which is an inversion of the old associations or visions of salvation. Keynes describes the effect on them by the Cambridge professor G. E. Moore:

> Nothing mattered except states of mind, our own and others people's of course, but chiefly our own.

---

[206] Algis Valiunas, "Shall We Fight for Kind and Country?" *Claremont Review of Books*, Volume X, Number 1, Winter 2009/10, 50.

These states of mind were not associated with action or achievement or with consequences. They consisted in timeless, passionate states of contemplation and communion, largely unattached to *before* and *after*.... The appropriate subjects of passionate contemplation and communion were a beloved person, beauty and truth, and one's prime objects in life were love, the creation and enjoyment of aesthetic experience and the pursuit of knowledge. Of these love came a long way first.[207]

The Bloomsberries were one of the first to start simply hanging out. They were progressive or looked forward to things to come. We see how this foreshadowed the idea of escape from the public sphere or the social body as we saw in *Titanic*.

Keynes and the other Bloomberries turned Moore's philosophy into a religion—one without morals though they were never explicit about this. The only kind of action they would admit was love.

They disdained social action such as politics, success, ambition, or wealth. It is easy to see how a solipsistic drug culture could emerge from this. E.M. Forster, in his essay, "What I Believe" declared his dislike for great men. He believed that:

They produce a desert of uniformity around them and often a pool of blood too, and I always feel a little man's pleasure when they come a cropper. One of the best things about democracy is that it produces, instead of Great Men, different kinds of small men—a much finer achievement.[208]

We see in this quotation two themes that we have seen repeatedly in the discussion of modernism in general; a disgust with uniformity, or being in character, and a desire for diversity and escape as an antidote. Churchill is contrasted strongly with all of this:

Churchill on the other hand emphasizes the moral

---

[207] Idem.
[208] Ibid., 51

heroism of empire, which brings nothing less than salvation to men who have never known the blessing of modernity. To bestow upon the primitive and ignorant the products of civilized intelligence is the richest gift one people can give another... British intelligence and British character equip the imperial soldiery to conquer peoples lacking those qualities, and to do so for their own good. Once the natives are vanquished in war, they are vouchsafed the healing benefits of peace.[209]

Churchill represents the dubious belief, common at the time, in inevitable progress. People believed that progress was hard-wired into nature, human nature, and history. (It was derived from Christian notions that history was headed inevitably toward the apocalypse or moral perfection in heaven. Another example is Frederick Engle's theory that under communism, the state would "wither away.")

The Bloombury group represents the collapse into subjectivity that we have seen repeatedly, and is a hallmark of modernism. As it was righteous to enslave your will to that of another, now we have swung to the opposite extreme and it is righteous to be solipsistic, completely free and emotionally expressive or a slave to your emotions.

This is an extreme example or expression of the inversion of Platonist psychology and politics. Instead of mind over body, like for Churchill, now it is body over mind, and this has only become more extreme in recent decades. (Simon Schama in his *History of Britain* said that during 1800 the English thought they could turn India into a Western country, but by 1900 they thought it was impossible. Even today, India is significantly poorer than several black African countries, and an American who lived there said that most things are done is sloppy fashion. India has the same national IQ as Black Americans.)

Modernists know at some level that all their high flown morality is motivated by a desire to forward pure selfishness. This is why they sometimes are disingenuous. They know they aren't interested in any kind of disciplined intellectual system that is part

---

[209] Ibid., 51-52.

of science. They simply want freedom, and to scream and rebel like a child, and revolt against a consistent understanding which might lead them to create absolute values and hierarchy that will marginalize the ego. Basically what we have done today is take the political model of freedom, which has some good rational, and applied it to social and cultural issues, which few before about 1850 would have supported. They knew at that time that if this kind of freedom was pursued it would lead to debauchery.[210]

In addition to the inversion of the mind and body, or culture and nature, we have also seen during the twentieth century an inversion of the nineteenth century's secular idea of progress. So instead of it being good to go from low to high, now it is good to go from high to low, as we saw in *Titanic* and Mailer.

During the earlier time, progress was defined as movement from primitive tribal social organization, as among Africans at the time, to complex Western civilization with its moral religion, elaborate legal system and abstract scientific knowledge. Hegel, for instance, saw slavery as a progressive institution for Africans because they were being acculturated into a more advanced civilization. We saw this with Churchill.

An example of this imagined hierarchy of "race" is shown in the film *Guess Who's Coming to Dinner* (1967). A Black woman objects to a marriage between a Black man and White woman because, as she says, "I don't want to see a member of my race getting above himself."

Today we have inverted this, and don't feel comfortable with meretricious whites getting above themselves; they must be socially humble and escape from themselves and find salvation in diversity and the blacks. Similarly, during the 1950s in the United States, African Americans embraced Western values. But starting during the 1960s, Blacks started to dress in African clothing and to adopt African names.

This was seen as progressive—the eruption of the primitive into the landscape of the civilized or cultured. So movement from low to high was maintained from the old scheme, it was just the

---

[210] James Morone, *Hellfire Nation: The Politics of Sin in American History.* (New Haven & London: Yale University Press, 2004).

moral worth of the agents that changed. We saw this in *Titanic*. So instead of it being good to go from low to high, now it is good to go from high to low. And this is savvy.

So here we are, chained at the rock bottom of the cave and talking to the shadows. In act two of Wagner's music drama *Tristan and Isolde*, the titular couple sings for about 30 minutes about how unreal and fake day or light is, while darkness is the preferred condition or real. Darkness symbolizes desire, which for Wagner and many today was more real than lucidity or mind.

Tristan sings in act 3, "The torch is extinguished! To her! To her!"And Isolde sings, "Unconscious, highest bliss!" We saw this in *Titanic* in the contrast between the two parties. Darkness and the unconscious, traditionally viewed as signs of evil, were viewed as rich in expressive value among the Romantics, and of course this is dogma today.

To show the power of hierarchy, both the nineteenth and twentieth century's concepts of "race" and imitation are structured by a Neoplatonic conception of hierarchy. Blackburn noted about Plotinus, a Neoplatonic philosopher, that:

> It is in contemplation of the higher, creative principle that the lower receives its form or impress. But it is also as reflections of the one cosmic Soul that individual souls exist, and their aim must be to direct their contemplation back up the hierarchy, eventually to obtain light and vitality by contemplative absorption of the One.[211]

We saw this tension between ideal and imitation in the class relations in *Titanic*. There the high should really imitate the low, and this is portrayed as the ideal to be aspired to. Cal needs to escape from himself and become real, like the blacks, as Mailer could have pointed out.

Another example of the elevation of nature is that, during the '60s, primitive art became elevated to fine art. Tribal art is irregular or assaulting, and so inspires savvy reverence and modesty,

---

[211] Simon Blackburn, *Oxford Dictionary of Philosophy* (New York: Oxford University, 2008), 280.

like modern art. Nowadays Westerners pay homage to tribal and modern art wherein their sense of the regular is destroyed, and diversity and justice triumphs. Recall how Picasso used distorted tribal art to attack the Classical tradition and to remake art into its sexualized and redeemed version. Classicism, as representing control, is just "brutality and darkness" but distortion and hysteria are good and promote "peace;" we saw what these values resulted in among the Vikings.

We see a similar fate for the human figure in art. Traditionally, it was considered the highest form of art, but today among academic modernism, it is stigmatized as commercial or low. This explains why in modern art the figure is usually presented as flattened and distorted or purified as in Byzantine art. One artist described a situation where he presented a drawing of a human hand to an instructor, and was criticized for it. He had succumbed to the temptation of beauty.

Another student presented a drawing of an ape hand, and this the instructor praised. The bestial and the irregular is the ideal today and offers a vision of purgation or salvation from Western culture in the same way that looking at a picture of an angel was once purging or morally uplifting. So again we see inversion in the relation between nature and culture, good and evil, just and unjust. The savvy malign as meretricious what we want to escape, and praise and move toward what offers "real" salvation.

The modernist inversion is also reflected in music. Modern music was ushered in 1907 with Schoenberg' *Pelleas und Melisande*. His 12-tone system attacked the beauty of traditional music and replaced it with noise whose only real value was redemption through subverting the dominant paradigm, as there was redemption or justice through subverting the body. Schoenberg described his system as the "liberation of dissonance." This is consistent with the other forms of liberation that were occurring at this time.

A professional musician recently observed that you don't get used to the large amount of dissonance in modern music. So the old dogma of learning and relativism is just a morality story to justify the drive toward particularism, rebellious noise and the justice of diversity. "Relativism" or consciousness of and insight into the social body, is presented by the savvy as moral insight, as the biodeterminism of evil, or the human inclination to hostility was understood by the savvy in moral terms. In other words, as the body was viewed as vicious, now the social body is viewed as vicious and both of course need to be subverted. Mahler said that, "A symphony should be like the world: it should contain everything." He was ahead of his time, with his savvy understanding of the new subversion.

The larger purpose is to subvert and escape the social body— controlling tonality and beauty in this case. This is the moral inspiration and justification for relativism. As subverting the body was moral insight, as we saw with the reformed prostitute, so the subversive value of relativism represents moral insight. So beautiful music is experienced as meretricious to the "educated," savvy or morally enlightened, as the body used to be experienced as meretricious. Modern culture has about as much intrinsic value as the ritual of viewing a medieval icon or dancing around a golden calf. It is nothing more than a vision of brute power that helps with escape.

Stravinsky's 1913 *Rite of Spring,*a ballet featuring a fertility rite and human sacrifice, also shows the inversion. The music's jagged dissonance and driving rhythms shocked most people and, according to the composer, caused a riot at the Paris premier. This is experienced today by the savvy as a good sign, or at least this is how the real "subversion" in history or the triumph of justice is taught in schools today. We saw this impulse with the art instructor's praise of the drawing of the ape hand. The French call the coronation of a King a *Sacra*, as in sacred. Similarly, the French often call the "Rite of Spring" *Sacra*. We know who rules today.

The parallel with modern dance is clear as both represented the liberation of noise. Aaron Copland wrote his *Fanfare for the Common Man* and *An Outdoor Overture*. One music historian said that around 1900 "The young composers saw in Debussy a new Moses who could lead them from the bondage of traditional tonality and to the promised land of new music."[212] Notice the

---

[212] Robert Greenberg, *How to Listen to and Understand Great Music*, 3rd edition, DVD lecture series (Chantilly VA: The Teaching Company, 2006).

use of the well known religious narrative of escape, also used by Martin Luther King, and the word *bondage* as in *confining*, a term we have seen regularly. The music of both Debussy and Stravinsky exemplify the collapse into subjectivity that we saw among the Bloomsbury Group and that only became more extreme during the 1960s. Jacques Barzun made the good point that in art today there has been nothing new since the 1920s.[213]

Similarly, as we saw with the romantics, the difference between the early nineteenth century and today is more a matter of degree then of kind. We today are only more low and diverse then they were during the early nineteenth century. The basic paradigms, high low, good evil, are the same.

One musicologist described German music as "moral,"[214] as opposed to the more ambiguous, sensuous and subjective music of the French. French music, going back to the middle ages, has always been more colorful. (This results from the influence of the language.) German music has a heroic discipline or inspires self control, and outgoing and ordered energy, like Beethoven's 5th, as opposed to French music which is more subjective or "touchy feely" to use a phrase popular in California. Beethoven is like Churchill, or out going, while French music is more solipsistic, like the Bloomsbury group.

During the eighteenth century, musical forms were commonly derived from stylized dance forms, opera or rationalist sources, like fugue, but starting in the early nineteenth century, literary and even the elements of nature start to inspire music. Beethoven's sixth symphony is subtitled *The Pastoral*. And while it does portray a storm, it does tend to have an idealized view of nature, not like what we saw among the Vikings and other primitive tribes. Mahler's Ninth Symphony was inspired by the composer's heart condition.

As described earlier, Mahler the child wanted to be a martyr when he grew up. It seems that when he actually had to face death, his bravery faltered. Few would describe his Ninth Symphony

---

[213] Jacques Barzun, *From Dawn to Decadence: 500 Year of Western Cultural Life* (New York: Harpercollins, 2001).
[214] Greenberg, ibid.

as rousing and heroic. It is more an exercise in self-pity, another recurring theme of modernism.

Nationalist composer Edvard Grieg wrote a piano piece entitled *Butterflies,* and Grieg once said, alluding to Beethoven, "I don't build castles in the sky." Similarly, the nineteenth century avoided large forms, like the piano sonata, and instead cultivated the miniature. The piano sonata is too much like Churchill. Of course since then we have been systematically destroying the castle of Western culture, or at least burying it in mud and pus in our rush to show how humble we can be before our brothers.

In the past century the involvement with nature has become an obsession. For instance, composer Olivier Messiaen notated the birdsongs in France and categorized them by region. He sometimes quotes this song in some of his music. And Finnish composer Einojuhani Rautavaara, went one further and recorded bird song and wrote orchestral accompaniments for this "music." Jon Leifs wrote a concerto for pitched rocks; I heard that later he regretted making the rocks pitched because it was too elitist. And certainly the percussion section in the orchestra has grown exponentially during the last century.

And Leifs, from Iceland, also wrote *Saga Symphony* based on the Icelandic sagas, the kind quoted during the discussion of the state of nature. Yes, we should all commune with the Vikings, as we should with the headhunters and the Zulus, complete with spears. The humility and gentleness that we believed we should express with ourselves, the savvy now believe should be directed to outside groups regardless of their characteristics.

As we have seen, nature was viewed as vulgar by the elite during the eighteenth century, and it would have been seen as inappropriate for music to be "polluted" by base and imperfect nature. When in college, I once played during a recital a nice piece of music on guitar.

I then repeated the piece but exactly one fret up on the instrument creating a terrible noise. I loved this, and the audience applauded. As the savvy applauded monks, rebels against the flesh, now the savvy applaud rebels against beauty or the social body. When Brahms heard the premier of Mahler's first symphony, he asked rhetorically, "Is this the future of music?" Joachim, the violinist who helped Brahms write his concerto for the instrument, said that the Sibelius concerto was "hideous and boring." Needless to say, this is not savvy.

Wagner once said, regarding his *Ring* cycle of operas, "I practice the art of transition." It is clear that modernists define themselves by their ability to simply do anything that is irregular, like unresolved dissonance and disjointed writing in general, as Joachim observed in the concerto. This is what defines "modern" music and is perceived by the savvy to be more real. So again we see the anti-aesthetic. Modernism is simple ritual rebellion and doesn't have anything really positive to say. It is simply "streaking" in art. It is not psychologically complex and expressively deep, and this is the source of the resistance to modern music among many rank and file concert goers.

Notice the equation in musical culture today between the amount of noise in a piece and the judgment of how modern it is. For instance, as composer Charles Ives got older he went back and included more dissonance in his earlier works. So, Schoenberg is more "modern" than Mahler, while Boulez is more "modern" than Schoenberg, etc. This idea of progress or escape, as we saw in the comparison of Debussy with Moses, is an aesthedicized version of the post-modernist philosophy of particulars and the politics of diversity; it is a high version of streaking and rock and roll, both also perceived to be "progressive" or more real as we saw nature portrayed in *Titanic*.

The fragmentation of form is also evident in popular or folk dance. In the eighteenth century, people danced in social forms resembling square dance or contra dance, and the savvy enjoyed this. Within a decade of the French revolution, the waltz roared into fashion, which critics described as "hugging set to music." Couples-based dancing remained the norm until the 1960s, when social dance fragmented completely and the savvy people started dancing individually or at some distance, with anyone who happened to be available. It is "hands off" today as the savvy don't want to be oppressed by anyone else. In a film from the 1960s, a character says, "This is the twentieth century; no one possesses anyone else." This is what defines savviness.

We see a similar fragmentation in the area of the family. In 1800, the average American family had 8 children. That figure steadily declined throughout the nineteenth century until it reached 2 children by 1940. There was a brief increase immediately after World War II, but by the 1960s it was down to 2 children again. With an emphasis on individual self-realization during the last two centuries, we see people less committed to a strong and demanding family life. So we see among the savvy the desire to escape entrapment.

It was once part of people's civic obligation to have large families, and the Biblical injunction was to be fruitful and multiply. Today, children are often seen as a nuisance that we want to escape from, those "little monsters." And recall here that children and the family are explicitly portrayed as evil in *Rosemary's Baby*. Again, we see the recurring motif of claustrophobia, as in the earlier discussion of Tolstoy and *Anna Karenina*. Commenting on the low fertility of upper-class people in the 1920s, Stoddard noted that, by promoting a strong eugenics movement, "People will think less about 'rights' and more about duties."[215]

He sensed what was going on; the slide to the individual. No one wants to be oppressed by a family today or at least they want to minimize it. In addition, God only had one child, and as it is unseemly to imagine God being harried by 8 kids, it is unseemly to imagine ourselves being harried by 8 kids. Both God and we today are above this characterization.

I once was doting on a baby in a restaurant, and said playfully to the parents that I wanted to have 10 kids, and when the family was leaving the mother said to me, "good luck with our 10 kids" and then she raised her top lip in disgust. Instead of the body being a disgusting imposition, now the social body is a disgusting imposition.

Parents and for that matter children and teens think that youth rebellion or the bottom-up movement is morally justified. This reasoning, as we have seen, is common in popular and

---

[215] Lothrop Stoddard, *The Revolt Against Civilization* (New York: Charles Scribner's Sons, 1923), 255.

academic culture. Rebellious youth is a popular idea and image in the West today, and the subject of many films. No wonder the savvy are resistant to parenthood.

If we put parents back in charge of children, like during the nineteenth century, then we will see the fertility rate start to increase. For the Puritans, the goal of child rearing was to break the ego of the child. This would make the practice of parenting more sane and inviting, plus have the benefit of lowering crime and cultural degradation. But this won't appeal to the savvy, not at least for awhile.

I personally love children and am very doting, but the present practice of permissiveness is clearly very destructive. Loving children is one thing but putting up with naturally bad behavior profits no one, including the child. They have to go back to learning their place in the family, community and world.

We have seen a consistent picture of the nature of modernism in disparate areas of life, like the visual arts, dance, popular film, music and political and social philosophy. As Chateaubriand said, "Without taste, genius is but sublime folly."

And he was an eye witness to the developments of all the new ideals and new culture. This describes much of the non-scientific intellectual and cultural production of the last 150 years. What is good taste? It is Classicism in art, Baroque in design and Romanticism in music. These styles have the maximum of expression while maintaining formal coherence.

Predictably, though, folly is the today's ideal. In one pop song the savvy woman sings, "Do you have street smarts, or are you just an intellect?"

A professor in the book *The Dumbest Generation* noted that there is a strong trend of anti-intellectualism among the young today.[216] On the side of a building in Rome was a large banner that read, "I'm with stupid….be stupid."

And a London department store used the same sentiment in an advertisement. A 30 year old female attorney who was raised and educated in California said that it's fashionable to be a fool today.

---

[216] Mark Bauerlein, *The Dumbest Generation: How the Digital Age Stupefies Young Americans and Jeopardizes our Future* (New York: Penguin, 2008).

This savvy anti-intellectualism creates, as part of the inversion of Platonism, both the anti-elitism in *Titanic*, and anti-Wagnerism, the sensation that his music is "heavy" or mentally oppressive. Most people just want to dance today, like before the golden calf, and don't want to try to think in any kind of systematic and deep fashion. Again we see the idea of escape from oppression. This is what the savvy are convinced of.

To show how much attitudes and values have changed, Blacks in Hollywood film during the 1930s were often portrayed as lazy and stupid, and this was considered funny. But only for Blacks, not Whites. (Though it should be mentioned that even at this time blacks were portrayed as better than what you see on the streets. You need to go back to the nineteenth century to find realistic portrayals of blacks.)

Nowadays, being lazy and stupid seem to be ideals for White Americans as well, at least among the savvy. Recall the element of imitation of an ideal in Plotinus's hierarchy. During the 1950s, blacks aspired to be smart, while today, whites aspire to be dumb and lazy, and it is common for the savvy to romanticize this. We saw this in one of the Billy Joel songs. Recall here the values and ideals in *Titanic*.

We will go into more detail on this subject of deference in the last chapter, *Modernism's Theology of Race*. The savvy do not want the mind and its regularities pressing down on anyone's freedom today.

It is critical to be out of character. For instance, a Danish writer published a novel about a woman who had a sexual affair with a gorilla. This epitomizes the extent of the modernist aesthetic inversion. The savvy West has gone from Homer's *Iliad* to a woman having sex with a gorilla. This is certainly more natural, humble and real. I'm sure the savvy readers of the novel experienced it as an escape and a source of redemption.

According to Vasari, Michelangelo's Medici tomb would suffice to re-invent the art of sculpture:

> On one tomb he placed Night and Day, and on the
> other Dawn and Dusk; these statues are carved with the
> most beautifully formed poses and skillfully executed

muscles and would be sufficient, if the art of sculpture were lost, to return it to its original splendor.[217]

There are times, like today, when it is appropriate to learn from history. We also need a Renaissance. Vasari was familiar with medieval art, so he knew that art was fragile and that it could die fast. Regarding the piety of modern art, what Vasari says about excessive moral zeal in art is informative:

> But I would not wish anyone to be mistaken and to construe that clumsy and inept works are pious, while beautiful and well-done ones are corrupt, as some people do when they see figures either of women or young boys that are a bit more pleasing, beautiful, and ornate than usual and who immediately seize upon them and judge them as lustful, without realizing that they are very much in the wrong to condemn the good judgment of the painter, who holds that the beauty of the saints, both male and female, who are celestial beings, surpasses that of mortal beings just as heavenly beauty surpasses our earthly beauty and our mortal works. But worse than this, they reveal their own infected and corrupted souls when they dig out evil and impure desires from these works, for if they were truly lovers of virtue, as they wish to prove by their foolish zeal, they would discern the painter's yearning for Heaven and attempt to make himself acceptable to the Creator of all things, from Whose most perfect and beautiful nature all perfection and beauty are born.[218]

As the beautiful was once praised because of its elevation from raw nature, the savvy now praise the ugly and irregular because of the elevation of raw nature. They love and praise the irregular, the particular and ugly because of its humble piety, just as they did during Middle Ages, as Vasari makes clear. Similarly, modernists scorn beauty as a gross indulgence of the social body, a

---

[217] Giorgio Vasari, Julia Bondanella and Peter Bondanella, trans., *Lives of the Artists* (New York: Oxford University, 2008.), 455-56.
[218] Ibid., 175.

claustrophobic "vulgar" temptation, meretricious, as we saw earlier from the art historian who criticized a piece of furniture as being vulgar. Beauty is now seen as a disgusting expression of the social body, like racism.

Janson, in his *History of Art*, says that realism in medieval art is a realism of particulars, and not of a coherent overall structure, as in Classical art. Of course, the tension between particulars and form, or nature and culture, is one we have seen repeatedly.

The drive today is toward particulars and diversity, or the redemption of the irregular and ugly, like drinking pus, and claustrophobic nature. This is all done by the savvy in the name of subverting the high, the mind or any higher type organizing principal. We saw this clearly in *Titanic*.

Michelangelo himself was motivated by a religious rejection of this world to attack art. In his *Rondanini Pieta* he portrays the Madonna and Christ in a manner that looks more like a Brancusi bird or a tree stump than as an example of celestial beauty. That this is an attack is shown by an important element in the sculpture. Next to the figure group is a beautifully described male arm.

It is fairly muscular and very realistic or beautiful, like his more famous works. Michelangelo juxtaposed an element of beauty next to something that looks essentially medieval and primitive. Nevertheless, the prominence of the figure group shows where his sympathies lie. Beauty is marginalized, and thus it is clearly symbolic of his past sins or his early preoccupation with the beautiful body.

We see this logic in another of his works. In the painting the *Doni Tondo*, the Holy Family is in the foreground of the painting, while some nudes, who represent pagan antiquity, are in the far background.

As the nudes represent past sins, the arm in the *Rondanini* represents the past sins of Michelangelo, or his preoccupation with the beauties of the body. So even in the short time span of the life of one man, art was able to meet a quick end, at least for Michelangelo; and it is no small thing that it was done by the hand of the man who did the most to show us the perfect body, as in the *David*. (A Michelangelo scholar approved of this interpretation of the arm.) As should be clear by now a new religion has formed in the West.

What makes it different from other religions is that we can see its birth, for its birth is well documented, unlike the other religions whose origins are lost in the mists of time.

As we saw in the discussion of Becker's *Heavenly City of the Eighteenth Century Philosophers*, people were beginning to use man and no longer God as the measure, so man was to some large measure becoming deified. This was clear in the quote from Robespierre that man was "divine."

But compared to statements from Hugo and others from later centuries it is fairly muted, though the actions were obviously strong in that it produced the whole era of violent "revolutions." On the other hand, there were no hippies at the time, so things became more intense as the inversion of Platonist psychology and politics became more extreme; as this happened man became even more deified and seen to be more powerful and self indulgent, as we saw with the Bloomsbury Group and the solipsistic '60s. (It should be mentioned here that the term "revolution" means to "turn around" and it is clear that that is what literally happened. Instead of seeing the state as a good and holy control on human's depraved nature, suddenly the state and the upper-class became depraved and needed control by good people. We have seen the long term cultural result of that logic, and Benjamin Franklin alluded to this in his quote on the potential social destruction of republicanism.)

In later political and cultural productions this higher or divine status was strongly projected backwards onto the revolution. We saw this in the quote earlier from *Les Miserables* when the revolutionary said that the revolution was a consecration of man. Another character said that the revolutionaries were "giants" (p. 1154) or in other words were super-human.

In the opera *Andrea Chenier* a character who participated in the revolution describes himself: "Pure, innocent and mighty, I thought myself a giant!" Purity! Will we ever escape it!

And another character said that the revolution was to "Transform all men in God's own image!" (act three). Many Frenchmen today consider the revolutionaries as heroes. One French woman said a few years ago that, "We had to fight for everything we have."

All of this imagery combined is stronger than Robespierre's statement, and stronger then the belief, popular during the revolution, in living and fighting for posterity. So as the inversion became more intense with political changes and liberalization of the culture, the deification became more extreme producing hippies, streaking and the solipsistic drug culture. Notice that Aristotle's God is a simple first mover who thereafter contemplates himself or is solipsistic. The individual and his subjective productions certainly have high status today. Similar speculation on the nature, formulations and origins of religion is visible in antiquity.

Euhemerus was a Greek writer during the Hellenistic period who wrote a travel novel that some have interpreted as having a theory of the origins of religion. A group of sailors in the uncharted Indian Ocean comes across an island. They land and discover a column on which the deeds of Uranus, Cronus and Zeus are recorded. This gives the novel its title, *Sacred Scripture*. The column describes how Uranus, Cronus and Zeus had been great kings, and had received worship as Gods from a grateful people.

The novel is typically interpreted as a justification for Hellenistic ruler cult, or as a secular explanation for the origins of religion. The parallels with modernism are clear. First you have the heroes of the revolution, who represent the ascendancy or rule of the individual. Then you have later writers like Hugo and the librettist of *Andrea Chenier* who explicitly turn them, and the individual into Gods.

Christianity did this in its relationship with the Old Testament. Recall that they interpreted it as a series of foreshadowing's of the New Testament, like Issac anticipating Christ. Similarly, recall here the characters in *Les Miserables* who believed that the men who fought in the revolution were "giants" and that the revolution was the "consecration of humanity." All of this was then projected backwards onto the revolution during the nineteenth century, and we saw this same process in *Sacred Scriptures* with the deification of the early kings.

As the early kings ascended to Godhead, so has the individual today. To put it another way, Hugo and others were writing foundation myths in the same way that modern feminist scholars today rewrite history to create for women some large role, a saintly "conduit between past and present," again with no foundation in the record, a foundation myth for modern feminism. This re-writing of history is a central activity for many academics or mythographers.

Why is this so easy for people? It reflects the mind on automatic. Recall the connection between self and mind and the group, and that the sense of agency could move back and forth. Similarly, if God could exist "out there" up in the clouds, then agency could be moved into the individual body, resulting in its deification.

Recall that, at one point to summarize my basic argument I say, "The problem today is not seen as pressure from base nature and the body, but social pressure in the mind." Now, Jones in his study, *An Instinct for Dragons* shows that a kind of African monkey has a cry that specifically warns conspecifics that a snake is near by, and a separate cry for eagles. Then there are the well known experiments with babies that show that they have an instinct to be fearful of snakes.[219]

So if you put this all together with the idea that in Western history the snake has been a strong symbol for evil, then what is clear is that humans are hardwired for the perception of evil, and so it is only a matter of were we define its placement. It can be more externalized, as I show in the discussion of our historical relationship with nature and outside groups of people, or it can be more internalized and distributed to peers, as I show happening in films like *Titanic* and the era of revolution. And of course, history shows clearly that humans are easily provoked into aggression and fighting. In history people kill each other over almost nothing as we saw in the state of nature.

This has clear implication for social engineering. We have to construct an external evil for people, which of course was always done, because if not then they automatically start to fixate on those near themselves. We saw this in the change from viewing social

---

[219] David Buss, *Evolutionary Psychology: The New Science of the Mind,* (New York: Allyn & Bacon, 2012). David E. Jones, *An Instinct for Dragons,* (New York & London: Routledge, 2002).

pressure as a good to an evil. First the state was viewed as good, but then evil. What appears to be the case is that we are hardwired for the perception that there is legitimate and illegitimate or threatening modes of power. At first, the individual was viewed as illegitimate, but state legitimate, but then the individual was viewed as legitimate, and state illegitimate.

In order to better understand the next chapter, on film, we need to stop and see how the Devil has functioned as a narrative character in the religious traditions as they developed in the West, starting in the ancient Near East. This has been done brilliantly by Forsyth in his *The Old Enemy: Satan and the Combat Myth.* Of course, we have seen repeatedly how the battle against evil is a prime moving force in modernism. This was clear in *Titanic.* I will quote and summarize the essential points from Forsyth to help get a bigger and more historically grounded picture. The battle against evil has been a driving force in Hollywood film since its beginnings.

Forsyth observes that "Satan emerged from the ancient mythological tradition, and he never quite shook off the signs of his origins. Indeed, it is my chief point of attack here that Satan is to be conceived not as the principle of evil but as a narrative character... Since the word *Satan* means "adversary", I follow the story in which the Adversary is most fully himself—the combat myth—from its earliest discernible stages in the third millennium B.C. until it became the framework of the Christian belief-system."[220]

Of course, "combat" is a very good way of describing the narrative thrust of *Titanic,* of good Jack against evil Cal. Jack did indeed win the love of Rose, while she spit in Cal's face. This is the stuff of high drama.

High drama is not new to recent history. As Forsyth observed, "The Castle of Wartburg probably still has a black stain on the wall of the room in which Martin Luther flung his inkhorn at the devil."[221] And Forsyth continues, "What is important is not the weapons so much as the fact that the story is told at all. Luther imagined his experience as part of the perpetual combat with Satan

---

[220] Neil Forsyth, *The Old Enemy: Satan and the Combat Myth,* (Princeton, NJ: Princeton University Press, 1987), xiv.
[221] Ibid, 3.

and his kingdom which was the core of his own and indeed of much Christian belief. By flinging ink at the devil, Luther was not only following the biblical injunction to put on the whole armor of God, he was reenacting the central Christian narrative. His act was an *imitatio Christi.*"[222]

So we see in *Titanic* that modestly dressed Jack is waging the eternal battle against evil hubris and its kingdom, quit literally. Certainly among the savvy, the devil is overbearing and inspires feelings of avoidance and escape. And by watching the film we are relieved that Jack is on our side and that goodness wins, like a Knight in shining armor in victorious battle against a dragon. This is something that we want to imitate and root for. For instance, many savvy women today certainly don't have much patience with men. And there is absolutely no patience among the savvy for "racists," people who indulge in the social body.

Forsyth aptly observes that "Satan's very existence is a function of his opposition to God, or to man, or to God's son, the god-man. But he may appear as tempter, tyrant, liar, or rebel, each time taking on the characteristics appropriate to his role."[223]

Recall we said earlier how when power shifted during the eighteenth century, divinity also shifted; hence, the upper class automatically became "tyrants," like Cal, and the adversarial Satan considering that they were already in opposition. So people went from a sympathetic perspective on the upper-class, as looking to them for guidance, to a hostile perspective and started to view them as tyrants and hubristic usurpers: their beautiful lifestyle became, among the savvy, at best, meretricious, as we've seen.

I believe that Forsyth would like *Titanic.* He observed "The Christian version of the plot is something like this: A rebel god challenges the power of Yahweh, takes over the whole earth as an extension of his empire, and rules it through the power of sin and death. He is the typical death-dealing villain who causes consternation among his subjects, and his depredations and cruelty make them long for a liberator. This dark tyrant, the "god of this world" as Paul called him, is eventually thwarted by the son of God

---

[222] Ibid, 3.
[223] Ibid, 5.

(or man) in the most mysterious episode of the Christian story, the crucifixion, which oddly combines both defeat and victory.

As Luther could testify, the struggle with Satan continues, however, and we wait still for the end of his story in the end of history. The function of Christ, in almost the technical narrative sense of function, is to be the potential liberator of mankind from this tyranny, while the function of Satan is to be the adversary in this Christian variant of the ancient Near Eastern combat narrative."[224]

In other words, people look to Jack for liberation—both personal and political—with his spiting, drunkenness and dancing, and with his clear association with the Democratic Party. And, he is a Christ-type that "oddly combines both defeat and victory" like drinking puss and then ascending to heaven. Jack is a character that the savvy can relate to today.

It is very common for the savvy to describe the importance of relevance. They want relevant politics and even stories, like *Titanic*. Today's savvy were not the first to discover the uses of relevance. As Forsyth observed, "Instead of narrative that is situated in the creative time of the beginning when the world was being formed, the narratives about Moses and Jesus take place in the recent past, when the world was physically as it is now.

Strictly speaking, this means that those formative stories are not myths, but legends…What distinguishes both Jewish and Christian religious systems, then, is that they elevate to the sacred status of myth narratives that are situated in historical time. Both therefore claim the continuing activity of God in history and so sanctify ordinary human time."[225] Certainly after viewing *Titanic*, or taking a modern history class, the savvy feel relieved to be living in the divine contemporary world, were good triumphs over evil, instead of the benighted nineteenth century. It is the contemporary world that is of greatest relevance just as the New Testament, with its plan for salvation, has greater relevance than the Old Testament.

Of course, what is of relevance in *Titanic* is the establishment of good order. For instance, Cal does commit suicide at the end, and Jack dies as a Martyr, like Christ so Rose can live. As Forsyth

---

[224] Ibid, 7.
[225] Ibid, 9.

observed, "The narrative is akin to myth in its concern with the well-being of the people and the establishment of orderly life, yet it shares also the common folktale characteristic of the difficult journey, the cleverness of the hero, a mysterious sleep, and magical helpers."[226] The savvy who watch *Titanic* are relieved that in their flight from society, and to establish good order, they have a magical helper.

As any one who has taken a history or sociology class can testify, the stories about the origins of evil can be very complicated, and usually never entirely clear or consistent.

Forsyth continues, "The narrative interests of these theologians are perhaps most clearly revealed when they discuss the apparently philosophical problem of the origin of evil. What they tried to do was to find narrative answers, to construct a story that would situate the devil in time and so explain their own relations to him and to his adversary, God."[227]

As any history professor can readily describe, at first there were the evil white males during the eightieth century, and all the subsequent stories of evil emanate from them. These professors will be quick to quote John, "[The Devil] was a murderer from the beginning, and abode not in the truth, because there is no truth in him". Yes from the beginning white men are doing all the murdering and lying against the virtuous women, Indians and Blacks. But there is a light for the savvy: there is Saint Thoreau, who is a conduit between past and present, and the historians look hard for as many of these as they can dig up, like a fragment of the holy cross.

Forsyth would understand my interpretation of cultural history and *Titanic* because he has seen this kind of transformation many times in history. He observed how, "External pressures are also at work in the process of narrative change.

New social conditions require fresh versions of stories, whether because an alien tale needs to be adapted to local conditions, or because an old story is no longer fully understood.

The rise of kingship is an obvious instance of this kind of pressure, and indeed has much to do with the popularity of combat

---

[226] Ibid, 11.
[227] Ibid, 14.

myths in general."[228] During the course of the last two centuries the "old tales" of the battle against sin were no longer understood, with our new inverted politics, and needed updating, so savvy James Cameron came up with *Titanic* and made a billion dollars. The old saying is "There's a fool born every minute." But at least they're savvy and an exemplar for the rest of us.

Of course, any professor today will definitely take heart from *Titanic* and immediately see similar enemies around campus who remind him of Cal, like those evil conservatives. As Forsyth observed, "Doctrinal adversaries were inspired by the narrative adversary..."[229] Ah yes, demons or "racists" like Rushton are potentially lurking everywhere. Temptation! Whites males! The Septuagint translates *satan* as *diabolos*, or "slanderer" or "opposing witness."[230] Rushton was banned from the classroom because he was a slanderer and an opposing witness. Certainly no righteous people would let anyone get away with murder.

So the larger point of this is that all of these preconceptions about the nature of evil existed in the culture and had an existence to an extent separate from the quantitative existence of bad people in history or those around us today. Certainly bad things were done is history, but there is a vast difference between this and how we reacted to it. Our reactions have been largely determined by preconceptions accumulated over millennia. This is clear in the fact of the many parallels between the combat myth and *Titanic*.

---

[228] Ibid, 17.
[229] Ibid, 18.
[230] Jeffrey Russell, *The Prince of Darkness: Radical Evil and the Power of Good in History*, (Ithaca & London: Cornell University Press, 1988).

Chapter Six: PC—The Greatest Show on Earth

> Let me put it this way: the five films nominated for Best Picture for 1975 were *One Flew Over the Cuckoo's Nest, Barry Lyndon, Dog Day Afternoon, Jaws,* and *Nashville*. Well, not the greatest ever made...[but] it was a pretty good year. I won't take the space to list the ten films the Academy scrounged together for Best picture this last year, because so few of them stand company with what 1975 had to offer.
>
> — David Thomas
> *The New Biographical Dictionary of Film,* 2010

As we have seen, film provides many examples of our new debased morals. This chapter focuses on several films and how they illustrate the creation and work of the social body, its encroaching evil, and how we rebel against it and escape. They are all about the struggle for a perceived justice. It works chronologically, starting with older films and working its way later in time.

In the silent film *The Eagle* (1925) Rudolph Valentino plays a Russian Robin Hood named Vladimir Dubrovsky. At the beginning, Dubrovsky is in the special guard of the Czarina. She asks to see him in private, and as part of a sexual advance, she kisses him. This he finds revolting, leaves the palace and goes AWOL. Out of pique, she issues a warrant for his arrest. Dubrovsky then receives a letter from his father that describes how an evil landlord has confiscated his father's estate, leaving him penniless. The father asks Dubrovsky to try to obtain assistance from the Czarina. This of course is impossible because Dubrovsky just walked out on her. This conflict is the last straw for Dubrovsky, and he dons a black mask and declares war against the landlord and his representatives who robbed his father, all the while trying to avoid arrest from the Russian Government. He is surrounded. As the rebel, he becomes known as the "Black Eagle" and he forms a band of loyal followers who help him to harass the landlord and his servants.

At one point, Dubrovsky robs a man who works for the landlord. So we see that the system or the social body is corrupt and that the only thing a man of virtue can do is fight against it. This is identical to *Titanic*, and is a standard theme in many films throughout the century. There is a music group today called "Thievery Corporation."

Rebellion is romanticized in the film for the savvy, as is common today, and as people in earlier times used to romanticize rebellion against the body and its corruption. Of course, social body rebellion derives from the older belief, as we saw how modernism has simply recast the battle between good and evil. Instead of the high against the low, it is now the savvy low against the high. Again, like in *Titanic*.

There is a historical example of people opposing the upper classes because of sexual transgression. One factor that inflamed the Parisian masses during the French revolution was that Maria-Antoinette crossed the border between virgin and whore. The French Kings had traditionally had their wives appear very plain, and the wives' role was as devoted mother and upholder of religion. In addition, the king was allowed to have a mistress that he could doll up, or who played the whore. This maintained the Madonna/whore dichotomy. Louis XVI made the mistake of dolling up his wife, and this mixing up of the traditional roles inflamed the moral senses of the Parisian people.

This was not the only cause of the Revolution, of course, but it was factor, as we saw with Dubrovsky and his reaction to the Czarina. And recall from Italian opera that the upper classes were commonly accused of sexual perversion, so apparently it was a free floating concept looking for a convenient or appropriate landing place given the new political views. (It should be noted that recent evolutionary psychology has identified that humans have both long-term and short term mating strategies,[231] and the traditional division between Madonna and whore seems to grow out of this.)

In another Valentino silent film that takes place in Algeria, *The Sheik* (1921), an Englishman says to an English woman, "I love you, let's get married." The woman responds, "Marriage is captivity, the end of independence." Recall here the example from *Sex and the City* when Carry Bradshaw is trying on a wedding dress, falls to the floor and yells, "I'm suffocating, I'm suffocating!" and quickly removes the dress. The second chapter presented many examples of society or the social body as confining or claustrophobic, and that inspires escape. The traditional cry "Babylon!" or captivity to sin became "Society!" the new sin or captivating source of corruption to rebel against and escape. Later on in the film the English woman is kidnapped by "the sheik" played by Valentino. At first, she resists him, but after they get to know each other, and he performs several heroic deeds, she falls in love with him. At the end of the film, they unite in love, and things point in the direction of marriage.

In the sequel, *The Son of the Sheik* (1925), Valentino plays both the original sheik, now age 50, and his own son. Most of the film is about the tribulations that the son undergoes over a woman, but toward the end of the film the father is holding his English wife in his arms, and she says wistfully, "Remember when you were young, and you grabbed what you wanted." She is alluding to her own kidnapping at his hands when they were young. It is clear that, although she resisted her kidnapping at the time, at some level she liked it. (Bride abduction is still practiced in some Muslim countries.) Her acquiescence contrasts with the opening scene of the first film where she rejects the honest advances of the civilized Englishman.

This is "captivity" but her literal abduction by a wild Arab is exciting. By the end of the second film, it becomes clear that she does not mind captivity, only a certain form of it. She does not want to be the wife of an uptight Englishman, like Cal, and chained to

---

[231] David Buss, *Evolutionary Psychology: The New Science of the Mind.* New York: Allyn & Bacon, 2012.

some dreary house in England. She wants to be in captivity to a wild man with a sword and gun strapped to his side and who lives in a tent in the middle of the desert and commands a horde of men. This is a more physical captivity or dominance, and less of a social captivity or confinement to the stifling social body, which is more cerebral or symbolic. Rose certainly didn't want to have anything to do with this, and this is inspirational for us today. We have seen the theme of the righteous, heavy body and its battle against the oppressive mind repeatedly in modernism. Instead of the body being a "heavy" burden, now it is the social body. If we were to ask savvy Tolstoy's opinion, we would know who the real man is—who is the one to get excited about.

In the context of our regular cultural values, we know which man represents the irregular and which is the hero. In *Anna Karenina*, Tolstoy portrays the urban elites as fools, while Levan, the farmer, is the real man. And recall women's rape fantasies here, and the growth of white women married to black men, who, it should be said here, have higher crime, and are prone to swagger to show off, and have this general image by association with the lower classes and wild Africa.

In a short, entitled *The Physique of the Sheik*, Valentino simply gets out of a car, changes into a bathing suit, lays out on the beach and shows off his nice arms. Of course this is very mild by today's standards for sexualized violence. Valentino was extremely popular with women, and when he died at age 28 it was a shock, and he was mourned by millions of disappointed, savvy women.

Another film about heroes is the World War One drama *All Quiet on the Western Front* (1930). It starts with a group of young German men in a school room being lectured to by a older man who goes into detail about the virtues of heroism, and that there is nothing sweeter than to die for one's country. The young men decide to volunteer for the army but soon learn that the training is hard work.

Twice while marching they must fall into the mud. Even before they have seen any action they get fed up with the training, and one of the men calls the drill sergeant a "filthy ape." This use of low imagery to a high context should sound familiar to the savvy.

As police today are pigs, and Cal is overbearing, so drill sergeants are apes. This whole situation is simply disgusting and demands correction or evasion.

The men decide to take revenge on the drill sergeant. At night when he is out by himself, they tie him up, put a sack over his head and dump him in some mud. He suffers at the hands of his own sins, a common theme in Christian and Greco-Roman morality, as we shall see.

In one of the first scenes at the front, a bunker frequently leaks dirt on their heads because of bomb explosions and, most horribly, at one point a swarm of rats invades the bunker. The men groan and complain throughout the scene. The first 45 minutes of the movie, before any military action, comprises scenes like this of horrible suffering. Of course, the under-current of the film has a tone of rebellion, and this often breaks out, even during eating scenes.

At one point, the film explicitly romanticizes insubordination. An officer comes into the bunker and demands to be saluted. The men ignore him. One pulls down his pants and aims his buttocks in the officer's direction. This is his salute. Of course those who are savvy, wise and righteous know to rebel against the corruption of the social body, the "tyrant" as we saw in Forsyth. You should never be dupe, or you will loose your immortal soul.

One of the most ridiculous scenes in the film is when a German soldier is in fox hole and a French soldier drops inside of it. The German takes out a knife and stabs him. Not sure that he's dead, the German starts to talk to him and eventually apologizes for the assault, and he even prays and apologizes to God for the assault. So he has misgivings about the entire war effort, or the social body, just as we always had guilt feelings about our sinful impulses.

During a lull in the action, the soldiers bathe in a river and some French girls come walking by on the opposite bank. The men start to yell in a flirtatious way and try to make dates. Another soldier who is on guard sees this and warns the men that they cannot cross the river. The men show the girls that they have food, and this gets the girls' attention, and who then agree to meet them later. That evening, there is a scene in a house with the men and girls eating and drinking, and clearly there is hanky-panky. The message is clear: make love not war.

This is depicted for the savvy as real, as opposed to the fighting which is the false consciousness of zealous nationalism or social anger or hate, one the deadly sins for modernism. This is what the savvy want to escape from, and into sensuality and solipsism as we saw among the Bloomsbury Group and the 1960s.

After over an hour and half of the horrors of war, the main character, Paul, finally starts to make explicitly anti-war statements. While on leave he visits the classroom of the teacher who convinced him and the others to join. The teacher encourages Paul to praise war, but Paul simply describes how horrible it is, and says, "When it comes to dying for your country, it is better to not die at all." The other students look at him with disapproval and call him a coward. Then he says what may be the thesis of the film, "Death is stronger than duty to one's country." As the suffering and death of Jesus were absolute horrors, and could trump duty to ones country and leaders, we see this logic working here, with the individual being Jesus of course.

As people used to plead on behalf of Jesus, now they plead on behalf of themselves. As it was horrible that Jesus died for our sins, now it is horrible that people die at the hands of the social body, or social anger and hubris, one of the deadly sins. This is the source of the evasiveness, complaining and cowardice throughout the film. As people strained to avoid the suffering of Jesus, now the savvy desperately want to avoid their own suffering, and do not want to be oppressed.

This is why people dance almost alone today. Traditionally, duty to one's country was seen as part of duty to God; as in "God and Country." The traditional hierarchy was such that national leaders and their orders were up there with God. Nationalism and religion were entangled for most people in the nineteenth and early twentieth centuries. With the rise of natural rights and popular sovereignty, we have seen religion bent to different purposes as is clearly illustrated by the film.

The film *From Here to Eternity* (1953), which takes place in Hawaii in the days before the Pearl Harbor attack, is not anti-war, which would have been nearly impossible in the years after the success of American forces in World War Two, but it is clearly anti-military. The impression one gets from the film is that the military embodies abuse of power. In the film, the Army is a surrogate for the social body. The film portrays the military hierarchy as corrupt to the point that it kills its own people. The hero of the film, Robert Prewitt played by Montgomery Clift, refuses to box for his regiment's team as the result of a contrite heart. So he's a good person.

The commanding officer tries to convince him to fight but Prewitt refuses. The officer and his underlings make life difficult for Prewitt as incentive to get him to fight. At one point, Prewitt is scrubbing the floor, and a low-ranking officer kicks over two buckets of dirty water, and then yells at Prewitt, "Clean it up!" Prewitt becomes angry, and refuses. The commanding officer orders Prewitt to apologize to the officer who kicked the buckets, but Prewitt says that it ought to be he that is apologized to. This is part of the strategy of the commanding officer to force Prewitt to box. Jesus always told us that virtue would be tested. Later, in his office, the commanding officer is arranging special punishment for Prewitt for disobeying orders, and says, "Men like him can't be treated decently, but must be treated like an animal." Of course, the savvy know here who is abusing power, and is thus an "animal," a "filthy ape," the overbearing social body.

While on leave, Prewitt's character meets Lorene Burke, played by Donna Reed. They fall in love, but Burke resists marrying someone of such low status. She says that she wants to earn money from her job, buy a proper house, join a proper golf club, meet and marry a proper man of status, and have proper children. Her reason for this is that "When you're proper, you're safe." The significance of this becomes clear near the end of the film.

Frank Sinatra plays Angelo Maggio, a character who likes to drink. At one point, Maggio gets into a bar fight with Fatso, a guard at the local stockade. Eventually Maggio goes AWOL and is sentenced to 6 months in the stockade, where Fatso beats him mercilessly whenever they are alone. The situation is enough to make you sympathize with the storming of the Bastille, or making a film like *Titanic*. Eventually, Maggio breaks out of the stockade but is injured in the process. He finds Prewitt and as he dies in Prewitt's arms, he tells of the abuse he suffered and how he spat in Fatso's face every time he was beaten. He describes how he escaped and perishes. He is portrayed as a victim of the military's cruel abuse of power. As the body made Jesus suffer, now the social body or social hubris, makes us suffer. The scene with the dead Maggio draped in Prewitt's arms resembles a modernist Pieta.

Prewitt then fights Fatso and kills him, but is injured in the process. While he is recuperating in Burke's house, the Japanese attack Pearl Harbor. Though injured, Prewitt decides to go back to the Army to help fight the Japanese. As he is leaving Burke's house, she becomes hysterical with fear for Prewitt's life. She describes that he is injured and that going into battle will open the wound; then she says that if he goes back the Army will put him in the stockade for Fatso's murder. She offers to marry him.

With this offer, we see that she has given up her shallow class aspirations and decided to be real, like a nun, or like the English woman in *The Sheik*, and the sexy girls in *All Quit on the Western Front*. The savvy can just imagine her drinking a bowl of pus to forward this glorious agenda. She then says, "The Army treated you like dirt" and "they killed your friend." At this point, it is clear that the abuse was not the responsibility of a few bad people but the entire institution of the Army. As the Virgin Mary grief-stricken over the death of Jesus, now Burke is hysterical with grief at the impending death of Prewitt at the hands of the social body. In the last scene, Prewitt is gunned down by a US soldier for not obeying an order to halt. In the end, he is killed, not by the Japanese, but by his own military. This vindicates Burke's hysterical concerns. As the savvy once understood that the body was sure death, so now savvy understand that the social body is sure death.

The modern Christian morality we saw in *All Quite on the Western Front* and *From Here to Eternity* generates today the same paranoid fantasy iconography as it did with old master paintings of hell. Today, as during the Renaissance, there is iconography representing the mortality that people will suffer if they follow their deep desires, believe in their social system and military, and satisfy its needs, succumbing to its desires.

The film *The Terminator* (1984) partly takes place in a future when the West's military defense systems have taken over and turned against people. The military computers kill everyone foolish enough to have believed in them and did not disarm—who did not repress their social body's hubristic desires. To make people suffer for their sins, the defense systems inflict mortality on people instead of protecting them and the interests of civilization.

As the glutton in Bosch's *The Garden of Earthly Delights* is devoured by a huge stomach on legs, the social body's military systems set out to exterminate humanity for having created them to socially dominate their good brothers, and kill Westerners for having succumbed to their social body. The savvy see that the West suffers at the hands of the sins themselves.

The film presents images of hell on earth to foreshadow the future damnation. In the *Book of Revelation*, the sins of our bodies cause the destruction of the Earth. So today the sins of the social body cause the destruction of the Earth. Mortality and its symbols are in full view for the savvy as a warning of what they will receive for having succumbed.

In Dante's *Inferno*, the gluttonous live on heaps of garbage under driving storms of cold rain, while flatterers are immersed in pools of sewage, and the sexually perverse walk burning stretches of sand in an environment as sterile as their attempts at love.

In *The Terminator*, the social body's urges dominate. People live in folly, so the wages of sin is total annihilation by the sin of social anger itself. People are killed and tortured by their earthly pleasures.

In response to the attack by the social body, exhausted, demoralized humans go underground to fight a losing guerrilla war, a war against the force of mortality that ceaselessly descends. The desolate battleground where people meet their mortality is strewn with the bones and skulls of the millions who have died at the hands of their own defense system, their sins.

In the arena where humans face death, their descent, symbols of their mortality are in view as warning to the ignorant and savvy alike. Closely framed images show tanks rolling over skulls and incinerating or burning people with lasers. People burn for their sins. People die for having sinned and believed in society's project of civilization and its defense, for living for this life. Those who live suffer endless pain inflicted by their own sins. The battle scenes do not depict battles like those in World War II films, but are stylized and symbolic of gloom and doom. Humans live underground, while the machines or the military control the surface of the earth. What is righteous is revolt from below, as we saw earlier. Only this movement is legitimate; the movement up of good against evil. People today do indeed enjoy getting down and dirty, as we saw in the state of nature.

If people had repressed their social body and disarmed, they would have had life, true immortality in the future. They would have gone to heaven instead of hell. Recall here how we have changed the meaning of "peace" as going from individual to collective. As Christians once needed to fight the body's desire to sin, everyone now must fight the social body's desire for a military, now and in the future—the military body, quite literally, in this case. We see this sentiment in embryonic form in *From Here to Eternity*. This battle against the military is a graphic, literal example of the battle that people must wage if eternal life is to be had. But of course the savvy know this. But there is a light: People can be saved from their sins through Jesus.

In the film, a robot-agent of the social body goes back in time to the present pre-apocalyptic era to kill Sarah Connor, a woman who will give birth to a boy who will be a super-leader of the humans during their future battle against the social body. To protect her and their future leader, the humans send Kyle Reese back in time to subvert the assassin. Appearing out of nowhere, he desperately searches for the woman, who is oblivious of the folly of her social body, unaware that she is going to be devoured by the social body in its future attempts to kill her, and ignorant of her sacred mission to give birth to the savior.

She is busy having a good time. Connor is just a regular woman, not "conscious" of her mission to give birth to the boy who will lead the successful battles against the social body in the future, who will save people from their sins and give them the strength to fight their sins. She is not conscious of the folly of her social body.

When Reese and Connor finally meet, he tells her of the sins of the social body and announces to her that she is to give birth to a son who will be the leader, the savior in the future, the man who will save people from their sin. She thinks that Reese is crazy as he seeks to raise her consciousness of her mission. After repeated attacks from the robot, she becomes convinced that the man came to protect and enlighten her. Together, they finally destroy the robot, the social body. The authority of the human body—the will to resist the temptations of the social body—temporarily triumphs.

The hero Reese dies in the process of saving the woman from herself, from her lack of consciousness, for her future and the future of mankind. He dies for our sins, but her consciousness of the sins of the social body has been heightened. In the final scene, the woman moves to a humble, alternative desert country, where people speak Spanish, to escape the social body and raise her son, the savior. She is pregnant as she drives a Jeep Renegade. She is a savvy warrior or rebel against society, as we saw in *The Sheik*.

We see the simple anti-war message of *All Quite on the Western Front* raised in intensity to a fantasyland narrative and iconography of anti-militarism. This is how we direct our anger and outrage today; outward instead of inward.

In the Bible, an angel tells Mary that she is to give birth to a Child who is going to be the Savior of the world. She is startled, protesting that she is of humble birth. Eventually, she is persuaded of her mission. In *The Terminator*, the man who appears and announces that she is to give birth has sex with her, and thus sires the savior.

This is an echo or humanization of the original Biblical annunciation scene where the Holy Spirit enters the Virgin with prompting from the angel. Recall that we like to get down and dirty today.

In the Bible, after giving birth, Mary hides herself and the child because the state (Herod) has given orders to destroy all baby boys born on the same day as Jesus: In *The Terminator*, the agent of the social body kills all women with the same name as Connor in an attempt to stop the Savior. "How early did persecution commence against Christ and his Kingdom!" as someone said during the nineteenth century. As most any savvy "professor" can testify today, the social body was rampant in history.

Each woman, Mary and Connor, gives birth to a boy who will save Christendom from their sins, the sins of either their human or social body. *The Terminator* is a modern polyptych: *The Slaughter of the Innocents, The Last Judgment, The Annunciation,"* and *The Flight into Egypt.* Until this century, people were largely illiterate, and Christianity and its narratives were people's basic education.

The sequel to *The Terminator* was appropriately titled *Judgment Day.* It tells how figures reflecting Mary, Jesus, and Joseph try to destroy the social body before "judgment day," as they refer to it in the film—that is, the day the social body takes over and inflicts hell on earth.

Some interesting differences in this film from its antecedent are that the Connor, Mary figure, has choices in her life (she has triumphed over her social body and is a hero as we saw in *The Sheik*) and a handsome, clean-cut policeman represents the stalking, evil social body. The Joseph figure (a re-programmed beneficent terminator robot) looks like a motorcycle gang member. The movie implies that people should not succumb to their social body and believe that evil looks evil and good looks good.

After all, the savvy claim that White men and the police are evil. Motorcycle gang members are beautiful, while the police are pigs, the evil agents of the social body. We do want to be like the Vikings today and get down and dirty. Sarah Connor has a more active role in this film, taking on much of the fighting. Her back-story says that in the past she tried to blow up a computer factory. In the first film, both of the main characters were blonds, but their son, the savior, in the second film appears to be part Asian.[232]

We see a blow for diversity, regardless of the facts, as with the emotional Scandinavian and restrained Italian in *Titanic.* There are almost no Blacks in the first film, not even as extras, whereas in the second film there are many, including one who is important to the plot. When Connor, the Mary figure, talks to the man responsible

---

[232] Editor's note: The child John Connor is played by Edward Furlong, whose mother is Mexican and father is Russian.

for creating the technology that will try to destroy mankind in the future, she says, "it is men like you who destroy life, while women create life."

The film depicts men as the evil social body, while women are good, representing the body. This is an inversion, because during the nineteenth century people believed that woman's more earthy role was suspect and evil while men, as agents of control of wild nature were good. So goes the way of the savvy.

At the film's climax, Connor and the good terminator robot destroy with axes the computer lab that will create the machines that will try to exterminate mankind.

This resembles the tactics used by Carrie Nation, a leader of the early temperance movement. Around 1900, she would go into bars and destroy them with an axe. She raised money for the movement by selling miniature axes and by the publicity that resulted from her prison time. Both women are heroes against evil: for savvy Carrie Nation the evils of the body, for savvy Sarah Connor the evils of the social body.

And recall here that Picasso, another savvy hero, chopped up the old classicism "with an ax." So we see how anger is now directed outward. In the film, Sarah and the good terminator fight desperately for their lives, and she is often almost hysterical with fear. Reflecting Christianity, the film's Jesus, Mary, and Joseph figures, by their example, inspire others in their battles against sin. This reflects that today modernists experience the military as an evil or fearful imposition and something to frustrate and escape.

A Christian song expressed the idea that belief in God was a conspiracy, and this sounds familiar. Certainly, during earlier centuries, the savvy thought they were in on something special and they helped each other, and part of this was to fight those on the outside. We see this same perspective in *Terminator*. The humans are in a war or conspiracy against the evil social body, just as they were in a conspiracy against the sinful body and the other enemies.

This perspective contributed to driving the competitive state system in Europe for a millennia, which of course often fell along confessional lines. This is indeed a powerful social psychology that we cannot ignore. We saw this in how we need to construct an evil for people or they start to fixate on those around themselves, like among the Vikings.

This idea about conspiracy helps to explain the difference between the left and right today and their perspective on each other. The left definitely sense that they are conspiring and in war against the right, while the right has more humble aspiration and is mostly just trying to figure out the right solution to problems. As I observed earlier, the savvy left view the right as evil, while the right considers the left just misguided due to "good intensions," as the people who burned evil witches had good intentions but were misguided.

It is worth stopping for a moment and note an interesting example of inversion in *Terminator*. In Christianity, the devil is associated with hell because of its malevolent subterranean aspect. So "low" is evil in this tradition and high is good as it is associated with heaven. Earth is literally in between and hence had a morally ambivalent status. In *Terminator*, the humans are underground, and, as we have seen repeatedly, is good, and the high is evil, as we saw in *Titanic* and elsewhere. So we see that *Terminator* inverts the values associated with high and low. This results from popular sovereignty. We also saw this with the Romantics and their drive toward the low, or the common, nature, particularism, and diversity. Recall the African tribe that does the gorilla dance; they saw this as high.

With this kind of inversion of symbolism in mind it is instructive to note Russell's discussion of color symbolism: "Blackness and darkness are almost always associated with evil, in opposition to the white and light associated with good. This is true even in black Africa. Blackness has an immense range of negative and fearful associations: death, the underworld, the void, blindness, night stalked by robbers and ghosts. Psychologically it signifies the fearful, uncontrollable depths of the unconscious. It is also associated with depression, stupidity, sin, despair, dirt, poison and plague."[233] Similarly, "Chaos is often represented as a snake, serpent or dragon."[234] As will became clear in the next chapter, *Modernism's*

---

[233] Jeffrey Russell, *The Prince of Darkness: Radical Evil and the Power of Good in History* (Ithaca & London: Cornell University Press, 1988), 10.
[234] Ibid, 11.

Theology of Race, now black people are "the light" and whites, like Cal, represent stupidity and death etc. Earlier we saw a clear parallel between the oppressive dragon and Cal.

In the earlier film *The Santa Fe Trail* (1940), an officer tells a group of junior officers: "We here at Fort Leavenworth are the only military installation between here and Santa Fe, and we are proud of that responsibility." Today, people would complain about being understaffed, victimized, and oppressed, and would conclude that they deserve danger pay.

In the film, the fort and the men who occupy it are inseparable: "We here...are the only military installation." The men are the military installation. The fort is an extension of its occupants and does not oppress them or bear down on top of them as in modern imagery. It does not have an adversarial relationship as in *From Here to Eternity* and *Terminator* and does not need to be escaped. It supports communal life against threatening outsiders.

Today, when the military wants to inspire people, it mentions that if they do not fight, they will be killed by the enemy—or worse, they will not receive their college tuition scholarship. The old, savvy perspective is that the interests of superior civilization and its defense are the interests of all, even non-Westerners because of the reigning idea of progress.

The film *Saving Private Ryan* (1998) is anti-war in an oblique fashion. It takes place during the Normandy invasion of World War II, so it would be hard to portray the American cause as evil, but the film's plot argues that there are more important things, as in *All Quite on the Western Front*. The opening scene shows the landing, and instead of the soldiers heroically running off the landing ships and attacking the Germans, the soldiers vomit and are cut to pieces by German machine gun and artillery fire.

Three or four scenes show limbs blown off and men lying in the water with their guts hanging out. John Miller, a captain played by Tom Hanks, has a hand that shakes throughout the film. The issue here is emphasis. Obviously there were many fatalities during the landing, but the allies were successful. The impression you get from the scene is that it was a failed cause. The scene would have been perfect for *All Quite on the Western Front*: war is nothing more than horror and futile loss of life. The savvy know the social body is only death, as we saw in *Terminator*.

The surviving men huddle behind a hill of sand and eventually penetrate the German line of defense. Once they have made a beachhead, the film cuts to a meeting of General Marshal and his staff. A Mrs. Ryan has lost three of her sons in the fighting, while the fate of her fourth and last is unknown. Marshal concludes that Private Ryan must be pulled out of the fighting at almost any cost. A special unit is formed from the Normandy force to save Private Ryan and is commanded by Captain Miller. Nothing at the beginning or end of the film says that it was based on true story, so we can take it as the product of the same imagination that produced *All Quite on the Western Front*. The plot implies that the entire war effort was put on hold for one person. For over an hour, the unit roams around the villages of Normandy looking for Ryan, occasionally fighting German troops.

Now one need not rely on the plot nor the action to see the film's preference of the individual over the collective war effort. Statements are to this effect. For instance, at one point Miller says, "I am willing to lay down my life and those of my men to ease the suffering of Ryan's mother."

At the end of the film he does indeed die with most of his men, but Ryan, whom they find, survives. At the film's mid-point, Captain Miller tells a soldier that one rational for a war action is that it can save more lives than it costs: "This is how you rationalize the choice between the mission and the man." The soldier responds, with a savvy look on his face, "But this time the mission is the man." As Jesus was the all-consuming mission now the individual is. Recall here John Stuart Mill's belief that the individual is above the state and is to be served by the state. It would be hard to find a clearer example of this philosophy than this film. Though, even most libertarians I don't think would be willing to lay down their lives for their "sacred" beliefs. They are mostly interested in hanging out.

A soldier in the film makes an even more emphatic statement when he says, "Saving Private Ryan was the one decent thing we were able to pull off from this God awful shitty mess. We do that then we all earn the right to go home." Now I think it is fairly obvious that defeating the Germans was more important and more decent, but not according to modernist philosophy. We could have lost Private Ryan, and if we had defeated the Germans, the war would still have been a success though apparently it would have been indecent. Decency, in the eyes of some today, lies not with survival of our institutions, the social body, but with the suffering individual—the Christ-type and model of decency. We know who is on top of the state today in their eyes.

At one point, to convince Ryan to quit the fighting and go home with the special unit, a man says to Ryan, "two men died to find you." Now this statement is amazing in light of the events at the end of the film. There is a large battle between an outnumbered special unit and a well armed and manned German unit. During the course of the fighting almost all of the Americans are killed except Ryan. So not just two, but over a dozen men are killed "Saving Private Ryan."

The film ends the way it began, with an implied heroic ethic. As people wanted to immolate themselves over Jesus, now it is over the all-powerful individual. This is what savvy modernists want to fight for today, and this prompts major currents in political thought such as among the libertarians, and in lesser degrees among most people, and prompts the mania over civil rights on both the left and right. Hence, we have the savvy ACLU defending the right of Mexicans to invade the United States. It is the decent thing to do, at least from one maniacal perspective.

As Louis the XIV glorified his reign in art and architecture, Hollywood and almost every liberal arts "professor" glorifies the rule of the individual. We will see this very powerfully in the next chapter, *Modernism's Theology of Race*.

In the film *Tears Of The Sun* (2003), a departing U.S. military unit cannot bring itself to abandon a destitute and threatened African people, and so it returns to rescue them. Recall here that as Christians wanted to fight for God, now the protagonists want to fight for Blacks, a Christ-type—"They suffer for our sins," as we will see in the next chapter. In an episode of *Friends*, Phoebe, Ms New Age, throws herself in front of a dart gun aimed at a monkey.

In another episode, she hysterically stops Joey from putting a dead Christmas tree into a wood chipper. The series makes clear that such actions by Phoebe express a form of devotion integral to her fanatical personality. In *Tears Of The Sun*, team leader Lieutenant A.K. Waters, played by Bruce Willis, gets misty when viewing a field of dead Africans.

He decides to help the Africans and come to their rescue. His unit inadvertently saves a king by their military actions. Waters certainly is a faithful servant. A Black soldier tells Waters, "Those are my people" as moral justification for helping them, and Willis adds that his men should fight, "for our sins," as if for redemption. So much for the "modern" world.

What is significant about this film is that it is pro-military, pro-war and even romanticizes death. What matters is what the soldiers fight for. When the cause is Blacks, or fighting for redemption from the sins of the social body, then fighting and death are portrayed in a positive light. When fighting is presented as the expression of traditional European nationalism, or any other form of social body self-centeredness, then it is just a horror, as we saw in *All Quite on the Western Front* and *Terminator*.

Another important element of the film is that the military unit helps the African group against orders from superiors. In other words, they are themselves rebels, rebelling from below in order to help the low. At one point, Lt. Waters says, "It's the same mission," to morally justify his rebellious action by drawing a parallel with the official mission.

Only the rebellion from below is righteous or morally justified at least for the savvy. If, in a different context, the military unit had gone against orders and helped the conservative Contras fight against the Sandinistas of Nicaragua, it would have been viewed as horrible by Hollywood liberals. It would have been in the interest of the United States, but that is just a horror. When Waters is asked why he does it, he responds that he "does not have it figured out." This statement is worth pausing over. This is similar to the statement from Rose in *Titanic* on how the Picasso has truth but no logic, and, most importantly, that going off with Jack, "makes no sense, but that's why I trust it."

It is clear that modernists on both the left and right do not know what they are doing, and instead are on automatic emotion, reasoning, and action, like an animal. Science, like evolutionary psychology, is nowhere to be seen in the modern world as it pertains to human nature, action, morals, and politics.

The end of *Tears Of The Sun* has a quotation usually attributed to 18th-century philosopher Edmund Burke: "The only thing necessary for the triumph of evil is for good men to do nothing." We see that the battle against evil, or at least a new notion of evil, is the driving engine or heart of modernism and its moralizing films and politics.

A more sophisticated and fantastic development of the same metaphor of evil from the social body is the movie *Alien* (1979). A ship belonging to a private company is traveling through space when it receives radio signals from a nearby planet. As part of the crew's contract with the social body, they must search for the source of the transmission or forfeit their pay. Against their best instincts, they land on the planet.

For "selling out" in this way, they are doomed. They have sold their souls to the Devil. We saw this in *Terminator*, and, like in *Titanic*, a large, private concern is involved.

The crew enters a derelict ship on the planet's surface and finds pods containing large, crablike creatures. One creature leaps from a pod and latches onto the face of a crewman, inserting a tentacle down the victim's throat and into his chest and stomach. His mates bring him back to the ship, where they attempt to remove the creature. However, after a day of failed effort, the creature dies and falls off.

The victim becomes conscious and appears to be normal, joining the rest of the crew for dinner. Suddenly the man collapses in convulsions on the table, screaming in pain as a baby reptilian monster eats its way through his chest to emerge and slither away while the terrified crewmembers watch. The baby grows within hours to become a huge carnivorous monster that stalks the crew and devours them one by one.

In an attempt to gather helpful data from the computer to fight the monster, a female crewmember discovers that the company had planned to sacrifice the crew in order to bring the monster back to civilization. With the aid of a White male (robot, unhuman) science officer, the company (the social body) brings evil into the world from the outside, with innocents falling victim. We saw this in *Rosemary's Baby* with the white male father bring the devil into the world.

They deposit evil into the body and back out again, creating evil in the world: monsters. The savvy know that the social body is evil, and succumbing to the social body creates evil in the world. If the crew had ignored the transmission, gone on strike, repressed the social body, then evil would have been frustrated. Westerners must be ascetic and deprive their social body to repress evil. The crew succumbed to the social body, sinned, and fell to Earth. Recall that in medieval art the dragon angrily consumes his victims. The dragon of the Vikings and then of the Christians has become the dragon of society.

In *Alien*, a powerful voice against going onto the planet is that of the Black male mechanic. He naturally resists the urges of the social body, but is ultimately victimized by it. To whom should the West listen? To evil White men or righteous, savvy and beautiful Black men? That is easy, "Black is beautiful" (just like the woman's hero in *The Sheik)*. Black men are hip to the real agenda, the evil with which White men want to infest people's lives. Middle-class White men are evil, while lower-class men, like in *Titanic*, and especially Black men, are heroes. In compensation, to lower themselves white men today have impulses to drink a bowl of pus.

I believe it is good to stop and revisit the psychology of the dragon because of the role, as an innate image of power, it has played in myth and political and ethical imagery in relatively modern societies. Recall that in Russell's discussion of color symbolism, that dragons and serpents are commonly associated with chaos and blackness. And recall from the discussion of Christianity in the chapter on the state of nature, how a French woman imagined, with her sins, snakes. So we see, like with Russell, an association between evil and snakes, which of course is very common in Christian iconography. The devil is commonly portrayed as or associated with a serpent.

Now recall that Jones, in his study *An Instinct for Dragons*, shows that we are hardwired for the image because of the evolution of predator avoidance among primates and hominids. In his discussion of the cultural and mythic expressions of the dragon, Jones says that it is common, around the world, for heroes to kill dragons, and anthropologists commonly categorize him as a "culture hero" who defeats the chaos of nature.[235]

Jones also notes that in many later societies, like in Asia and England, the dragon becomes a domestic or political symbol. So the power is harnessed to the creation of good order, an order on the wild individual. We can see how modernist inversion is expressed in predictable ways in dragon imagery. As we saw in *Titanic* and *Alien*, the dragon represents the evil state, the "chaos," with the displacement of evil we have seen, which is defeated by a nature hero, not a culture hero.

As we have seen, culture is the enemy. So instead of the French woman imagining herself to be an evil dragon, now we imagine upper class white men, the military and private business as the evil dragon and that need to be defeated by good nature. Instead of the domestic or political dragon being a vehicle for order, now it is threatening with our new perspective on the state. In both *Titanic* and *Alien*, the nature heroes slay the dragon of society or the social body. Richard Wagner, in his opera *Siegfried*, also used this inverted value when he portrayed the nature hero Siegfried as slaying the dragon of evil society. This is clear evidence that we are hardwired for a conception of legitimate and illegitimate power, or good and evil, as mentioned earlier.

To return to the film, another important difference between the old and new process of evil is the kind of presence that evil has in the body. Two 19th-century creations, Frankenstein's monster and Dracula, derived from Christian tradition of witches, goblins, and ghosts, and so were inseparable from their evil. Evil permeated the very fiber of their bodies. In fact, evil was their bodies, and the savvy knew this. Frankenstein's monster had the brain of a crazed murderer, and Dracula was compared to a wild animal.

---

[235] David E. Jones, *An Instinct for Dragons*. (New York & London: Routledge, 2002), 94.

The plot of the 1931 film version of *Dracula* is a good example of how people at the time thought about evil. Dracula has no reflection in a mirror and can take on the form of a bat or a wolf. He is dead and evil and so cannot stand the sight of either daylight or the cross. Dracula's evil is contagious. The people he bites become vampires themselves.

This derives from the popular idea that emotion was contagious temptation. At one point Dracula tries to dominate a man, but the man resists, and Dracula compliments him in his strength to resist the power of Dracula. (Women uniformly succumb.) The same man eventually figures out what Dracula is doing and drives a stake through his heart to kill him. When Dracula is destroyed, the spell that he has over people is broken. With this in mind, consider that in 16th-century France, 50,000 so-called werewolves were executed. Suspects were men with hair between their eyebrows who kept to themselves. The savvy people took evil so seriously, that it generated collective fantasies or images and dictated church and government policy. Witch trials also come to mind here. If one recalls the behavior of the Vikings, these responses seem less ridiculous. They represent a kind of over-reaction.

At the beginning of the *Dracula* film, the first person that the vampire bites says, with a possessed tone of voice and look on his face, that he will be loyal to Dracula, and that Dracula is his master. The person has become a slave to evil or sin. We saw how this idea was transformed in political theory during the eighteenth century by the idea that the lower classes were good and needed freedom from the enslaving evil of the upper classes. As the slogan in Dracula is "Freedom from evil or death," the political slogan starting during the eighteenth century, was "Freedom or Death."

As Dracula was depicted as subhuman or inferior, so is the upper class today as we saw in *Titanic*. The phrase, "great blond beast," was used to refer to Germans during the Second World War. College student draft deferments were suspended during the Vietnam War, and Charles Murray in his recent book on education said that smart students are not superior, just lucky.[236]

---

[236] Charles Murray, *Real Education* (New York: Crown Forum, 2008).

Anti-elitism has become ever stronger during the past century, even among conservatives like the military and Charles Murray. Dr. Murray may be caving in to the hate mail he received for co-authoring *The Bell Curve*, which describes how intelligence determines social class or status.

As we saw that it was evil for Whites to offend Blacks, now we see that it is taboo for smart Whites to get uppity with dumb Whites, or for the upper class to get uppity with the lower. Recall here that most wealthy people are democrats because they want to be politically fashionable or seen to have the proper morals and high status. They drink puss. Today, the high identify with the low, instead of the tradition whereby the lower classes tried to improve themselves by imitating the upper.

We see this reversal in the deference relationship between White and Black Americans. Victor Hugo's class bashing universal love so strenuously argued for in *Les Miserables* has triumphed. Who would want to impose misery on anyone? Of course to believe otherwise would be succumbing to the social body which is seen as evil, like the Nazis.

Regarding the prospect of resurrecting eugenics policies, one writer said, "that went *down* with the Nazis" [italics added]. Nowadays, the elite are the "great blond beast," subhuman or low, while everyone loving each other, regardless of characteristics, is "high," righteous or sublime in order to defeat the social body, as we saw in *All Quite on the Western Front* and *The Sheik*. For centuries the West had been taught that we can only defeat evil by love, for each other and Jesus. Of course, Hugo collapsed this and the "love" has been spreading out to a wider circle ever since, which of course follows empowerment and deification.

The film *Rabid* (1977) translates the tale of Dracula into the new Christian moral causality of social body determinism. The movie opens with a meeting of male plastic surgeons plotting to become the "McDonald's of plastic surgery." The head surgeon leaves the meeting and performs an experimental method of plastic surgery on a woman. The procedure is faulty—evil—and she goes into a deep coma. After waking, she has grown a small set of jaws in the area of the incision.

When she has a hunger for blood, she embraces her victim and the jaws come out. The people who are victimized, including the doctor, become rabid, but then die. She eventually escapes the hospital and proceeds to infect the entire city.

Again, the message is that the social body creates monsters, evil in the body and in people's lives. When the woman begins to understand what she does to people, she cries in protest, "But it's not my fault!" She is a victim of the urges of the evil social body. The social body causes evil to which people fall victim. "Society made me do it!" says the criminal.

Bram Stoker's Dracula was innately evil and therefore was logically created from the innately evil body. If today's society creates human evil, then logically it should also create Dracula, and the savvy know this. As Jesus said that sinful actions are just the outward sign of what people are inside, the evil actions of the *Rabid* lady Dracula are just the inward sign of what she is outside.

For the new Christian monsters, evil has a quantifiable presence in the body. The innocent body can be opened up, and evil can be viewed and removed. What was once human folly is now a quantifiable mental disorder or mental victimization. "The Devil made me do it" has turned into "Society is in me and made me do it." Today, people must go to a psychologist—a modern priest—to purge the evil from their minds. In *Dracula* evil is contagious, and in *Rabid* we see that the social body is contagious. People's impulses come from out there, from social institutions like class, gender, and "race." As described earlier, with the redemption of sex and the body by the 1960s, the displacement of evil and agency was easy to make because of the connection between felt emotion and the emotions of the vocabulary of body images in the mind and those of our peers.

The dragon of society is seen as pure evil, as are the men who create it. Evil emanates from White men, makes people's lives imperfect, and permeates their bodies. White men are the source of people's mortality. They are the dragon.

The causality of evil in *Alien* is identical to the model of moral causality in *Rabid*. In both films, the imperfect plotting social body puts evil into people, only to have it emerge from and create evil in the world. Not only is the causality identical in both films, but the physical process that creates evil is also identical: evil is placed within people, and then literally protrudes from the body.

As in the old Christian schema, the body is an important point of evil in these films. But how the body obtains that state has become complicated for mythmakers, creating a need for narrative to explain how the body comes to the condition of evil, how it is victimized by the social body.

The savvy know that the body is innocent or beautiful, but the state, larger business institutions, and White males who are their active agents are evil. The new narrative of the victim is why modern films seem sophisticated compared to the traditional stereotyped portrayals of pure evil bodies.

The film *Ghost in the Machine* (1993) shows displacement of evil. A psychotic killer dies in a MRI machine, and his spirit goes into the machine. He then spends the rest of the film conducting a reign of terror against people through their machines; for instance, a man is burned to death by his microwave oven, and another is burned alive by a hand dryer. We see that people do not kill people, but machines do.

The reasoning is similar to *Terminator*. It also generates the mania for gun control. The NRA combats this with the slogan that "Guns don't kill people; People kill people" but this obvious assertion goes against our intuitions today. Recall here that people believe that there are "bad cities," "bad neighborhoods," "bad schools," and that there is "gun violence."

Similarly, the disaster film genre came into existence during the 1970s. Two well-known examples are *The Poseidon Adventure* (1972) and *The Towering Inferno* (1974). The technological structures in the films—a ship and a skyscraper—while appearing safe, turn out to be, respectively, a whirlpool and an oven that close in on people and become their tombs. The savvy know that the social body only spells doom so it is best to not be a dupe. The films are about people's escape from evil.

In *Alien*, the monster's main opponent is a woman. The savvy believe that women are on the cutting edge. At the end of the film, the woman triumphs against the monster of the social body. In both *Alien* and *Terminator* women play a decisive role in defeating the social body, just as they have this role in the popular imagination in combating the social body in politics.

Today women are more progressive than men. There is even a recent book by an irate White male entitled *In Fifty Years We'll All Be Chicks*. As men used to dominate women before the twentieth century because women were viewed as earthy and more emotional, today women dominate because they are more progressive or in tune due to their association with Earth and the emotions.

Nowadays men are seen as subhuman or male chauvinist pigs like Dracula. At some level women fear men as they fear death or entrapment, and have impulses to escape, instead of looking up to men as they did in the nineteenth century. As we have seen, this fear is a common theme in *Sex and the City*. Again, we see a reversal or inversion.

Sex is commonly portrayed in different ways in film history, either representing the old notion of evil or the new notion. In *Flesh and the Devil* (1926) Greta Garbo is portrayed as an evil Eve type who leads innocent men to their doom. She dies an ignominious death at the end. After making several of these kinds of films, she went on strike and refused to play any more "silly women" as she described it. So MGM simply reversed good and evil and made her good and the men evil. This is clear in *Susan Lennox: Her Fall and Rise* (1931). Here Garbo is good, an innocent victim, and the men who persecute and pursue her are evil and subhuman beasts. There is a similar redeemed status in *Love* (1927) where she plays Anna Karenina, who also tries to escape.

A similar contrast can be seen in two Cary Grant vehicles: *Hot Saturday* (1932) and Hitchcock's *Notorious* (1946). In the earlier film a young woman is engaged to a man who subscribes to the old Madonna/whore dichotomy. At the same time she is tempted by a playboy, played by Grant. During the transition to the more sexy option, she is persecuted by all the staid middle aged women in her small town.

At one time the movie screen has four suspended "talking heads" of gossiping middle aged women trying to make life difficult for her. At one point she is even fired from her job for her loose behavior. So she clearly feels bared down upon from evil society. Of course, the last scene shows her escaping with Grant, driving out of town in his luxury car. So our new notion of salvation and righteousness triumphs as the savvy woman escapes the stifling nineteenth century.

In contrast to this is Hitchcock's *Notorious* (1946) which is about a young woman, Ingrid Bergman, who is a notorious promiscuous party girl, and whose father collaborated with the Nazis. Her father is convicted of espionage, and commits suicide in prison. The federal government sends an agent, played by Cary Grant, to recruit her to be **an agent** to help penetrate a Nazi group in South America. As he is coaching her on how to be an agent, they fall in love, and this is portrayed as problematic for Grant because of her loose past.

Most of the film she is on the defensive, and trying to exonerate herself and her father by service to the government and to Grant. So this film is traditional in that society is good and Bergman, a woman, is evil, and she looks to service to society for redemption and salvation. She is nearly killed by the Nazis, but Grant saves her for her heroic service. She is not only saved by service to society, but she is redeemed by love, another common nineteenth century idea. We have inverted this today as now to be loose is good, while to be a house wife is morally questionable, and these women are on the defensive.

It makes sense that during a crisis like a large war Hollywood would regress to traditional values. Obviously, this would help get people in line for the self-sacrifice of war. *Hot Saturday* is known as a "precode" film, when Hollywood played fast and loose with sex and morals. This came to an end about 1934 with the introduction of the production code and its restricting rules about sex. Though as we saw in *The Philadelphia Story* (1940) the modern rejection of the virtue ethic occurred during the more restricted period of the code. Though in this film, sex is more toned down than in *Hot Saturday*.

So it is clear from these films that during the entire period we could vacillate between the two perspectives. Put another way, it was a transitional period, before we made the complete conversion during the 1960s when evil was largely expunged from the body, and lived a vigorous life in society as can be seen in most post 1960s films.

A film at the top of the inversion list is *Gran Torino* (2008). Clint Eastwood plays Walt Kowalski, an elderly Korean War veteran who initially hates non-Whites in general and in particular his Asian neighbors. A young man in the Asian family, named Thao, tries to steal Kowalski's Gran Torino car but Kowalski stops him. In compensation, the Asian family makes Thao work for Kowalski. Kowalski and Thao become friends, and at one point Kowalski says that he has more in common with the Asian family than he does with his own "spoiled, rotten family". This shows a major transformation for Kowalski in his attitudes to non-Whites. Kowalski also says that he is proud to have Thao as a friend. At one point Kowalski starts to offer Thao advice on dating, and goes so far as to offer Thao the use of the Gran Torino for a date. In addition, he changes his will and leaves the car to Thao. Such is Kowalski's response to the man who tried to steal his car. Something very strange is afoot in the West today, like drinking social pus.

Thao is beaten up by an Asian gang, and Kowalski takes revenge by beating up one of the gang members. As we have seen, Whites are depicted as subservient to non-Whites, identify with them, and have impulses to work and fight for them. Kowalski starts to identify with the Asians, or with his captors. In psychology this is called the Stockholm syndrome. A well known example of this occurred with the kidnap victim Patty Hearst. She was kidnapped by a terrorist group, and she started to help and to agree with them. We see Kowalski undergo this same process during the film. Of course, this film represents in miniature the transformation in Whites' relation with non-Whites during the course of the twentieth century.

At one point in the film, a priest describes how it is sinful to kill during war, and later Kowalski admits that killing Asians during the Korean War has tortured his soul ever since. At the beginning of the film Kowalski rejects religion, but toward the end he has a conversion experience. In preparation for what will be in essence a suicide provocation of the gang, he goes to the priest and confesses some venial sins of his youth. Before going after the gang, he gives his silver metal earned fighting in the war to Thao. Kowalski goes to the house of the gang, provokes them, and they gun him down. The police discover that he was unarmed.

The confrontation was self-sacrifice or compensation for his sins of killing during the war, and, likely, for his guilt feeling for a lifetime of racism or succumbing to the social body. This is evident in his giving the metal to Thao. Thao is the true hero, while Kowalski is just a miserable and condemned sinner, who can do no more than work, fight, and die for his master. In essence, the film shows the transformation of the traditional heroic battle against sin and the devil into the battle against in-group self-love, worthiness, or vanity; and by implication, a condemnation of out-group hostility, elitism or racism.

Clint strikes a suicidal blow against feeling worthy, the condition he was in at the beginning of the film. As we were in a state sin before Jesus, but then redeemed, we were in a state of sin before the coming of the non-whites, but now we are redeemed, but only if we accept them, of course. The savvy know this.

His death also exemplifies the sinner suffering for his sins, and even suffering at the hands of the sins themselves, though it probably would have been better if the Klan had killed him for being a "race" traitor. But his conversion to Christianity and moral conversion to multi-racialism complicates his status at the end of the film. He is clearly no longer a simple sinner being punished. There is an element of martyrdom in his death, and thus an element of the imitation of Christ or being a Christ-type, which is what martyrs are.

That it was a suicide would elicit pity in most viewers, and this is a primary emotion in Christians' experience of Christ's passion or death. That Kowalski dies to redeem the sins of the social body is shown by one strong piece of symbolism. As Kowalski lies dying on the ground you see in his hand a military decoration he earned killing Koreans in the war. War is an example of out-group hostility or feeling worthy relative to the communists, so is thus a sin of the social body. His death/suicide, evoking pity, redeems himself or the social body of its original sins of war. After all, we can trace all racial tensions to earlier stages of history, right? To our original sins? At least according to modernist dogma.

That social body modesty is a driving force in modernism is shown by a quote from Susan Sontag: "During the last years Vietnam has been stationed inside my consciousness as a quintessential image of the suffering and heroism of the weak. But it was really America the strong that obsessed me—the contours of American power, of American cruelty, of American self-righteousness."[237] The social body! Temptation to hubris! War is certainly no exercise in modesty. As can be seen in the opera *Lohengrin*, only the King and God get to be judge or righteous. Today Whites must defer to and be judged by non-Whites.

Notice that it is common for non-Whites to judge Whites, while the reverse is seen as racism, or insubordination, as Kowalski suffers from at the beginning of the film. Kowalski's racism represents a sinful era of history, like the Old Testament, before the coming of the non-White redeemer who teaches Whites the virtue of social body modesty. The film is about the progress of an individual soul from sin to salvation through martyrdom or imitation of Christ. Of course, the viewer is supposed to see his own struggles for virtue and salvation mirrored in Kowalski's struggle and transformation. Whites have spent so many centuries being reprimanded by authority figures, that this is what feels good and natural in almost any form, even if it means suicide or death. Of course, this death was always viewed as the wages of sin.

It is helpful to stop and notice that the viewer's relationship to Kowalski is similar to the Catholic's experience of saints. For instance, in the Italian Renaissance painting *The Madonna and Child with Saints Sebastian and Roch*, in the Ringling Museum in Florida, Sebastian looks lovingly at the Child so as to help guarantee his intercessory role for the viewer.[238] We see a similar intercessory role for Kowalski. He looks lovingly at Thoa, to help guarantee for the viewer his power to ward off evil, and for redemption of the sins

---

[237] William A. Rusher, "Will They Ever Learn?" Claremont, California: *The Claremont Review of Books*, Volume IV, Number 2, Spring 2004, 22.

[238] Virginia Brilliant, *The John and Mable Ringling Museum of Art* (London: Scala Publishers, Ltd, 2010).

of the social body. From having viewed the film twice I can attest that it did indeed have purging and comforting effect on me.

I think it should be mentioned that the star of this movie was not an obscure actor, but one of the most famous actors of the last 50 years, and who came with a very strong and heroic background in film. In his early films he was the stern cop in *Dirty Harry*, who hunted down dangerous criminals and snuffed them out with his huge 44 magnum.

This is a bit speculative, but I can't help but think that Clint Eastwood made *Gran Torino* to compensate for the ethno centrism of his early films, and now directed his heroic energy to forward the new vision of social righteousness and salvation. Of course, this is predictable, as all of our institutions now support "diversity," and as we will see, even at the cost of scientific knowledge, and even survival. This new vision is what the law, or "justice" now enforces, so Eastwood should indeed get in line and support the cause. The law is helping whites to escape their new sinful nature by the new vision of social modesty and even suicide.

This is why evolutionary science plays almost no role in modern politics and ethics. The traditional definition of heresy was treason against God, so of course with a new God it now has a new definition; science often reflects negatively on non-whites. One academic institution said that they would not support research that was "racist." Welcome to the new divine right dark ages.

Modern entertainment has not progressed beyond the medieval morality play. As should be clear, this is a very old impulse. In Spain during the sixteenth century, a woman went to the Inquisition and insisted that she was a sinner, and should be punished. They reviewed her sins and concluded that she was okay, and dismissed her. A few months later she came back and insisted that she was a terrible sinner and requested to be executed. They dismissed her again. She came back a third time and made the same claim and insisted that she be executed. Realizing that the situation was hopeless, the Inquisition acquiesced and burned her at the stake.

While describing a film, a well known black actor said, during a stand up comedy routine, "And all the white people were killed…isn't that great," and then the audience laughed. Now one might be tempted to attribute this to a group or race based animosity, but put into its full cultural context we see this is not the case; he is expressing a moral vision of the righteous punishment of sin that has driven the West for a millennia. Sin is simply defined differently today, and in such a way that inadvertently empowers non-whites. The black actor is simply telling whites what they want to hear, and in fact he has internalized this from whites or their institutions as we saw in *Gran Torino, Tears in the Sun* and our entire education system.

As of 1950 both whites and the better educated blacks pretty much thought the same ethically, and it was these blacks that led the civil rights movement, a movement that many whites responded positively to. We saw this moral perspective in the fact that middle class blacks have been killed for "acting white" or for a condition to be escaped or attacked. During the 1950s in the United State more whites killed blacks than blacks killed whites, but this inverted starting during the 1960s and through today.[239]

Almost all cultural and political developments of the last 50 years simply resulted from the accidental combination of historical developments and psychology. 90% of the culture today is simply on automatic. Even the entire welfare state is driven by a huge moralizing fantasy. We also saw this automatic ethical reasoning in the film *Tears in the Sun*, and will see it powerfully in the last chapter, *Modernism's Theology of Race*.

While *Gran Torino* took us up to heaven, the film that gets the award for hitting rock bottom is *Dances With Wolves* (1990). This film is certainly a great blow against feeling worthy.

Kevin Costner plays Lieutenant Dunbar, an officer in the army during the Civil War. He requests posting to the Army's westernmost fort. It turns out to be two mud brick buildings that are abandoned and falling apart. He is the only person there. That the military would assign an officer to an abandoned fort seems unlikely, but this is necessary for the rest of the plot. Left to his own devises he makes friends with the local Indians. Had he been with

---

[239] Marvin E. Wolfgang & Franco Ferracuti, *The Subculture of Violence: Toward an Integrated Theory in Criminology* (London: Tavistock, 1967).

other soldiers he would have been forced to keep his distance. This breaking of atonement and salvation is of course intolerable for the savvy today.

An early scene shows that Dunbar is not a gung-ho 19th-century White man. Before Dunbar's journey, another officer asks him, "So, you're an Indian fighter?" Dunbar responds, "Excuse me?" An element of ambiguity is thus introduced into Dunbar's character. Except for Dunbar, the protagonist, all the other Whites are portrayed as stupid and crazy, but mostly vicious. For instance, the officer who assigns Dunbar to his post says, "I've peed in my pants," pulls out a gun, and shoots himself. This could almost be right out of Bosch. Sin or the social body is just insanity and suicide.

When Dunbar arrives at the abandoned fort, he describes the surrounding countryside as being "Like no place on earth." Such hyperbole is common in the film to forward the modernist agenda. The film is propaganda from beginning to end, but that is the norm today, and especially in our academic culture, as we've seen. Even Nazi film makers would have blushed at some of the tactics used. After Dunbar meets his first Indian, he describes him as "magnificent." The first view that we have of an Indian camp is accompanied by majestic music. This is a real vision of grandeur and purity. Here is the goal of life, according to the film, and Tolstoy.

Dunbar finds an injured White woman dressed in Indian clothing. He does not inquire how she got into this position and if she would rather go back to civilization, but merely takes her to the Indian camp and leaves her there. This is her true home and where Dunbar himself will eventually end up. Back at the Indian camp, the savvy White woman says that she likes it there and is afraid that civilization will take her away. She has escaped from civilization and is happy to have achieved salvation and justice.

Before we progress with the main plot involving Dunbar, we must stop and review two small scenes early in the film. One shows an unarmed man, who has stopped to eat lunch, killed by Indians even though he has made no threatening gestures. The Indians shoot him full of arrows and scalp him. In the other scene, the Indians massacre a peaceful family of farmers who posed no threat. Those two introductory scenes are amazing in light of what happens later in the film. Most of the film shows the Indians as innocent victims of encroaching civilization. The essential brutality of the Indians, while portrayed, is never allowed to interfere with the propagandistic purpose of the film. It probably does not occur to most viewers that there is something wrong with these murders, so accustomed are they to masochistic social modesty from Hollywood. This is how much the West hates itself today. It just feels right, as similar perspectives of righteousness, modesty and justice have for centuries.

After a few contacts with the Indians, Dunbar writes in his journal that the Indians are not, as he has heard, beggars, thieves, and "boogie men." Indeed, the film portrays them as sweethearts. (Recall here the rate of violence among tribes, which was well above whites during the nineteenth century.) Later, Dunbar becomes their friend and hunts with them. When they reach the bison herd, they find about a dozen dead in the field without their skins. They were killed by soulless White hunters. This whole situation is clearly unjust. At least one Nazi film implied that Jews were soulless.

Dunbar starts to participate regularly in Indian life and even exchanges an article of clothing with an Indian. Dunbar says that it is a "good trade." Back at the fort, Dunbar dances around a fire Indian style and praises the Indians for their strong sense of community. As a narrator, Dunbar says that one day there will be "too many White people" in the area. Pollution! The Indians rename Dunbar "Dances with Wolves" because they saw him playing or dancing with a wolf.

With his new name, Dunbar says that he has discovered who he really is. In religious conversion people commonly change their names. St Paul changed his name from Saul, and there are many examples of this in history. Recently, a white woman changed her name from Chadwick, to Chad. And she told me that her favorite film in *The Sheik*. *Dances With Wolves* depicts Dunbar's conversion as an act of modesty. Through the White woman, Dunbar learns to speak the Indian language. As the result of this intimacy, he marries the White woman. This is a good example of reconciliation through sex, a tactic used in the animal kingdom. By three quarters of the way through the film, he wears Indian clothing and is almost assimilated. This purported modesty increases as the film progresses.

During a visit to his camp, he discovers that it has been occupied by a fairly large military force. They think that he is an Indian, beat him and take him into custody. At first he agrees to speak English and tries to explain the situation, but the military personnel are hostile and accuse him of treason and "goin' injun." After a few minutes of this, he starts to speak in the Indian language and says that he will refuse to cooperate with the military. He is a savvy rebel against sinful social vanity. They say that they will ship him back to another, larger installation and have him tried and hanged. As a military escort takes Dunbar back for trial, a group of his Indian friends attacks the unit. One of the Indians is wearing a US military hat. This shows us who is righteous and who ought to have sovereignty. It resembles Walt Kowalski giving his metal to Thao in *Gran Torino*. The entire military unit is killed. During their fighting the White soldiers have crazed looks on their faces and are portrayed as vicious while the Indians are portrayed as noble.

Dunbar is reunited with the Indians, his saviors. His escape has been a success, but only with the help of his redeemers. He is dependent upon them. When Dunbar gets back to the Indian camp, he and his wife passionately kiss. They love one another in God or through the Indians, as is the truly righteous thing. Their love has been blessed by the Indians. The West now looks to the Indians as a model and for redemption, as the film has made clear. (A grade school teacher in California reported that the kids just love the Indians. They are the very picture of wild progress and redemption.) Dunbar says in a meeting with the Indians that it was good that the Indians killed the soldiers. In this film we see again militarism used in modernist or propagandistic purposes as in *Tears of the Sun*. Killing is fine as long as you kill the right people—representatives of Western civilization. Pollution! As we saw with Victor Hugo.

In one of the last scenes, Dunbar talks with an elderly Indian man. The Indian says that the old Dunbar no longer exists and that now he is an Indian. He has been reborn, as Dunbar implies two or three times in the film. As Christians wanted to imitate Jesus, now modernists want to imitate Indians. Dunbar describes the old Indian as an "extraordinary man." Again, hyperbole is used as propaganda and to forward modesty. Indians built teepees from animal skins and shot wooden arrows, while Western civilization built the Eiffel Tower and sent men to the moon, but this film presents the Indians as extraordinary. Western accomplishments are simply meretricious. Even Nazi filmmakers would have had difficulty following this act.

Modern liberals are almost as intolerant as the Nazis; they just believe in demeaning a different group: Westerners who dispute the modernist agenda or the social body in general. Also, another difference is that the left don't have direct control of the police. If they did, we can guess what would happen. Recall here that the early modern monarchs felt they had to control themselves as servants of God, but that "the people" know no control like this and so tend to by very tyrannical. To them, there seems to be something virtuous about suicide, the destruction of the drive toward sin or our sinful, immodest natures, as there was something virtuous about medieval flagellants.

The last scene in the film portrays the military pursuing Dunbar and the Indians into the snowy hills. The film implies that Dunbar and the Indians escaped. Of course today people like to hear stories of how people escaped from the Nazis. Text at the end of the film says that the Indians eventually came under White rule, and that "the American frontier was soon to pass into history." What is implied is that as long as the West was wild or irregular it was alive, or real and rebellious like the English woman in *The Sheik*. But when it was settled or pressed down upon it was killed, and made a relic of history. It is no longer "The greatest place on earth." It became subject to captivity, and needed to escape, and this impulse very much drives high and popular culture in our relation to nature and primitive people in general. The savvy want them to come to the West today, as we wanted to make pilgrimages to the holy land for redemption and to defeat the unjust body.

Reversion to savagery and dancing around is righteous and understandable to modernists. It is an example of social modesty. If dancing with wolves is an ideal, then the animal act of modern dance, and the rest of modernism, makes sense, in a dark and nonsensical sort of way. Traditionally, the progressive goal of popular culture was assimilation to God, now it is assimilation to non-Whites. This is the clear lesson from *The Sheik, Gran Torino* and *Dances With Wolves*. This represents the vision of social modesty and virtue. It explains why *Dances With Wolves* and the others, is seen as progressive. We see the psychology of dependent rank here with whites obtaining a perceived empowerment which is comforting.

What is clear is that this film represents an inversion of the West's perception of its relation with nature. As we've seen, wild nature was viewed as evil, and peaceful civilization and culture represented goodness. Now of course this has been reversed, and this perception is common, as we have seen in *Titanic* and elsewhere. But the aspect of inversion in the relation between heaven and hell in medieval history showed, as we saw, that this was actually an easy transition.

The plot of *Avatar* (2010) is almost identical to *Dances With Wolves*, with humanity representing Western civilization and blue aliens in the role of Indians. The human hero, Jake, joins the natives in the jungle to fight against the evil forces of humanity. Jake's former superior officer at one point says to Jake, "So what's it like being a traitor to your race?" This is a rehash of the modernist social humility or unworthiness that we saw in *Wolves*. The human race is unworthy to be fought for. As the ideal was to be a traitor to yourself, now it is to your species or the social body.

There is Bach's Cantata, "A Mighty Fortress is our God." If you want to get inside the fort, or in this case the jungle, then you need to be a traitor to your race, at least if you are White. Imagine that if there was a war between non-Blacks and Blacks, and a Black went over to the side of non-Blacks. Do you think Hollywood would make a movie romanticizing this? In other words, is it at all conceivable that God would fight on the side of the Devil? Not in this inhuman world. So the bad news is that we are not gods, but the good news is that this represents the victory of mind. The Greeks observed that people were prone to self-deification, but this can and must be resisted.

As should be clear by now, what in part drives modernism are very strong patterns of emotion. Of these, the emotions of heroism and fidelity can be seen among apes. Seeing these among apes helps get them in focus among humans. It is common among apes for an individual to fight for or defend an individual with which he is familiar, or for which he has sympathy. This is such a powerful emotion among apes, that it has been found that an individual will defend a human he feels sympathy for against another unknown human.

This is the case even if the known human starts the fight.[240] Notions of sympathy and fidelity trump the human idea of justice. As we saw in the films, and in Susan Sontag's feelings about Vietnam, whites now have strong feelings of sympathy for non-whites. Put this together with all the other ethics we have seen, and you have a suicide culture. In addition, whites now think that non-whites are their leaders both ethically and politically.

This entire scenario can be seen at work in modernism's theology of "race," in the next chapter. As Christians wanted to be faithful to God and had sympathy for Jesus, now white Americans show deference towards Blacks. This emotion trumps normal standards of justice. For instance, I once was speaking with a South African woman, and I said to her, "Since Apartheid came down, 30,000 Whites have been murdered by Blacks." She glared at me and simply said, "Their rights." Seeing that she defended Blacks at all costs, I dropped the subject. A study found that a White woman is ten times more likely to be killed by her spouse if married to a Black man than married to a White man.

I sent this information to a savvy White woman, and she thought that it was fine. Similarly, an organization published a study that found that half a million White Americans are attacked every year by Blacks.[241] When the organization held a press conference to release this fact, only one newspaper reported the statistic. All the other newspapers were too savvy to fall for this temptation.

---

[240] Frans De Waal, Chimpanzee Politics: 25th Anniversary Edition. (Baltimore: Johns Hopkins University, 2007).

[241] New Century Foundation, *The Color of Crime*. Download available at: www.amren.com.

As with the South African woman, those in the media want to defend Blacks at all costs; we also saw this with the military unit in *Tears in the Sun*. Academics in criminology and elsewhere know about this, but do not talk about it publicly for fear of being accused of racism. The savvy dogma today is to be faithful to Blacks no matter what, or no matter what human ideas of justice might be in other, larger, contexts. (For instance, insurance companies charge high risk groups of people higher rates. They generalize, out of a sense of justice and the necessity for survival.) We have seen heroic impulses of Whites in other contexts, such as in the films *Tears of the Sun*, and *Avatar*. It got a big push by Hugo, who in *Les Miserables* portrays the lower classes as Christ-types and worthy of pity or sympathy. This was gradually expanded to include not just the poor but, as we have seen, pretty much all non-Whites. We saw sympathy and "justice" united in *Gran Torino*. So being faithful to our new rulers means destroying the social body, or ourselves. This is what defines justice.

The impulses of sympathy and the moral idea of being a traitor to yourself or to your own culture and race combine to create a toxic perspective. This helps to explain the apathy of many savvy Americans in response to their country being invaded by high crime and hostile Mexicans. With little sense of civic survival left, the West's days are numbered unless it can break out of its masochistic prison.

Chapter 7: Modernism's Theology of Race

"In times of rapid change, experience could be your worst
enemy." –J. Paul Getty

"Society made him do it!"
—Almost any attorney

U.S. society today displays a dominance hierarchy, with
non-Blacks smiling at Blacks to appease and atone. Even a
fraudulent accusation of "racism" can wreck a career, whether
academic, business, or public sector. Courts have ruled it a crime
or violation of federal regulation to "racially" offend someone,
even when the offense is entirely in the eye of the accuser. Fear of
such accusation makes non-blacks walk on eggshells when in the
company of African Americans. During the *ancien regime*, there
was the same rule by fear.

As society once passed judgment on African Americans
and everyone else, now African Americans have the power to pass
judgment on whites. Those African Americans who "play the race
card" do so precisely because it works. Accusation alone suffices
to convict. This is reminiscent of the following fragment of Greek
poetry: "It is not granted unto men to fight the gods, or to pass
judgment: no one has this right."[242] Similarly, in Pericles's Funeral
Oration he said that "The blows of the enemy we must bear with
courage: those of the gods, with resignation."[243] Most whites today

---

[242] M. L.West, trans., *Greek Lyric Poetry* (Oxford: Oxford University, 1993), 138.
[243] H.D.F. Kitto, *The Greeks* (London: Penguin Books, 1957), 142.

are resigned to Black hostility. To deny an accusation of having caused "racial" offense brings terrible retribution. The following nineteenth century description of the status of criminals resembles how anyone accused of "racism" is seen today:

> He was a convict; that is, the creature who, on the social ladder, has no place, being below the lowest round. After the lowest of men, comes the convict. The convict is no longer, so to speak, the fellow of the living.[244]

Nowadays, anyone accused of "racism" is beyond the pale or outside of proper civil discourse, or in other words are so low as to be not human. He is part of the thingness of social body evil. Traditionally, the savvy knew it was important to avoid bad people and keep good company or find salvation in notions of class, gender and race. We saw this in the woman's notion of being proper in *From Here to Eternity*. Now we romanticize bad people, and this is "good company" and the savvy are fearful of anyone who questions the wisdom of liking bad people or who points out that the blacks, for instance, have very high crime.

The people who do this are just "things," or "racists" to be reviled. It is taboo to pass judgment on the African-American community by mentioning its flaws, such as high crime rates, low test scores, or low net worth compared to income. The blacks are seen as in this quotation from *Les Miserables*: "God has his instruments. He uses what tool He pleases. He is not responsible to man."[245] As the power of God was highly gratifying, so now the power of the blacks is highly gratifying as we saw in the discussion of dependent rank and sexuality.

This deference explains why modernists apparently hate Western culture. They falsely equate African-Americans with non-West or anti-West. Instead of the modernist hating himself, he hates the next best thing, Western civilization itself, because of the connection that exists in the mind. (This is probably what killed Rome after Christianization.) An example of such self-effacement

---

[244] Ibid., 1216-17.
[245] Victor Hugo, Charles E. Wilbour, trans., *Les Miserables* (New York: Modern Library, 1992), 1216.

can be found in a scene in the film version of the eighteenth century novel *Dangerous Liaisons* (1988), where a man and a woman are talking. The man says, "But I just don't feel worthy." The woman responds, "But it is when you don't feel worthy that you become worthy." Similarly, a character in *Les Miserable*, after confessing his crimes says, "It is by degrading myself in your eyes that I elevate myself in my own."[246] Modernists today become worthy when they hate their own civilization, or feel unworthy in the face of non-Westerners. To consider oneself unworthy is the sure sign of social virtue today. We saw this clearly in the film *Dances With Wolves*.

I once said to a White man, "Black neonates can turn themselves over within hours of birth, while a white baby can only exercise the same motor skills at 4 to 8 weeks." He responded, "Whites are lazy." Contemporary culture is one huge spiritual exercise. A book written by an Australian referred to "Australasia" in a promotional blurb. Whites certainly know their place today; to be out of character.

Contemporary culture has the same basic structure as in the past, but inverted. Earlier, the individual was evil and the state was a controlling good, and the theological structure was based on this. Today, the individual is good, but the state, i.e. the nineteenth century, is evil creating the evil social body of class, gender and race to be "purged."

We have the same Christian structure and culture as traditionally, but build on this inversion. So instead of Christ being a victim of our sins, now the blacks, women and trees etc are victims of our sinful social body and to be pitied, loved and fought for.

Pop singer Katy Perry was both engaged and married near the same lion sanctuary in India. As going on pilgrimages to Jerusalem and viewing relics during the middle ages were viewed as relevant, so now is getting married in India near a lion sanctuary. (Perry was raised as a conservative Christian so it was easy to add India and tigers to the pantheon.) The Teaching Company had a cruise to South America that featured lectures about nature and Indian art.In Albany, California there is a *Sticks Framing*, a low image. And references to low nature are very common in popular

---

[246] Ibid., p 1205.

and even corporate culture. It is interesting that the old, derogatory term for the country side was "sticks." While this term could still be used and understood today, it is clear that our values are changing. So we see how the divine is helping to support the inversion of Platonism or the raising of the low to a high status. Nature, like the blacks, is now a guiding ideal.

So all that has happened during the last century is that the evangelical culture of the nineteenth century has become reconfigured, and produced modern political and cultural taboos, on both the left and most of the right. The only difference between today and the past is that instead of moving from sin to salvation, now we believe in moving from salvation to sin. In other words instead of wanting to escape the conflicted world and move toward heaven, now we want to move away from stifling heaven, "civilization," and toward dynamic nature and hell. This is the new vision of exciting salvation. We saw this in *Dances With Wolves*.

A journalist recently wrote, "The chaos at home—a place intended as a quiet oasis far from the desert storm of an international career—doesn't faze Polenzani. If anything, he seems to be drawing deeply from the mayhem."[247] So instead of feeling repugnance and disgust in response to crude and vulgar people and nature, now we rejoice in it as we saw with Perry.

This impetus is the source of bowing and scraping from academics towards non-West. They find endless evidence of the superiority of non-Western cultures.

Any academic who rejects anti-Western dogma and depicts the accomplishments of Western civilization risks being fired. Praising Western thought is rarely countenanced and usually dismissed with a skeptical sneer. The temptation to injustice! Certainly the savvy know to scorn this.

Such rejection of rational thought recalls how Christians once responded to the temptations of the body or to the confinements of sin. This, in turn explains African-American deification at the hands of modernists. It resembles the ancestor-deification of Hellenistic cities. As previously mentioned, the Vikings once worshiped trees

---

[247] James C. Whitson, "Putting It Together," *Opera News*, jan. 2013, vol. 77, no 7. p. 19-20.

as images of endurance. Similarly, modernists worship African Americans as images of endurance.

When Nelson Mandela was released from prison, a White South African said, "He's our God."[248] Twice I've read him described as an "icon." A journalist for *Newsweek* described U.S. President Obama as "sort of God."[249] A cover of *Newsweek* portrayed Obama as an Indian God and with the title "God of All Things."[250] A painting by New York-based artist Michael D'Antuono features Obama with outstretched arms and a crown of thorns on his head, and is entitled "The Truth." (During the eight years of the presidency of George W. Bush, not once did I read a journalist, on either the left or right, say he was god.)

At the 2012 Democratic national convention, a news story reported that a group distributed literature describing Obama as Jesus. In the film *Bruce Almighty* (2003) a Black male actor plays "God." A black man was recently arrested for murdering his family, and he reported that he was Jesus and the police were Satan.[251] (It is easy to see how you can get John Wayne Gacy's perspective on his raping and murdering of boys from this narrative of innocent victimization by the evil one.)

In the film *Ghost* (1990), the ghost of a White person is resurrected in the body of a Black person in order to realize a relationship of love. This film was so popular it was made into a musical which was broadcast nationwide. As Jesus and his miracles was a revelation to be broadcast, so the blacks and their miracles are a revelation to be broadcast. Those who suffer for the sins of society are thereby elevated to divinity, and the savvy know this.

In the film *Like Mike* (2002), a black boy jumps leap-frog fashion over a white boy. We certainly know who's in charge today. A common chant among black civil rights demonstrators during the 1950s was "We shall over come." If you modify this slightly it

---

[248] National Public Radio, 1990.

[249] John Bolton, "President Obama's Foreign Policy: An Assessment," *Imprimis*, October 2009, Volume 38, number 10, page 2. Reprinted by permission from *Imprimis*, a publication of Hillsdale College.

[250] *Newsweek*, Nov. 22, 2010.

[251] Ian Jobling, "The Crime the Media Chose to Ignore," *American Renaissance*, 16, no. 5 (May 2005), pp. 11–12.

becomes, "We shall come over." This form of tyranny savvy whites clearly enjoy, in contrast to their control by the evil social body which only leads to damnation. There is a book entitled *Slavery as Salvation*, so savvy whites enjoy going into social *work*. This is what defines escape or salvation. We saw this with the reformed English prostitute and how she romanticized her slavery as salvation from the pit.

A good example that we are a new dark ages can be seen in the recent François Girard production of Wagner's opera *Parsifal* at the Metropolitan Opera. He greatly emphasizes sin, blood and Teutonic torture, while the traditional production, by Schenk, that it replaced, was much more beautiful and toned down. Girard said he wanted to create a "contemporary" interpretation. So he certainly thinks we live in the dark ages.

Similarly, fidelity to the manifestations of God in African Americans, and loathing of Western civilization are the essential savvy virtues. This explains why so many recoil in horror at any mention of the government-sponsored racism of the Jim Crow era. Who could possibly enjoy hearing stories of the Crucifixion of Christ? This would simply be monstrous.

Modernists take on the responsibility of others' suffering. They are prone to feeling guilty about the Third World's higher aggression levels and African Americans' former status as slaves.

The savvy protest that almost everything suffers for the sins of Western civilization. Some believe that trees suffer for its sins. Others believe that whales suffer. Some are more ambitious and try to prove that the ozone layer suffers for their sins. They believe that it is impossible for whites to suffer for the sins of African Americans, because obviously African Americans suffer for the sins of the West and, like Jesus, African Americans are innocent. Modernists see African Americans as Jesus-like. "How they suffer!" There is no greater heresy than to claim that African Americans are collectively guilty of anything, as it was incomprehensible to imagine that Jesus was responsible for His own suffering.

As it is painful for Christians to think of turning their backs on Jesus, so it is painful for modernists to think of turning their backs on African Americans, trees, whales, and so on. This would stop the progress to redemption. The vision of suffering is why modernism, when not raging against the sins of the West, is usually on the verge of tears. Modernism is driven by a vision of a number of angry Christ-types.

To them, Western culture is guilty. Modernism yearns for redemption and looks to the trees, whales, and African Americans for redemption and renewal through communion. If one person kills another, then a modernist will point to the killer, become misty, and say, "See how he suffers for our sins!" Then, "What can we do to help him?"

This condoning perspective is different from the traditional one. After raping and murdering 33 boys during the 1970s, John Wayne Gacy said, "I see myself more as a victim than as a perpetrator...I was cheated out of my childhood." He complained that the media were treating him like "an asshole and a scapegoat."[252] The thingness is external to himself. He probably had a degree in sociology.

As Anderson describes in *Sin:* "through his suffering, Christ was paying off the enormous depts incurred through human sinfulness. For those who saw punishment as means of raising currency to pay down the dept, it was important to magnify the suffering of Christ" [like images of Him tortured on the Cross].[253] So those guilt ridden sociologists like to dress up the blacks with those harrowing stories which of course give them, and everyone else, a license to kill. This kind of romanticizing of the evil impulses gives black men the moral glow that in part inspires white women to say things like "black men are real men." This obviously is not a coincidence. Physics always want to drag metaphysics down to its own level.

Anderson points out that during the history of the writing of the Bible, the conception of sin was changed from a weight to a dept; with this change, the source of compensation was more easily moved from the sinner to another source, like Jesus.

---

[252] Jonathan Gottschall, *The Storytelling Animal: How Stories Make Us Human* (Boston & New York: Houghton Mifflin Harcourt, 2012), 171.

[253] Gary A. Anderson, *Sin: A History* (New Haven & London: Yale University Press, 2009), 9.

For instance, Jesus pays off our dept, but it would be more difficult, or at least less poetic, to imagine Him carrying our weight. People like poetic justice. So it is easy for whites to displace, and magnify the "suffering" of the blacks and so for them to become Christ-types. (Anderson also makes the good point that the transference from weight to dept heightened the sense of culpability.) The Hebrew phrase *nasa awon* can mean both the state of culpability, or to bear the weight of sin, and, in addition, to bare away the weight. So because of this association, and combined with the psychology of wish fulfillment, it is easy to see the potential for displacement. People are hardwired to escape from the sense of threat, even when the threat is just. For instance, bank robbers almost always try to escape from the police.

Modernists get their logic from the Bible. Therefore, conceptually, modernism and classicism are essentially identical; they reach different conclusions only because they see cause and effect working in opposite directions. For example, modernism sees social policy creating homicidal tendencies, or human imperfection, as we saw in the fight in *Titanic*, while the traditional view sees homicidal tendencies creating social policy as can be seen in the nineteenth century.

In modernist imagination, the West suffers at the hands of its sins—as in Hieronymus Bosch's *The Garden of Earthly Delights*. In the famous medieval painting, a glutton is devoured by a huge stomach on legs. A sodomite is impaled by a Demon bird. A musician is tortured by his harp. Such reasoning sometimes appears in Classical myth. For instance, the Greek hero Neoptolemus commits homicide at an altar, and is himself later killed at an altar. And the mortal Semele falls in love with Zeus and demands that he show himself in all his glory. So he turns himself into a thunder bolt and this of course incinerates Semele. Similarly, Actaeon is out hunting with his dogs, and accidentally sees Artemis bathing. She' becomes outraged and turns him into a stag, whereupon his dogs devour him.

These myths show how concerned the ancients were with morals. The use of this logic today, as we shall see, shows the depth it has penetrated in our culture. For instance, Western civilization erodes the ozone layer, so it suffers. Westerners cut down the trees, so they suffer. And African Americans attack Whites because of the sins of the West. The West suffers at the hands of its sins. During the mid-twentieth century, the Hays film censorship code required that fictional sinners suffer for their fictional sins. The concept of sin followed by retribution is the source of modernist apocalyptic prophesies, like global warming. The film *The Day After Tomorrow* (2004) exemplifies the fear of sin. After years of unabated global warming, the greenhouse effect wreaks havoc around the globe in catastrophic hurricanes, tornadoes, tidal waves, floods, and, most ominously, the beginning of the next ice age. It is a warning of the fruits of social hubris or of feeling worthy. We also saw this in *Terminator*.

Two different large corporations promote among their clients going paperless in business transactions. On their websites the symbols for this service is a leaf. So a leaf is a symbol of saving the environment or virtue. Similarly, Jesus was a symbol of salvation, saving the environment and virtue.

The West's sinful social practice must consume them, so modernism rages against Western culture and criticizes society's temptations. Society's false desires cause the sufferings of Christ-types and take people off the righteous path of loving communion with trees, whales, and African Americans. In other words, such false desire or "false consciousness," breaks the bond or atonement between the West and its various suffering servants, redeemers, and saviors, as in Christian tradition the false desires of the body broke the bond with Jesus. To modernists, the trees have arrived to redeem humanity if humanity will just accept them. Those who turn their backs on the trees are evil. As Christians once were to love one another in God, to gain a higher strength, modernists love one another in the trees. I once saw a picture of a group of hippies dancing around a tree. During the course of the twentieth century, Christian fundamentalism declined, and so the left rose to fill the psychological vacuum for absolutism.

As impulses from the body were once seen as false and drove Christians down the wrong path, modernists see impulses from society as false because they drive people down the wrong, meretricious path. The feeling of attachment that drives modernism is displaced desire for communion with a redeemer. Modernists desire redemption and look to the trees, whales, and African Americans for redemption and renewal through communion if they can just break society's grip. As there was a larger purpose for loving Jesus, now there is a larger purpose for loving the blacks.

The savvy think that African Americans suffer for Western civilization's sins, but that if whites accept Blacks and the West's guilt, then their sins will be forgiven and modernism will be righteous. Modernism's felt righteousness creates their hair-trigger sensitivity and placating yearning. They want to get right with the Lord and to attack anyone who gets in their way. As people wanted to fight for God, now modernists want to fight for the blacks. We saw this in the *Tears in the Sun*, the film about the US military unit that fights for a group of Africans.

This impulse inspires *demonstrations* from modernists. As whites had hope in God, now they have hope in the blacks. As whites didn't want to give up on God, now whites don't want to give up on the blacks, regardless of sense data. The strength of these emotions is well illustrated by a comment by Bernini about his papal service: "This, and nothing less than this, is what the gravity of this situation, proper service to the pope, and my personal reputation all require; and I wish to give each its due, even at the cost of my own life."[254] This is how most feel about service to the blacks.

Jesus was "friend of sinners." Similarly, the blacks are the friend of the whites. During the nineteenth century, if you loved Jesus you were a good, sensitive person, but if you didn't like Jesus you were a bad person. Today if you love the blacks you're a good, sensitive person, but if you don't like them, you are a bad person. It's that simple.

It is common in history that when one set of gods defeats another, that the defeated are then made demons.[255] This of course can be seen in God's defeat of Satan, and, today, with the black's

[254] Franco Mormando, *Bernini: His Life and His Rome.* (Chicago & London: University of Chicago Press, 2011), 340.
[255] Jeffrey Russell, *The Prince of Darkness: Radical Evil and the Power of Good in History* (Ithaca & London: Cornell University Press, 1988).

defeat of the whites. As the blacks were demons, so now the whites are demons, and the best that the whites can do is fight for their righteous masters as we saw in *Gran Torino*. As blacks used to bow and scrape before whites, now whites bow and scrape before blacks. There is a book entitled *Slavery as Salvation* and St. Paul uses this image several times. As this relationship with God always just felt right, now this relation with blacks just feels right. As whites used to rejoice in God, now they rejoice in the blacks. As whites used to sing the praises of God, now the blacks. Whites certainly don't have much of a survival instinct left, or it has been redirected.

The civic dimension of this can be seen in ancient Athens. In their myth, Athena beat Poseidon in a fight, and so she became the patron deity, or the one that the Athenians were dependent upon. Among chimpanzees, a male becomes the dominant by beating and intimidating other males. Similarly, now that the blacks are in charge, it is common for academics to portray the blacks in history as triumphant. They love slave revolts, for instance. This is a vision of justice triumphant. And there is the popular image of the "church militant."

In the 1960s, trees and African Americans were added to the modernist pantheon and suddenly modernists found themselves surrounded by the unredeemed or heretics. As Westerners were once Christian warriors, modernists suddenly felt compelled to become warriors for the trees and African Americans and to work for their political elevation. Hence, they attack whites that are unredeemed or cut off. A white dares not break with the blacks in public.

Before 1960s, the body was the morally problematized object and seen as the location of agency. During the 1950s and 1960s, with the academic redemption of the body, notions of human agency or emotional motivation and evil were displaced to the public sphere, creating the modernist critique of social, governmental, and technological evils that are people's doom. As Christians had previously raged against the body, modernists now raged against society.

As Christians were once vigilant against impulses from the body, modernists now are vigilant against impulses from the

251

social body. As Christians were once in a constant state of protest against the body, modernists are now in a constant state of protest against society. The cry, "Babylon!" became "Society!" As the body had caused global warming, today the social body causes global warming. As the body was seen as the source of temptation and pollution, today the social body is seen as the source of pollution and temptation—the temptations of race and gender, for instance: "Don't you succumb to the urges of race and gender: that's the social body," says the modernist.

Hence we have the fear of biological determinism. This is a "temptation" and a slippery slope to hell. The displacement of agency was a frequent concept in Homeric Greece. As Classical scholar E. R. Dodds noted in *The Greeks and the Irrational*, "unsystematized, nonrational impulses, and the acts resulting from them, tended to be excluded from the self and ascribed to an alien origin."[256] The belief in "society" is a form of animism and, as we have seen, results from the connection in the mind.

The concept of society as beyond human agency is a modernist invention that turns policy from a reflection of people's desires into an evil imposition that creates desires. Classicists, on the other hand, believe that the social body is a fiction, and that traditional policy—that is, policy before the 1960s—reflects public desires.

As Christians had purged or expelled the body, modernists expel the state. Modernists feel that society hems them in, and they want to be liberated. As Christians wanted to be rid of the body, modernists now want to be rid of the social body, society. They believe in social reform instead of body reform. They displaced into the public sphere the metaphors they previously used to understand the body: "Don't succumb!" The urges of the social body are the source of all imperfection, suffering, and death. Society made him do it!

In artistic representation, Jesus is usually portrayed either as triumphant, erect, and alert, or as suffering in bleeding agony. Modernism's view of African Americans vacillates between these

---

[256] E. R. Dodds, *The Greeks and the Irrational* (Berkeley: University of California, 1951), 17.

two conceptualizations. When an African American is seen sleeping on the street, he is experienced as suffering for our social body's sins. When an African American is in college, he is seen as triumphant over whites sins—a vision of Resurrection and Heaven. African Americans are burdened with the sins of all mankind, but they will be resurrected if modernists can just purge the social body and defeat it with love and communion. This is what defines goodness and justice today.

Suffering occupies a prominent place in the Judeo-Christian imagination. The Jews suffered, the prophets suffered, Jesus suffered, the apostles suffered, and the martyrs suffered. Jesus warned Christians that they must be prepared to take up their cross and suffer. In addition, in Greek myth, Prometheus and Odysseus are long-suffering. Christ was the first archetypical victim in Western culture and today's victim archetypes are modeled on Him.

A recent TV advertisement about preventing violence said, "Violence has warning signs." It then showed a picture of a Hispanic boy with a tear running down his cheek. How he suffers! It is clear to the savvy that they suffer at the hands of the sins themselves. In response, a common chant of modernism is, "They're going to change! Be Resurrected! If we can just crucify the social body!" As the Devil once conspired against Christians through the body, today the social body conspires against modernists and their various victims through the body. We saw this in film. A bumper sticker during the 2004 national election read: BUSH/SATAN. Modernism never tires of alleging that Western culture is the primary medium of the social body, and thus is the source of all suffering and deviance in the world.

Christians once inspected, contemplated and mourned the rejection, wounds, and sufferings of Jesus, and hoped and worked for better days. Similarly, modernists today inspect, contemplate, and mourn the rejection, wounds and suffering of the trees and minorities, and hope and work for better days. Thus, many of the savvy feel drawn to social work instead of finishing schools, as did the elite in traditional Western culture.

Two recent books on feminism have titles that draw from Jesus imagery: *Reviving Ophelia* (1995) and *Ophelia Speaks*

(1999). Jesus was first revived and then he spoke and pointed the way to redemption. Women were first released from the bondage of the social body, and now they speak pearls of wisdom, charms for redemption. The powerful emotions of modernism should make one suspicious. The obsessions of the 1950s turned into the obsessions of the 1960s.

That Christianity can blend into feminism which in turn can be a medium for women's newly reemerging sexuality can be seen from a woman's self-reporting about her rape fantasies. She said explicitly that: "I blame my recurring rape fantasy on the fact that I'm a feminist."[257] She certainly would have liked living with the Vikings.

So we see here again that modernism is simply Christianity turned into a fertility religion or pattern of values that expresses or promotes emotion instead of inhibiting them. We saw a similar process of blending, and the promotion of emotion in the pornographic treatments of the Christian narrative paintings, like the Deposition. We see this same process in white women morally justifying their sexual attractiveness to ethnic men. It is now a righteous good instead of a damnable evil.

In this situation, ethnic men are really just a pawn in the game of promoting the inversion and emotion. As goes the status of emotion, so goes the status of ethnic men, as can be seen by comparing whites' ethics and pattern of self-reporting about ethnic men from the nineteenth century to today. And this perspective pretty much applies not just to white women but also to white men. At the level of self-reporting there is not much difference.

Pagden reported that by the early eighteenth century, the power relationship between Spain and her colonies was becoming inverted, and he quoted Montesquieu to illustrate it: "The Indies and Spain are two powers under the same master, but the Indies is the principal one and Spain nothing but an accessory."[258] And Denis

---

[257] Ogi Ogas & Sai Gaddam, *A Billion Wicked Thoughts: What the Worlds Largest Experiment Reveals About Human Desire* (New York: Dutton, 2011), 113.

[258] Montesquieu, *De l'espri des lois*, XXI, 22, 1949-51, II 648. Quoted in Anthony Pagden, *Lords Of All The World: Ideologies of Empire in Spain, Britain and France, c. 1500-c. 1800* (New Haven & London: Yale University Press, 1995), 152.

Diderot said, "Europe will one day find her rulers from among their sons."[259] This has indeed come true.

A film title, *Malcolm X: Soldier of Righteousness*, reflects when Christians were soldiers of righteousness against the body. Similarly, there is a book entitled *Redemption Song: Mohammed Ali and the Spirit of the Sixties*. During the 1960s, modernists asked African Americans what kinds of sacrifices were necessary to make them happy, to atone for white guilt, to redeem the West. As Jesus was reviled but proud, similarly gays and African Americans were reviled, but starting in the 1960s it was believed that they should be proud—gay pride and Black pride. *Ecce homo* means "behold the man," so starting during the 1960s, modernists pointed to African Americans and said, "behold the man." An image that loomed was that only a monster would partake in the flagellation and stigmatizing of Jesus, succumbing to the conspiring social body.

As Christians were once concerned about the progress of Jesus in their lives, today the savvy are concerned about the progress of the African Americans in their lives. As Jesus was good news for white women, now black men are good news. In this sense, modernism is progressive. If one proposes anything that gets in the way of that progress, modernists fly into a rage as they feel moral redemption or salvation slipping away.

As people were always checking up on each other to make sure they loved Jesus, now they are always checking up on each other to make sure they love the blacks. After all, this is progressive or a good thing, at all levels. As Jesus was the plan, the blacks are the plan. As it was "praise the Lord," now it's "praise the Blacks." As we people were supposed to be strong in God, now they should be strong in the blacks, and reject temptations to do otherwise. There is a website called *nigger mania*.

There have been an endless number of commentaries written about Jesus and whites relationship to him. But at the end of the day what matters is that you love Him. Similarly, endless numbers of commentaries have been written about the blacks and

---

[259] Guillaume-Thomas Raynal, abbe, *Histoire philosophique et politique des etablissemens et du commerce des Europeen dan les deux Indes,* 10 vols. Geneva, 1781, p. 233-4. Quoted in Pagden, Ibid, p. 167.

whites relationship to them. But what matters at the end of the day is that whites love them, and there is a tension between these two modes of being and feeling.

Modernists need African Americans and the other victims for progress to occur. The universities have abandoned the study of the human condition (Classical studies, for instance), and are now devoted to the study of the various victims and their progress against society. Dinesh D'Sousa calls the movement of the 1960s the "Victim revolution."[260]

The universities have regressed to being medieval or religious institutions. During the Dark Ages, Roman roads were viewed as the product of the black arts. Similarly, today modernism views the biology of human variation as a black art because it stops progress. As noted earlier, one professor proposed making research into human variation a crime. As the body was once stigmatized or banned, today the social body, which stops progress, should be banned. As Christians were once angry with the body, today modernists are angry with the social body. Before the 1950s the religious cowered and said "God is angry at us." Starting during the 1960s the savvy cowered and said, "African Americans are angry at us," and thus desired atonement.

The more violent African Americans become, the more this excites modernism, because it is divine retribution. One can imagine Jesus casting sinners into hell. A book titled *Green Rage* justifies terrorism by environmentalists (as if Christian warriors). Modernism supports violence as punishment for sin. This of course has great appeal to white women.

At this point we need to ask that if whites want atonement why aren't they moving into black neighborhoods? First of all, just as the radicals among the Christians become monks and nuns, the radicals among the whites do indeed move into black areas, but this are relatively rare. As the majority don't want to move into a monastery, the majority don't want to move into black neighborhoods. But on the other hand there is most definitely the longing and love for blacks and the desire for atonement. I think we

[260] Dinesh D'Sousa, *Illiberal Education: The Politics of Race and Sex on Campus* (New York: Vintage Books, 1992), 1.

can find the answer with some ancient examples of this issue. The ancient Greeks believed that the gods were vindictive and quick to anger, and so you want to avoid them. Similarly, the Jews always approached God gingerly because He was prone to anger. We see this with the blacks. Whites know that the blacks are quick to point out their sins and are quick to anger. So whites tend to avoid the blacks. When whites talk to blacks it is common for the whites to have a slightly self conscious look on their faces. As people don't feel entirely comfortable with God, whites don't feel entirely comfortable with blacks.

The way this avoidance is said in polite company is that the white family wants to avoid "bad schools." This is code word for too many blacks and Hispanics. It is wrong to condemn blacks, so they condemn the social body, or the "schools." It's the teacher's fault that blacks like to swagger around, carry weapons and use them.

As is even more obvious, the entire situation is, in the big picture, white's fault. But the savvy only have this glorious revelation or see this "fact" in their more philosophical moments or when they are in a sociology class. Whites suffer at the hands of the sins themselves. So at this point the savvy start to, again, recognize a preciousness to the blacks, just as Jesus, and his punishments represented justice and were, in some sense, precious in that they were educational. As Jesus was the councilor, so now are the blacks, and the savvy want atonement.

Studies have found that women like intelligent men,[261] so considering that white women perceive black men to be wise, this makes them even more attractive, in addition to being *real* men. With black men white women get the whole package. They get their moral, epistemological and sexual instincts satisfied. A woman's studies professor once said that women think with their bodies. Didn't people believe during the nineteenth century that women were emotional and couldn't be trusted?

The issue of atonement raises another aspect of whites' experience of the blacks. As having five crucifixes on every wall in one's house would cheapen the entire experience, so being

---

[261] David Buss, *Evolutionary Psychology: The New Science of the Mind* (New York: Allyn & Bacon, 2012).

surrounded by blacks would cheapen the experience. It would be just too much of a good thing. As whites like to savor the savior, they like to savor the blacks, one at a time, and put each one on a pedestal. Hence you tend to see just the more middle class ones in the media as part of the elevating white wash. I think that this is an important part of the experience, and we do indeed want the get across the whole experience for whites of the "*real* men." As God was impressive, so are the blacks. We always seem to come back to the same, basic issue, don't we?

Because of the violence and debauchery of modernism, it contains what Classical scholars would call a Dionysian element. Several scholars have noted the similarity between ancient Greek religion and contemporary modernist religious culture. As Classical scholar Martin P. Nilsson noted:

> There [is] seen…a seventh figure clad in a Dionysiac costume—boots and fawnskin. He is Iacchos. Iacchos is a personification of the Iacchic cry heard in the great procession, which went from Athens to Eleusis in order to celebrate the Mysteries. The gay revels, the merry cries, and the light of the torches in this procession were reminiscent of the festivals of Dionysus, and the name of Iacchos suggested the second name of this god, Bacchos. So Iacchos was represented in the likeness of Dionysus.[262]

Thus, modernists portray African Americans in the likeness of Dionysus, as irresponsible hedonists, a view shared by much of the public. I once saw a book entitled, "*Why Black Folks Like to Yell.*" In the San Francisco area, I have twice seen African Americans yelling with hostility at each other on the street, and savvy white bystanders simply smiling. As Classical scholar David Sacks noted, the Greek gods are concentrations of energy.[263]

Similarly, modernists see African Americans as mindless concentrations of energy, as well as suffering and screaming victim

[262] Martin P. Nilsson, *Greek Folk Religion* (Philadelphia: University of Pennsylvania, 1972), 47.
[263] David Sacks, *A Dictionary of the Ancient Greek World* (Oxford: Oxford University, 1995).

archetypes. Modernists have heaped the West's sins upon African Americans, who creak under the weight. The religious motivation for the indulgent emotions of modernism is reminiscent of the religious festivals of ancient Egypt. As David O'Connor noted regarding the festival for the arrival of a god:

> Such festivals were occasions for public participation and rejoicing, and they established an important link between the deity and its community. Food and drink were distributed to the populace, and ordinary rules of decorum were often ignored. As one scholar has described it, the behavior of the participants was "excessive and unrestrained, be it eating, drinking, sex, or all three at once." These activities were probably associated with that "induced, ecstatic state" thought to facilitate communion between humans and the gods, or between the living and the dead.[264]

With the redefinition of African Americans as redeemers, modernists started, as part of their attempts at communion and imitation of ghetto culture, to eat, drink, take drugs, and have unmarried sex. A recent Christian song included the phrase, "I want to live like there's no tomorrow." We can see how this sentiment for immortality is expressed in modernism by the desire to commune with the powerful image of the fun blacks.

The savvy look on and yearn for redemption, especially when so much fun or revels are to be had. For modernism, the joy of redemption correlates with the fun of the body. Thus, the savvy look for redemption to the trees, African Americans, whales, and so on, with smiling joy, and seek connection or communion with God, the "all-powerful" and the "all-fun" concentration of energy.

Modernism also spawns exaggerated environmentalism. As Christians once dreamed about Jesus and the angelic perfect body, today they dream about the redeeming perfect bodies of nature and the blacks. The savvy feel revived by nature. As Christians are refreshed by the connection with Jesus, the savvy are refreshed by

---

[264] David O'Connor, "Architecture of Infinity-The Egyptian Temple." *Archaeology Odyssey*, September, 1999, 46–47.

connections with trees and African Americans, whom they see as somehow more primitive or earthy. Thus, the savvy often start to beam when they are in African Americans' company. In making a connection with African Americans, they feel progress and the enhancement of justice and power.

As Jesus was "the heart's desire," similarly trees and African Americans are the heart's desire for the savvy. As Christians used to be lost in Jesus, now the savvy are lost in African Americans. One White girl said to me that African Americans are her favorite people. It was odd that Asians were not her favorite. In the Bible, a fallen woman cleaned Jesus' feet with her tears, and so He forgave her sins. I once saw a White televangelist kneel and use his tie to clean the shoe of an African American preacher so that the televangelist's sins would be forgiven.

As Christians were once dead to the world and alive in Christ, the savvy are now dead to society and alive in African Americans, trees, and whales, and seek their moral resurrection through these agents. As Jesus had more than one vote in the lives of Christians, an African-American lawyer suggested that African Americans should have more than one vote during elections. Both of these examples show wisdom and justice, the justice of power for the savvy.

One savvy professor described multiculturalism as "summoning," just as Jesus was summoning. Modernists are summoned to make progress. Christians say that Christianity is not a religion, but a relationship. Similarly, the savvy say that their ideology is not a belief system but a series of relationships that summon them to the goal of progress, redemption and atonement. If a white has not accepted African Americans as special, he is viewed as evil. He rejects the summons and turns his back, and so is cut off. As Christians once looked to Jesus for guidance, the savvy now look to African Americans. As Jesus was in charge and made the summons, today African Americans are in charge, and the savvy listen to the summons for progress.

In ancient Athens, to help achieve political acceptance or power, the tyrant Pisistratus dressed a tall woman as Athena, put her on a cart, and marched behind her up the Acropolis, demonstrating extreme or literal atonement. During the 1960s, modernists dressed African Americans as Jesus, and marched behind them down the street. Cleopatra crafted the image of Mark Antony as the god Bacchus in order to achieve certain political ends. Similarly, today the savvy have crafted the image of African Americans as suffering servants in order to achieve certain political ends—their own political empowerment and libidinal satisfaction.

There is no question that the African-American community suffered collectively during the Jim Crow era. So it was easy to attach this suffering to the sins of the West to be able to formulate a modernist political strategy. This reveals the heart of contemporary political discourse. Religion is the heart of culture and politics. As the heart pumps blood to the extremities of the body, religious belief pumps power to people and groups of people.

During the 1960s, the savvy ascended to the moral high ground by crying out, "They suffer for our sins!" Listeners thought: That sounds compelling. They must be right. African-American blood is shed for our guilt. African Americans are the suffering servants. Whites are evil, and African Americans are innocent or good. Whites must commune with or accept African Americans to be redeemed, for progress to occur. It is the social body that takes us off the righteous path. Such reasoning has been sinking in deeper ever since and completely dominates every college campus. Many academic departments today criticize the social body and try to figure out how to repress, subvert, and transcend it: "Subvert the Dominant Paradigm!" yells the savvy.

Christians are awed by Jesus' suffering and resurrection and all that these mean to them. Modernists often feel reverence and attachment when in the company of African Americans because of how African Americans function in the narrative of modernism's moral and physical regeneration.

The moral standing of whites depends on the condition of African Americans. The resurrection or enculturation of the latter, the defeat of the social body, will facilitate the resurrection, both moral and physical, of the former. Although few modernists are eager to associate with African Americans on a basis of friendly equality, they want to work for the image of suffering in their mind's eye, so they go into social work. In their minds, when the social body has been defeated, and African Americans become acculturated and are no longer hostile, the Apocalypse will subside, and Heaven will triumph. As God could be appeased, so can the blacks.

With the displacement of evil and human agency to the public sphere, not only trees and African Americans are Christ-types, but many others strive for rhetorical victimization as well. The savvy are eloquent in their suffering or victimization by the social body—by their parents, for instance, the source of imperfection. We saw this with John Wayne Gacy.

The savvy have displaced the Jesus victim narrative onto themselves and onto objects in their environment. The individuals or groups that have the best victim credentials attract the most attention and sympathy. This results in competition between people and groups to see who can produce the best proof of victimization and so be qualified to receive the largest sacrifices: "We're righteous so we're entitled!" chant the savvy. This is the reasoning behind government entitlements. As Jesus was entitled, so are we.

Because the savvy suffer, they think that they are justified in being demanding and abusive, expressive of their aggression. As Jesus was justified in being outraged against the body or sin, so the savvy are outraged against the social body that causes suffering and imperfection. The savvy whispers to themselves, "I suffer and feel angry because of the social body, because of employers, technology, belligerent acquaintances, nuclear energy, and so on."

During the 1970s, a businessman said, "People need stop crying and to start sweating." As technology is a modernist specter of evil, similarly an unfriendly neighbor is evil and worthy of attack. Criminals justify their actions with narratives of suffering.

This theme, lack of personal responsibility plus innocent victimization by external forces, is a common way of framing experience of the world. Dr. Thomas Sattler, a dermatologist, says that it is common for people to attribute skin problems to stress. The social body causes our wounds and justifies our anger. An African American speaker said that African Americans are irresponsible parents because of genetic engineering by Whites. The answer *must* be the *social* body. The savvy blame society and so justify aggression.

The example is typical of the causality of popular thought. Recall the socialization of sin.

Today, it is easy to justify aggression. All one has to do is play the victim card, no matter how trivial. A woman spilled hot coffee on herself at a McDonald's restaurant, sued, and won. This new moral schema of being victimized promotes fertility, or anti-social rebellion, in people's interpersonal relations, the medium for the intrusive social body. Once in a restaurant, another diner said to me, "If you find a hair in your food, sue their pants off!"

We see this justification for deviance in ancient Greece. The Greeks believed that the god Hermes would steal cattle at night. So when this happened, farmers would say, "Ah, Hermes." Similarly, today when a crime happens, the savvy say, "Ah, society." This is an example of the animism noted earlier.

One sign of the new metaphysics of fertility and social body rebellion is that today modernists say that every child is above average and demands to feel good or empowered instead of adhering to a standard, and feeling accomplished in that way. According to modernist dogma, traditional social standards are the social body, create imperfection and suffering, and should be repressed. Modernists often attribute academic weakness to an inability to take tests. It is clearly the social body's fault, just as it causes our skin problems.

Today, the savvy allow no one to say anything that does not make people feel good or fertile. If you propose that someone needs to live up to standards, the person will often react with anger. This is the source of modernist leveling. Modernism says that because we suffer, our desire to attack those who cause our suffering is morally justified. Modernists justify every negative urge with the narrative of suffering, instead of that narrative compelling them to adapt themselves to standards, as was traditional.

John Stott describes how Christianity inspires such a sense of heroic urgency within modernism. He writes:

> Christianity is a rescue religion. It declares that God has taken the initiative in Jesus Christ to deliver us from our sins.... There is no conquest without the Cross.[265]

---

[265] John R. W. Stott, *Basic Christianity* (London: Inter-Varsity, 1971), 81, 86.

The savvy confirm that they are trying to rescue people from their sins of succumbing to the hubris of society and urge them to accept any one of the modernist redeemers. With this acceptance and empowerment through dependent rank comes heroic status, enabling one to conquer anything. We see this idea in ancient Athens. As Classical scholar Martin P. Nilsson noted:

> [A god] came to Athens in 420 B.C., being introduced by Telemachos of Acharnae and received by the poet Sophocles, who because of this was made a hero under the name of Dexion, the Receiver.[266]

Similarly, the savvy have much heroic energy because they have received the gods, are in a state of communion; in Christian context they are redeemed and righteous. As one Christian observed, "When you are saved, you are King!"

So modernists point to classicists and exclaim, "You're still in your sins!" and "We're Kings because we're righteous!" or empowered.

Once the savvy has received his savior, he does not want to let go. We see this sense of attachment in newly Christianized ninth-century Germany. The Heliand was the telling of the Gospel for that German population. The author felt compelled to make concessions to the pagan religion of his audience. In the scene when Roman soldiers come to arrest Jesus, the Heliand portrays fierce swordplay to defend Jesus.[267] (Swordplay is not in the original.)

In a spirit similar to Germanic heroism, in the United States today fierce resistance arises when a lumber company tries to harvest trees. Radical environmentalists put metal spikes in trees to ruin chainsaws and injure loggers. And one can imagine what would happen if the police removed blacks from white areas.

There is another similarity between medieval religion and modernism. In the Middle Ages, Germanic peoples retained a pagan belief that dangerous elves would harm people and livestock,

---

[266] Martin P. Nilsson, *Greek Folk Religion* (Philadelphia: University of Pennsylvania, 1972), 94.

[267] G. Ronald Murphy, *The Saxon Savior* (New York. Oxford University, 1989).

so the church developed a set of Christianized charms or chants to combat them. Similarly, white males, who are seen as today's social body, are viewed as harming things. They harm whales, trees, ozone layer, and, of course, African Americans. As the Catholic Church developed chants against the elves, the savvy have developed chants against white males, to ward off the social body, the source of threatening evil.

In antiquity, people often compared gods to make a point and to clarify their natures. For instance, Plutarch said that Dionysus resembled the Egyptian god Osiris. Similarly, in the 1960s and '70s, when feminists tried to make their points, it was common for them to say that women were "like Blacks." Feminists made this comparison in order to help clarify women's nature as fellow suffering servants—as "The Goddess," as described on a bumper sticker. They, too, were to be part of the same Pantheon, to be received as redeemers, revered, liberated, and viewed as beautiful. More recently, homosexuals who view their gender preference as ethno-political self-identity compare themselves to African Americans in seeking the same deference, privilege, and coercive power. Homer also uses displaced mythological narrative to create vivid characters. As Classical scholar Seth L. Schein (1984) noted about the *Iliad*:

> The freedom with which Homer transfers to Patroklos and Hektor mythological motifs and dramatic roles traditionally associated with Achilles and Memnon has suggested to some scholars that these two characters are creations of Homer.[268]

Similarly, the creation of the oral and written myths of the suffering of African Americans, women, and homosexuals is the result of the free-associative imagination of modernism.

Anything that can be assimilated to a Christ-type usually is. We see this with the holocaust. Evidence that the savvy experience the holocaust as a Christ-type is the strong reaction today from some western governments to individuals who deny that it happened.

---

[268] Seth L Schein, *The Mortal Hero: An introduction to Homer's Iliad* (Berkeley: University of California, 1984), 27.

A movement called Historical Revisionism tries to minimize the holocaust. The historicity of the holocaust is undeniable, but it should be subject to normal critical review, without its critics being persecuted and imprisoned, as they are in Germany. As denying Jesus could get you killed in the early modern era, denying the holocaust today can result in prison time from some governments. Incidentally, these perspectives on the Holocaust are not mutually exclusive. The Holocaust can still be a Christ-type even though it actually happened.

Composer James Whitbourn wrote a coral piece called *Annelies*, which sets selections of Anne Frank's diary. The ad for the recording had only one journalist's blurb and it simply read, "Woundingly beautiful." This kind of imagery in discussions of any of the official victims is very common. I believe that there are indeed good lessons to be learned from the Holocaust, but they very likely will have negative side effects if they exist in a mythic context. As having a mythic knowledge of nature produced little in the way of material benefits, having a mythic knowledge of human nature and conflict will mostly produce dysfunction, as we have today.

This ambivalence about the Jews helps explain the vacillation of the savvy on the issue of the Jews and Israel. In the context of the holocaust, Jews are victims, and everyone wants to defer to and rescue them. In the context of the conflict between Israel and Palestine, Jews are oppressors, and the savvy are critical of Jews defending themselves.

Because the savvy experience everything as either a Christ-type or the anti-Christ, they cannot formulate consistent foreign policy. There is a conflict between the historical victimization of the Jews and their modern image as oppressors, and the savvy cannot work its way out of the dilemma. All a group need do is show their wounds, as do the Palestinians, and the savvy accept their victim status. This tends to usurp historical claims, as from the Jews. Because the standards to achieve victim status are fairly low, the savvy spends time running back and forth.

In *Les Miserables*, there is a scene where a young couple is in love and sitting on a bench. The woman leans over and the outline of her bosom becomes clear. The man turns his gaze away to avoid exposure to the body. We see the same thing today in modernism's relation with African Americans. If the savvy hear an unpleasant fact like, for instance, one in three African American men will eventually spend time in prison, he or she will not face it, and will turn the gaze away from this temptation from the social body. Negative thoughts about African Americans come from the social body, so are heresy to be banished from our minds. The traditional definition of heresy was treason against God.

Modernists so want to see African Americans as great that they have created a show for themselves. Most of the African-American middle and upper class is a product of government hiring, the military and racial quotas.

The *New York Times* recently reported that 20% of employed blacks work in the public sector,[269] so that is probably close to half of the black middle class, and then you have the hiring in the private sector based on racial quotas. If you combine these sources, it is most of the much vaunted black middle class. We certainly can't take the chance of letting "god" falter as it would reflect negatively on our own judgments, aspirations, and deflate us.

This impulse can be seen in history. The ancient Sumerians would dress up one of their gods, take him on boat rides and feed him lavish meals. In ancient Athens, the people made a 40-foot statue of Athena made of gold and ivory. And the huge Gothic Cathedrals are "houses of God." So today whites dress up the blacks, feed them lavish meals, take them for rides, and build housing for them. My soul doth magnify the Lord! The natural human impulse is to dress up and make a spectacle of where ever perceived power is. Through dependent rank, there is indirect self-empowerment and righteousness as we saw with Sophocles.

As the heart pumps blood to the body, religion pumps power to people. God and religion are fundamentally about universal power, so human or earthly power is seen as a subset of this. Tinkering with religion always results in changes with human values and politics. As we saw in the chapter on violence in the

---

[269] Timothy Williams, "As Public Sector Sheds Jobs, Blacks are hit Hardest." *New York Times*, Nov. 28, 2011. http://www.nytimes.com/2011/11/29/us/as-public-sector-sheds-jobs-black-americans-are-hit-hard.html?_r=1

state of nature, love can be as destructive an emotion as hate if it is not handled correctly. Paradoxically, "love" can result in more hate. Contemporary universal love is based on universal hate and contempt for whites, as the "original sinners" against "God". So again we see inversion.

Another example of inversion is between the contrast between human and animal. We used to think that humans were high and animals as low, as without reason. Now of course it is the reverse. What matters is that they suffer or have emotions. I saw a recent internet ad for clothing, and it portrayed dogs in sweat shirts, and the caption read: "Which animal are you?" This is what people aspire to today as we saw in the novel about a woman who has a sex with a gorilla. And I have noticed that people today are much more attached to their pets than 40 years ago.

Before the 1960s it was common knowledge that as gorillas have flat noses and black skin, these are also characteristics of Africans. It was also known that as chimpanzees don't have chins and foreheads, the Africans tend to have small chins and sloping foreheads. And I have noticed that blacks tend to have rounder heads than whites. It was also common knowledge that the blacks have brains that are, on average, 5.5 cubic inches smaller than whites.[270] For instance, Darwin, in *The Decent of Man*, refers to the "lower races." Plato, in his Dialogue *Phaedrus*, describes how the soul is like either like a good horse or a bad horse; the good horse has an aquiline nose, while the bad horse is snub nosed, dark, and physically distorted.[271]

Plato must have heard the same stories we hear today. Recall from the state of nature that as apes swagger through the jungle, many black men swagger through the urban jungle, and tend to have a thick or dumb look on their faces. One study reported that there was little difference between the tool use of Tanzanian Chimps and Tasmanian aborigines.[272] Recent studies report that during the

[270] J. Philippe Rushton, *Race, Evolution and Behavior* (Port Huron, MI: Charles Darwin Research Institute, 2000).
[271] Plato, Stephanus 19.
[272] W.C. McGrew, Tools to get food: The subsistants of Tanzanian chimpanzees and Tasmanian aborigines compared. *Journal of Anthropological Research*, 43, 247-258.

nineteenth century it was common to portray the blacks as ape-like,[273] while whites or "Greeks" as they were called, were portrayed as higher up the evolutionary scale with Asians in the middle.

Even though blacks look a lot like gorillas their social lives are more like chimps. This was probably also detected by whites at least at an unconscious level. People in general have strong emotional reactions to how others behave. Chimps live in groups, as do African tribes. In contrast, gorillas live in small nuclear families. Now chimpanzee males do not pair bond with females to any significant extent.[274]

And males and females look for food independent of each other, and males do not provision females. In Africa husbands and wives keep their money separate, and polygamy is common among primitive African tribes.[275] So like chimps, ties between males and females are loose. In contrast, because of the long cold winters in the Northern hemisphere males needed to provision females, and this selected for greater emotional closeness between men and women and greater consciousness among males to protect and provision females.[276] So we see that both in terms of what blacks look like and how they behave, they are indeed less evolved and this general idea was well know before the recent deification of blacks.

These biological facts help to explain aspects of whites' experience of the blacks. A full 10% of American blacks have IQs above 110. So a fair amount have some thinking abilities, and these are the ones you see working at the post office, and teaching in education and black studies departments. These are the ones that have fairly intelligent looks on their faces, and the ones you see at the expensive restaurants. So when a white sees a black at one of

---

[273] P. A. Goff, J. L. Eberhardt, M.J. Williams, & M.C. Jackson, (2008). "Not Yet Human: Implicit knowledge, historical dehumanization, and contemporary consequences." *Journal of Personality and Social Psychology*, 94, 292-306. Morone, James. *Hellfire Nation: The Politics of Sin in American History.* (New Haven & London: Yale University Press, 2004).

[274] Jane Goodall, *The Chimpanzees of Gombe* (Cambridge Mass: Harvard University Press, 1986).

[275] Rushton, Ibid.

[276] Richard Lynn, *Race Differences in Intelligence: An Evolutionary Analysis* (Augusta, Ga: Washington Summit Publishers, 2006).

the better venues, the white is struck by the fact that, though the black looks like a gorilla, he does not act like one. In the context of modernisms theology of race, this is highly gratifying and even edifying.

It is a picture of redemption and salvation; after all if this black can do it, so can most of the rest, or so most of the Republicans think. The Democrats have a different perspective in that these individuals act white and so have sold their souls to the devil. They are in character, and boy is it wrong. They have been taken over by aliens, whites' alien nature. Not as much gratification to be had there, especially for white women. So Republicans agree that whites deserve chastisement, but this is better than the Democrats, who believe that whites need to be exterminated, either directly or by intermarriage, to make the world right.

The advocates of inter-racial marriage are motivated by a desire to eliminate problematic whites, not non-whites. This is shown by the fact that if a black resists interracial marriage, this is viewed as a form of righteousness and putting the inferior whites in their place. While if a white opposes interracial marriage, this is viewed as evil usurpation that needs to be crushed. Whites need to be assimilated to non-whites, and we have seen this logic many times. As whites were the ideal, now non-whites are the ideal or the "cure" to the alien disease. As blacks were the alien, even to themselves, now whites are the alien, even to themselves. As the apish body was alien, now the apish social body is alien. So again we see inversion of good and evil in the context of the distinction between nature and culture.

In the myth of King Minos a woman has sex with an animal, but there is no Greek myth about a man having sex with an animal. Recall the novel about the women who has sex with a Gorilla. With our new notions of racial righteousness, we now view these impulses and views on nature in a sympathetic light. Whites now view their own animal nature and impulses in a more sympathetic light. "What animals are you?" said the advertisement.

This basic logic generated the values and sense of urgency in *Titanic*. As the fall of Jesus to the predatory body was lamentable, now the fall of Jack to predatory culture is lamentable. Cal is just a mindless, wild ape, a brute. In the ideal world, Cal would become like Jack or be assimilated. So we see how narratives of the destruction of the social body, instead of the body, completely structures the culture. It is unconscious, and so is not the product of a conspiracy. It is a natural outgrowth of the entire tradition combined with recent intellectual developments, like sexual liberation and the attack against beauty or the perception that it is evil.

As we have seen these are related, as the latter results from the former, or the displacement, and, when combined with the tradition, create the modern moral and cultural scheme to eliminate the social body or whites. Add the heroic tradition in this context, and you literally have a suicide culture as we saw in *Gran Torrino* and *Tears in the Sun*. As we wanted to destroy the body, now the social body. I don't think the situation can be made any clearer as I have been able to combine all the basic elements of the Viking, Christian and Platonic traditions.

Before Europe discovered the New World, it was commonly believed that people in other parts of the world were monstrous, like being dog headed. One recent historical study simply attributed this to an over active imagination. But there is a better explanation that is less speculative. Brian Fagan is a retired anthropology professor at the University of California, and he reported that the ancient Egyptians thought that the Africans were monkeys.[277] Now Greece was always very focused on Egypt. So if the Egyptians knew this then so did the Greeks and hence Rome. And of course it was Rome that created much of the academic and popular culture for later history. So it is easy to see that "monkey people" could easily be transformed into "monstrous people." This is particularly the case when one recalls that contacts between different groups are often spontaneously hostile, like between groups of animals.

Fritze describes how, for the European colonists, "the native Americans were supposedly pre-Adamitic or co-Adamitic human which raised the ominous possibility that they were not created in God's image, i.e., possessed of a soul. Such a condition meant that Native Americans were simply intelligent animals but animals

---

[277] Brian M. Fagan, *Human Prehistory and the First Civilizations*. Audio-tape lecture series. (Chantilly, VA: The Great Courses, 2000).

nonetheless, and so could be exploited accordingly. High-minded people like Bartolome de Las Casas vociferously rejected such an approach and argued persuasively that the Native American were as fully human as Old World people."[278]

Recall here that you can sense intelligence by language, and so the whites who first contacted the Indians would have sensed their diminished mental abilities. (The Indians have the same low IQ as American blacks.) In addition, the wild behavior and primitive living conditions would have been an enforcer of this image. Notice that one European was "high minded" or above the social body; as we were to be above the body, now the social body. The same study admits that the Indians lived in the Stone Age, but no where is this kind of thing portrayed as negative.

At first Europeans consistently thought that the Indians were inferior and so to be marginalized or even killed. But the same study describes with joy how, "A few people were more open-minded. Alvise da Cadamosto developed a very positive opinion of the natives of West Africa that he visited.

The same observation applies to Cabeza de Vaca as his respect and affection for the tribes of Texas…grew during his many years of wandering. Saint Francis Xavier dearly loved his Japanese flock while the castaway conquistador Gonzalo Guerro went completely native and became a respected and intensely loyal member of the Maya community that adopted him."[279] Twice Fritze describes how because of the colonial contact the world is now "one."

And no where is it mentioned that adopting Western ways was good, at least in the long run, for the natives. The most he can say with pride is that some of the Westerners "went native." At no time did he denigrate the bad ways of the Indians, but, in contrast he consistently portrays the Europeans as monsters. So instead of the natives being monsters, now the Europeans are, and this fits the pattern of inversion we have seen.

This is consistent with the white wash of the blacks you get in the media. You only see the more highly evolved ones. Similarly,

---

[278] Ronald H. Fritze, *New Worlds: The Great Voyages of Discovery, 1400-1600.* (Westport CN: Praeger, 2002), 237.

[279] Ibid, 237

the Metropolitan Opera in New York recently put on Wagner's *Ring* cycle of operas, and the singer who played Alberich was black. Now this character is normally portrayed as subhuman and cowering, which was Wagner's intention, but one critic asked of the Met's portrayal, "Why so noble?" Obviously, they didn't want to have a black act like what you see on the streets. Whites are animals, not blacks.

I believe we should stop and examine a problem that sexual selection and evolution apparently poses. Genetic similarity theory predicts that whites should have little interest in other races, but as white female sexuality shows this is not the case. It is the difference itself, that black men look and tend to act like apes or have this association or general image, that is the point of attraction. On the other hand, these same qualities in the women, like the higher aggression, make them unattractive to white men. Men like modesty, not higher aggression. So using genetic similarity by itself to understand race does not satisfactorily solve the problem and may even be questioned because of female sexuality. If we take the sexes separately, we can help solve the problem.

It has been shown in experiments that, compared to women, men are much more sensitive to the appearance of children and adults, with a significant preference for individuals that look like themselves.[280] This is adaptive as men are less sure of paternity, and so use visual cues of children and adults to determine relatedness.

So if we modify genetic theory and say it is more powerful in white men, then we can reconcile the historical preference for segregation and recent developments in sexual selection: white men are much less interested in black women than white women are interested in black men.

During the nineteenth century, white men were in control, and combining genetic alienation with the revulsion to sex and the bestial emotions in general, they instituted segregation. Recall that Morone reported that during the nineteenth century, whites feared the stimulation from the blacks or that they themselves would

---

[280] Eugene Burnstein, "Altruism and Genetic Relatedness," David Buss, ed. *The Handbook of Evolutionary Psychology* (Hoboken, N.J.: John Wiley & Sons, 2005).

succumb. When segregation ended, white women immediately started to regress to a state of nature, or to the sexuality we saw among the Vikings, while white men, because of genetic and gender alienation, still keep their distance. Another factor is that men are the primary victims of violent crime, so when aggression levels start to rise, it is men who get edgy, while women just think that men are becoming more exciting. We saw women's preference in the comparison of male types in *The Sheik* and elsewhere in the state of nature.

Men historically were considered to be the medium of control and power and the civilizing influence on women. As one man put it, "Men are the empire builders." For instance, Wroe, in her recent study on Orpheus, reported that Eurydice was his "lower self" and this was the common conception of women for most of history.[281] So we see that women, with recent empowerment started to live their nature that was known to most of history. Put another way, women have to internalize constructive social values from men. And the nineteenth century proves that they can.

It is men who are the primary victims of violent crime so they are the ones who have the incentive and consciousness to get people under control. As we've seen repeatedly women lack this consciousness on their own as they have no natural internal or external motivation. External motivation has to be constructed for them, as it was traditionally through dependent rank. I have spent the last 10 years reading most of the standard works on evolutionary psychology, and I have not come across any significant evidence against this basic scenario or interpretation of early and recent history.

In general, the whole growth and life cycle for the individual before the twentieth century was considered one of acculturation into civilization or constructive and peaceful behavior. Marriage and family were considered part of this. We saw this in the film *From Here to Eternity*, when Donna Reed says, regarding having a proper family, that "When you're your proper, your safe." Of course, today, with the inversion and black influence, we now need to become more wild or "hip," at least at the level of self reporting

---

[281] Ann Wroe, *Orpheus: The Song of Life.* (New York: The Overlook Press, 2012).

and attitudes. So the social pressure is to act more like Vikings, and these ideals are reflected in the huge increases in crime starting during the 1960s.

So it is clear that whites' human brain and nature is built upon the ape-man brain and nature; and we saw what whites are capable of thinking as righteous and sexy during the discussion of the state of nature. This is what we have to respond to with our human nature, and this basic fact was understood during the nineteenth century. As beautiful Raphael paintings don't grow on trees, neither does extremely virtuous and constructive behavior. So if you take away the social controls, you get backsliding, as we have seen during the past century in most spheres of life.

The traditional hierarchy of race of course has been inverted in the last century. Now whites are the "thingness" of alien evil while blacks are just sublime and invite celebration and intimacy, and this celebration creates the righteousness surrounding inter-racial sex, marriage and adoption.

For instance, a black artist exhibited a painting in a Berkeley café of a black male in the lotus position and levitating while surrounded by a hallow of light. A recent book is entitled, *Angles of Ascent: A Norton Anthology of Contemporary African American Poetry*. The blacks are just heavenly today. There is a recent film called *Dumb and Dumber*, and both exemplars of stupidity in the film are white males, not blacks or women. Recall here that in Hollywood film during the 1930s, it was common to portray the blacks as lazy and stupid.

Now of course we portray whites as stupid, and evil, as we have seen, because we also thought that stupidity was a form of evil. The Devil was dumb. In addition, stupidity was seen as the expression of a lack of consciousness of the bodies' innately sinful impulses. As the body and the blacks were low, and the mind and whites were high, now the body and blacks are high, and mind and the whites are low. What animal do you want to be? Whites are just things that can be treated in any way, and even killed. People are quick to make excuses for this. This is understandable. As it was evil and suspect for the devil to try to defend himself, now it is evil and suspect for whites to defend themselves.

Yahoo posted a story about a group of girls at a restaurant, and their bill had "fat girls" written on it. They complained to management and apparently yahoo thought this was a crisis and even reproduced the bill in the story. Now recall that half a million white Americans are attacked every year by blacks, and that only one newspaper reported the statistic. So it is fine to attack and kill whites, but don't call the one of our redeemers "fat" or ape-man. This is big news.

Jennifer Eberhardt is a black psychology professor at Stanford University, and she has a Ph.D. from Harvard. She wanted to know if whites still associate blacks with apes, so she designed an experiment to see if her white undergraduates unconsciously associated blacks with apes; and indeed she discovered this. She was "shocked" by the results. She asked her subjects if they knew that during the nineteenth century blacks were considered ape men, and the students consistently reported ignorance of this. So Eberhardt concluded that the negative associations were so ingrained that it penetrated the unconscious and was thus transmitted.[282]

It should be said that a recent psychological study has found that whites have in their amygdala a small viscerally negative response to blacks.[283] Whites have negative responses to threatening animals like lions and gorillas. The origins of this are obvious, but is automatically attributed to the social body, so no one is allowed to voice it in public, as they did before the 1960s.

Of course, the blind veneration of blacks is so intense today that it never occurred to Eberhardt that blacks do indeed have these characteristics, and that behavior would be an enforcing factor. The correct answer must be the *social* body and not the physical body. The latter is heresy or succumbing to the social body.

Certainly professors are paragons of virtue today, like the rest of the "elite," so "indulgent" or heretical thoughts would

---

[282] P.A Goff, J.L. Eberhardt, M.J. Williams, & M.C. Jackson, (2008). "Not Yet Human: Implicit knowledge, historical dehumanization, and contemporary consequences." *Journal of Personality and Social Psychology*, 94, 292-306.

[283] E.A. Phelps, K.J. O'Connor, W.A. Cunningham, E.S. Funayama, J.C. Gatenby, J.C. Gore, & M.R. Banaji, 2000. Performance on indirect measures of race evaluation predicts amygdale activation. *Journal of Cognitive Neuroscience, 12*, 729-38.

not even cross their minds. Of course the taboos have been so completely internalized that most are not even aware of it.

For instance, a white anthropology professor who read the first edition of this book reported that he was not aware that whites had to defer to the blacks. Of course sometimes it is explicitly stated.

A black professor, Lucius T. Outlaw, in "Reconstructions in Academic Philosophy," described the new state of wisdom: "The intense struggles at an increasing number of colleges and universities in the United States to establish Black studies programs…made very poignant the political, as well as the epistemological, significance of the production, justification, *legitimation*, and *mediation* of knowledges within and by institutions of higher education, and of the significance of using knowledges for emancipatory social transformation in service—or not—to peoples and classes on the short end of the political-economic stick" [emphasis added].[284] So the evil or deviance is an external "thingness," a stick, and is not internal to the constitution of the blacks.

So as the relevance of Jesus was "poignant" and the mediating power in knowledge and the struggle for the freedom from evil, so now are the blacks, their divine rule and their interests, as the new Christ-type. Anyone who gets in their way is automatically dammed or expelled from Paradise. You can't buck the new censorship, as many have discovered, like Prof. Rushton, who was banned from the classroom.

From the portrayal of life in the book *Chivalry and Violence in Medieval Europe* it is clear that violence and power has to be understood or categorized as either legitimate or illegitimate. Knights would frequently be violent, and rob and rape, but it was part of larger power structure that was perceived to be legitimate, so no one really thought too much about it, except some clerics, who tended to see it as sinful. One can imagine that the clerics had to be very careful criticizing knightly violence as it could be seen as treasonous.

---

[284] Lucius T. Outlaw, Jr. "Reconstructions in Academic Philosophy." *Proceedings and Addresses of the American Philosophical Association*. November 2012, Volume 86, Issue 2, p. 104-124. Newark, Delaware: American Philosophical Association, 2012, p. 111.

One can see the clear parallels with today. Those who feel that there is something wrong with exposing humans to the abuses of the non-whites, and the dysgenic consequences of the present value system, express this gingerly, if at all, as they know that these views go against the state religion and power structure. As we saw at the beginning of this chapter, these individuals are easily and quickly attacked, and this is viewed as legitimate. If these individuals defend themselves, it is viewed as illegitimate usurpation or violence as we saw with the example of the devil and God. About the most one can do in polite society is mention "reverse racism." Of course in this characterization one is using the modernist perspective on the blacks as a kind of bench mark or legitimizer.

So "violence" is very much in the eye of the beholder as we saw in the Yahoo story about the "fat" girls. If a black attacks a white, this is understandable or a non-issue, at least to some extent for many, like knightly violence, while if a white attacks a black, this causes an uproar as it is viewed as a revolt of the evil and so—justly controlled—underlings. The popular portrayal of history is that whites are evil demons and blacks are innocent victims, and that blacks are in great danger of white predation, but the fact is that a black male is 6 times more likely to commit an interracial violent crime than a white male.[285] The biggest casualty in this situation, from the point of view of the long term, is the science of human variation. This is *prima facie* treason for all the theo/power reasons stated.

What helps to get the social psychology of treason in focus is seeing it among non-human animals. Among many group living species, for an individual to be expelled, in a state of nature, can be a death sentence, and so this can have a huge impact on the evolution of individual and social psychology. This psychology of attachment is well documented among feral chimpanzees.[286]

This same psychology makes people very conformist orientated and fearful of marginalization, ostracism and expulsion.

---

[285] New Century Foundation. *The Color of Crime*. Download available at: www.amren.com.

[286] David Buss, *Evolutionary Psychology: The New Science of the Mind* (New York: Allyn & Bacon, 2012). Jane Goodall, *The Chimpanzees of Gombe* (Cambridge Mass: Harvard University Press, 1986).

For instance, much of the plot of Wagner's opera *Lohengrin* centers on individuals going to extreme measures to regain group membership and high status. Ostracism is commonly viewed as grounds for revenge, but this of course is usually viewed as illegitimate, as it is in the opera.

This is such an important part of human psychology, it plays an important role in the Judeo-Christian drama. The Devil rebelled against God, and he was expelled, and so became the king of the lower, alien world, and, most importantly, death. Because he is an outsider and an underling, he is simply laughable, stupid and subhuman, a thingness, and it is usurpation for him to try to defend himself.

The implications of this are clear. Whites are the outsider, the "thingness" of alien evil that encroaches on the good people who are on the inside of the legitimate group based power structure. During the middle ages, foreigners were commonly understood to be "Dogheaded."[287] So as outsiders they were subhuman and could easily be killed, as indeed was the common practice when it came to outsiders. Similarly when some anthropologists were leaving by plane from a New Guinea tribe, the tribal men asked the anthropologists to drop some large rocks on a neighboring tribe. Of course, these impulses are coextensive with the anthropological and historical record. Today in the West, of course, whites have similar, liminal status, like beggars.

Whites have to constantly prove themselves to the powers that be by bowing and scraping at the appropriate times and to the appropriate people. The outsiders can't rebel and are easily attacked and even killed. And no one can intellectually challenge the situation in the halls of legitimate power and discourse. To do so would be "shocking" and would result in immediate ostracism. Who wants to make the case for the devil, for being on the outside? Who wants to point out that the king has no clothes?

A recent magazine ad showed a picture of a famous black boxer, and his child-age grandson wearing boxing gloves. The caption simply read, "Some stars show you the way." Whites have

---

[287] Robert Bartlett, *The Natural and Supernatural in the Middle Ages.* (Cambridge: Cambridge University Press, 2008).

a clear idea who to follow today to escape their sinful, alien nature. And this veneration explains why blacks are commonly presented in the media as smart and competent, instead as what you tend to see on the street.

About 85% of Nobel Prizes in science and economics have been won by white males. Women have won 17 times and the Japanese have won 16. The rest of the world is almost zero. And I think it is important that of the female prizes, only 5 were in chemistry and physics, while the other 11 were in physiology or medicine and 1 in economics. So women are more interested in the body than things that are disembodied.

Regarding Asians, a Vietnamese math professor at an American college reported that whites are more creative than Asians. You see blacks on Yahoo headlines all the time, and 80% are athletes, and the rest are entertainers and criminals. So like women, blacks are very body orientated in part because there is not much of an alternative. Feminists do like to compare women to blacks because of their similar "social" disabilities. A psychologist reported that women have more types of emotions than men, and they feel them more strongly.[288]

I recently was speaking with a young female psychology student and she said that what she was interested in was feelings. And recall that a woman's studies professor said that women think with their bodies. Outside of jealousy, anger and sex, men are not very emotional. And this difference in temperament was often pointed out in history.

Recall during the discussion of the state of nature that traditionally we associated good behavior with culture, while bad behavior with wild nature, and that whites today have lost the traditional sensitivity to "bestiality." With the inversion we now like and romanticize wild behavior, and people who have a "wild" look. One example today of the traditional sensitivity to crude nature is how many, especially among of urban populations, respond to rain. When walking outside in the rain, people often lower their head and contract their body expressing discomfort. Similarly, whites used to "contract" or show disgust in response to the greater physicality

---

[288] Nigel Barber, *The Science of Romance* (New York: Prometheus Books, 2002).

and threat of blacks; whites were responding to tendencies of both the black's behavior and look. With the inversion of values, whites now contract or show "shock" in response to the old culture based, "racist" value system.

Those old responses are now considered treasonous, so we celebrate nature and being wild as a relief. Instead of rejecting our base nature, we now celebrate it as part of a strategy of rejecting our high or more mental nature, the social body. Of course, as we've seen, by doing so, whites achieve redemption. Katy Perry, Christen Stewart, Emma Stone, and Angelina Jolie all dye their naturally light hair dark. This is the morality tale about the battle against evil that we live today. I think this whole scenario or story has outlived its usefulness. It is clearly dysfunctional.

When whites celebrated culture, then they celebrated their own behavior, look and power interests: the triumph of the high over the low, or of good over evil. This, in part, generates Nordicism, which is the belief that blue eyed whites are somehow better than brown eyed whites.

For instance, a recent production of the ballet *Sleeping Beauty* shows this kind of color symbolism. For the first 2 acts, when evil is confronted and defeated, the dancers have normally colored hair.

The third act portrays a wedding celebration and celebration of life or goodness, and this is represented by white wigs for the dancers. Evil is represented by dancers dressed in black and dancing in a disordered fashion. So we see that with the triumph of good over evil, there is a similar triumph of color and behavior.

And recall that Russell in his study of evil observed that the color black was universally associated with death, while white was associated with light and good, and this was case even in Africa.[289] Regarding Noridicism, it needs to be said here that evidence shows that this is aesthetically based, as there is no data that blue eyed people have higher IQs than brown eyed whites, at least in Western Europe outside of Southern Italy and Spain.[290]

---

[289] Jeffrey Russell, *The Prince of Darkness: Radical Evil and the Power of Good in History* (Ithaca & London: Cornell University Press, 1988).
[290] Richard Lynn, Personal communication, 2011.

Racial characteristics can have any number of different kinds of associations and appeal, and some can blend into moral ones strictly with visual kinds of associations as we see with Nordicism.

One explanation of Nordicisism is that sky and sun worship are common among tribal people, and the sky is blue and the sun white or blond. So people naturally want to venerate these "high" features, and recall that we associate power with high things like mountains. The Romans would sometimes guild their statues, and the Incas would sometimes cover their kings in gold dust. So unless it can be proved that blue eyed people have higher IQs or are more creative, this preference is easily attributed to purely aesthetic issues.

Another factor is that for survival reasons, the mind often works heavily by association. In other words, brown eyed whites are associated with the blacks and Hispanics. This is naturally off putting, and I, personally, sense this association, and I have brown eyes, and so does my father. So the association is strong, and so the association needs to be broken. A full 25% of Germans have brown eyes and hair, and then there are the northern Italians and French and so on around Europe.

A Christian radio station in California ran an ad for a movie called *Christmas Angel,* and it had a young girl go into an empty house, and she says, "Are you the Christmas Angel?" And a middle aged, black woman says, with a lower-class accent, "Do I look like the Christmas Angel?" I believe this is a question that we all should ask ourselves today. Do they look like the Christmas Angel? Nature and the blacks are just divine today, and are even colonizing Christmas. And the San Francisco Symphony has a Christmas concert called "The Colors of Christmas" and it always features black performers. There are almost zero blacks at regular classical music events.

Recall here that Foucault believed that culture is a pattern of control. He is clearly right about this, but he is wrong to portray power as arbitrary. In the world of science there is more at stake than egos and emotion. In the case of whites, it is the future of the human race.

Lets get a good look at an example of the pure fantasy that is driving the culture. Below are selections of lyrics from the Barry Manilow song *Day Break* (on his greatest hits CD):

"Singing to the world, its time we let the spirit come in, let it come on in…everyone is caught in the spin…we've been blinded by pride…blinded with fear…but's its daybreak if you want to believe…let it shine around the world…singing to the world, what's the point of putting it down, there's so much love to share, I'm singing to the world, don't you see that it all comes around…the feelings everywhere…we've been closing our eyes…"

All of this imagery and ethics existed during the nineteenth century, but applied to the virtue ethic between whites. Now of course it is felt to be applied to non-whites resulting in the common impulse of universal love. This is so powerful it blinds scientific knowledge.

A good example of this mania driven blindness regarding race came from the president of the American Anthropology Association. I wrote him the following email:

"I took a physical anthro class about 15 years ago and there seemed to be some important missing info in both the textbook and lecture. What I have noticed is that the blacks are clearly less evolved. For instance, as Gorillas have flat noses and black skin, so do the Africans. And, as chimps don't have foreheads and chins, the Africans tend to have small chins and sloping foreheads. And about 60 studies have found that blacks have brains that are on average 5.5 cubic inches smaller than whites. And as apes swagger through the jungle the blacks often swagger through the urban jungle. So my basic question is, whether most anthropologists are aware that the blacks are ape men and just don't talk about it, or are most not even aware of it? Is this the first time you have heard about this? Pls inform."

This was his response:

"Sir, you are tragically misinformed. I strongly courage you to review the material produced at our website, "Understanding Race" (http://www.understandingrace. org/home.html) to gain a better *sense* of the anthropological perspective on human variation and the evil, hate-filled ways in which pseudo-science has used the concept of race for inhumane purposes." [emphasis added].

Sense is the operative word here. I looked at the website and apparently they are fact averse. Maintaining the right sense of love and virtue, redemption and salvation is what is important, just like during the last dark ages. Notice that the writer, who has a Ph.D., has a strong sense of sin and the narratives necessary for redemption.

Recall how Faust felt oppressed by the evil body and wanted elevation. We see this moral or existential impulse in this response. The writer wanted liberation from evil, subhuman death. He also felt oppressed and wanted to rise above. He felt cut off from an empowering relationship of dependant rank. His response was mostly moral and not intellectual. Recall how in the film *Ghost*, the ghost of a white person is resurrected in the body of a black person. As Faust wanted liberation, so does our "Ph.D." There is essentially no difference between the moral sentiment of the Barry Manilow song and the moral sentiment driving the "science" of the American Anthropological Association and the rest of the even more corrupted liberal arts.

On the website on race the Ph.D recommended was the picture of a white woman holding a black baby to her breast. We all simply need to love one another today and this is moral of the story that the "universities" are devoted to propagandizing. No wonder that I kept dropping out of school when I was young. If you're interested in learning about reality, you're certainly not going to find it there. In Stalinist Russia it was against the law to attribute characteristics of grain to genetics. The morally and politically correct answer had to be from the environment or the social body. It looks like Marx wasn't the only sick child of the enlightenment.

So the moral fantasy of subordinance to our new masters is all that counts today. This is where salvation is found, just like during the nineteenth century. Anyone who deviates from *the* revelation, the Gospel truth, is subhuman. So the blacks are not subhuman, but "racist" or insubordinant, "dog-headed" whites. So again we see inversion, as we saw with Diderot. Whites know where to find their leaders today. What is righteous is whites' subordinance to nonwhites or of culture to nature. We saw this same battle in *Titanic*.

One might be tempted to think that the views on race during the nineteenth century and today are completely different, but if one takes apart their respective views, they have much more in common then is commonly assumed. What the left believes today is that black behavior results from their treatment by whites. So, first of all they believe that there is a causal relationship between the whites' treatment and black behavior.

The nineteenth century also believed that there was a causal relationship between black behavior and whites' treatment, but they saw causality moving in the other direction: not from whites to blacks, but from blacks to whites. Or in other words, the behavior of blacks caused whites to treat them the way they did by different distancing tactics like segregation. A white person who was raised in the Jim Crow south said that the motive for whites was mostly avoidance. Whites didn't have much interest in seeking out blacks for any purpose outside of work. So both the left and right are working with the correlation of black behavior and whites' treatment, they just believe that the causality works in opposite direction from each other.

So there isn't much difference between the nineteenth century and today on race; just direction of causal movement, and love instead of hate as animating the relationship. Recall here that anthropologists have known since the 1950s that the blacks in the US act the same as do the blacks in west Africa, so clearly the more consistent view in this situation is that black behavior caused Jim Crow and the different repatriation movements.

Let's get a precise picture of the potentialities of the blacks in the United States; a third of one percent, or about 110,000 out of 35 million, have IQs above 125. 10% have IQs between 110 and 125, and 90% have average to below average IQs.[291] Now about 12% of blacks have college degrees, which is what you would predict based on their IQ distribution. So take 2,000 from that 110,000 and put them into each urban area, and you would indeed occasionally see a genuine, competent black professional, but the common mistake

---

[291] Richard Herrnstein & Charles Murray. *The Bell Curve: Intelligence and Class Structure in American Society* (New York: Free Press, 1994).

is to generalize from this impression to the entire black community or their potentiality. The vast majority of blacks are worthless, and this was understood before the 1960s. So the old generalizations were correct, and this was scientifically founded by the early to mid century with the new IQ tests.

During the 1960s an American college sent a physics professor to recruit a black science professor from among the black colleges, and the professors at the black colleges reported that none of their students qualified for the position. This is what he found among the colleges, which is where the smartest of the blacks are to be found. 90% of blacks are basically worthless, which is what the nineteenth century observed. But most blacks beam with confidence, as do apes, and most whites find this gratifying because of their new pro-emotion value system and because God was charismatic. Primatologist Frans de Waal reported that he has never seen a chimp exhibit guilt. Recall the situation where the Chimpanzee threw the kerosene can. The old saying was, "The devil looks good" or is meretricious.

The yellow pages is a big book full of offers; if you open the book you will likely see an ad with a picture of superman. If you have faith and follow the procedure, you will obtain a benefit. If you don't have faith the procedure will break down. It's a take it or leave it situation. The bible is a big book full of promises. If you open the book you will read about superman. If you have faith and follow the procedures, you will obtain a benefit. If you don't have faith, the procedure will break down and, historically at least, the authorities would come and get you. Today of course, religion is a take it or leave it situation. Similarly a university is full of "professors" who describe our sins, and who provide the offer of redemption; in their sermons they will tell you stories of the ominous, threatening and charismatic blacks, Mexicans and Arabs, our new magical leaders. If you have faith in their stories you will obtain a benefit. If you don't have faith, the procedure will break down and the police will come and get you. It's not a take it or leave it situation.

Recall the chimp that ascended to dominance by throwing a kerosene can. His conspecifics started to support him after this impressive display. Similarly, when a group in the world wants to rise in status in the West they come here and knock over a building. This impresses people and many become committed to the cause. So we see that with the rule of the low, we do indeed have impulses to follow the low today.

Today the entire traditional Christian culture and all the biblical narratives are built on this new idea of escape or moral movement toward the dynamic world. Instead of seeing the primordial threatening predator, or evil, in sex and wild nature, now we see it in stifling heaven and civilization, and so have feelings of avoidance. This is why the left and right mostly agree on the recent social developments. They only disagree on details, not on fundamentals. Very few want to go back to the kind of high moral and cultural standards of the nineteenth century and their social, aesthetic and political implications. This is automatically experienced as "racist" and, instead, most whites look to blacks for salvation.

This distorted perspective creates the ludicrous "wisdom" in academia about the blacks. Let's quote Outlaw again, who is a Black philosophy professor at Vanderbilt University. After listing a group of black writers like Du Bois and Toni Morrison, he says, "I continue to be deeply impressed by the creative thoughtfulness, by the philosophical agility and insightfulness, of so very many of these articulate thinkers.

I am reminded all the more that, contrary to the conclusions drawn regarding the philosophical thoughtfulness of Black folks not yet institutionalized in canonical curricula throughout most of our discipline, the no-longer-to-be-denied truth is that black folks, encountering White folks, *have been compelled to philosophize*. Survival and endurance of conditions of racialized and gendered colonization, enslavement, and oppression—not conditions of leisured freedom—*compelled* more than a few African and African-descended person to philosophize, almost daily, even on what seemed the most mundane of occasions; were compelled to consider the most fundamental existential questions: Continue life during what would turn out to be centuries-long colonization and enslavement, of brutal, brutalizing, and humiliating gendered and racialized oppression? Or, seek "freedom" in death? Suffer despair until mad? Or, find resources for continued living through surreptitiously nurtured appreciations of the sacred and beautiful, or irony and tragic comedy, while cultivating hope and patience aided by discoveries and creations of beauty and humaneness in the midst of the physical and soul-distorting psychological brutalities of enforced impoverishments of condition of oppression that were not in any way "mundane" living? Die at one's own initiation? Or, capitulate to dehumanization?"[Emphasis in the original].[292]

Outlaw then went on to describe how this situation inspires all the singing and dancing. This quote is only half of the paragraph. This is certainly a vision of redemptive suffering. Most feel the need to embrace it. This helps to explain why this quote is from a lecture given before the American Philosophical Association in Washington DC. It was not published in some low end book.

A recent book published by Yale said that the condition for slaves was better than that for day laborers in France.[293] These kinds of facts don't catch on because they are not consistent with the visions and values of atonement that are driving the culture. As only evil people didn't respond to the visions and stories of the suffering Christ, only evil people today don't respond the visions and stories of the suffering blacks, and instead just laugh at them and talk about apemen. This is horrific, like the nineteenth century is horrific.

And recall the subhuman values and living conditions of the tribes in the state of nature, and how they like to sing and dance in Africa. I'm sure that Outlaw would also see great philosophizing there too. As we saw in the discussion of the biology of race, these values are only subhuman for whites, not blacks.

I guess at some low level these fantasies make sense for whites because, craving charisma, it is a more compelling vision to see this in recent history and today than in a book written 2000

---

[292] Lucius T. Outlaw, Jr. "Reconstructions in Academic Philosophy." *Proceedings and Addresses of the American Philosophical Association*. November 2012, Volume 86, Issue 2, p. 104-124. Newark, Delaware: American Philosophical Association, 2012, p. 123.

[293] Anthony Pagden, *Lords Of All The World: Ideologies of Empire in Spain, Britain and France, c. 1500-c. 1800* (New Haven & London: Yale University Press, 1995).

years ago. The visions of the blacks are living among us today while Jesus is long gone.

This is what we have been reduced to today, and we have seen the theme of the low almost constantly in this study. But this "vision" is not experienced as low, but high, another theme in our study. As Jesus' suffering was elevated and elevating, so now is the blacks' perceived suffering, and whites want to embrace them, animating a relationship of empowering dependent rank for whites.

Now that we have a good understanding of the historically specific movement of modernism, I think we can step back and confidently say that the way the world was both culturally and politically roughly at 1800 was an institutional reflection of whites' desire to protect themselves from bad people, like the Indians and other natural populations, and the desire for men and women to ensure by law that they obtained their desired reproductive goals in a constructive fashion. (For the nature of sexuality, see Buss.) So what the left has done is simply to objectify all of this, and claim that it is an evil imposition that needs to be thrown off. This fundamental impulse, one for perceived survival or predator avoidance, is the force that has driven all the fancy ethical and ideological debate, like the rise of historicism, of the last two centuries.

Chapter 8: Conclusion — A Scientific Electorate

Life is best shared through story, and art is the medium
through which we illustrate it.
—Rudolf Bekink
Netherlands Ambassador to the United States, 2012

Euripides paints men as they are; I paint men as they
ought to be.
—Sophocles

It should be the highest ambition of every American
to extend his views beyond himself, and to bear in mind
that his conduct will not only affect himself, his country, and
his immediate posterity; but that its influence may be coextensive with the world, and stamp political happiness or
misery on ages yet un-born.
— George Washington

I know of no safe depository of the ultimate powers
of the society but the people themselves. And if we think
them not enlightened enough to exercise their control with
a wholesome discretion, the remedy is not to take it from
them, but to inform their discretion by education. This is the
true corrective of abuses of constitutional power.
— Thomas Jefferson

Recall from the introduction the professor who said that the
Greeks understood things with a clarity that we have lost. Now

we see why. Modernism, as we have seen in the films, is so lost in fantasy that we are stumbling around and do not know which way is up or down. The Greeks knew that groups and individuals were different, unequal, and often in subtle ways that needed careful thought. All we understand today is the urgency to enslave whites to non-whites, as whites wanted to be slaves to Jesus. Recall that there is a book called *Slavery as Salvation*. This is what defines goodness, wisdom and insight today. Not subtle.

While a few professors in evolutionary psychology and primatology have made progress in understanding the human condition, their insights are mostly published in textbooks and journals. Though some trade books have been published, like by Richard Wrangham, David Bussand recently, Steven Pinker's *The Better Angels of Our Nature*. The implications of their scientific findings for race and gender are too politically incorrect to find common currency, especially among liberal arts professors. But it's a beginning, and I hope that my book will help us down the path to real evolutionary wisdom, as opposed to just more fanaticism.

I recently was speaking with two people who had psychology degrees, and neither of them had heard of Steven Pinker, though he is a professor at Harvard and a leader in evolutionary cognitive psychology.

During the 1970s, 25% of people thought that the problems with the blacks had a genetic aspect, while today that figure is 3%.[294] This is how effective the taboos are. One professor said that Harold Bloom's book *The Closing of the American Mind*, while a good seller, had no impact on liberal arts departments. As it took a full two centuries to overthrow the virtue ethic, it will probably take a similar effort, though not necessarily that much time, to overthrow the far more comfortable and mythic dogmas of modernism. Communication is faster today than earlier, and literacy rates are higher.

In chapter one I was able to describe and defend humanism in art in about 40 pages, while to describe the fantasy of modernism took about 6 times as many pages. The right answer is always simple

---

[294] Steven Pinker, *The Better Angels of Our Nature: Why Violence Has Declined* (New York: Viking, 2011).

and clear while the wrong answer can go on forever. For example, there is only one right answer to the problem 2+2. The number of wrong answers is infinite.

Werner Jaeger was a Classics professor at Harvard during the early to mid twentieth century. In his *Paideia: the Ideals of Greek Culture* he makes the ethnocentric claim that only the West has culture. In other words, it was the Greeks who discovered the balance between form and content described in chapter one. While other groups stumbled from one fantasy to another, as we see in the fictional tribe in *Avatar*, and simply tried to massacre their neighbors, the Greeks were the first to discipline the mind and body and to coordinate them. To be specific, the Greeks discovered what we today call high culture. High culture, as we have seen, results from a rationalization of nature, as in the paintings of Claude, and the body, as in the art of Michelangelo. This objectivity also resulted in science. Non-western people either live more in the body, like most tribes, or in the mind, like the Eastern religions. The Greeks and their cultural descendants, Western civilization, were the first to strike the right balance. We live our lives surrounded by the benefits of this in science and technology.

Culturally however, things are different today. Most have all but abandoned high culture as an ideal. By inverting Platonism, placing nature over virtue, we have regressed to savagery, as also can be seen in *Dances with Wolves* and *Avatar*. Today's moral structure, as seen in film, is self-destructive or irrational. It reminds you of the Potlatch ceremony practiced by indigenous peoples of the Pacific Northwest Coast. It was originally a gift-giving tradition. But it turned into the custom of burning their belongings in order to show their wealth and generosity. This sounds strangely familiar. We saw this very clearly in *Tears in the Sun* where the US military unit fought for the blacks because of sins of whites. We still have minds and bodies, but they are largely dislocated from a goal of enlightened unity. Depending upon context, either our bodies jerk our minds around, or our minds jerk our bodies around.

We need to reestablish the right balance, but of course with the mind discovering and forming the rules. If we follow only our instincts, as most do today, we descend to barbarism. As Victor

Hugo was quoted in chapter one, "Proportion his song to his nature, and you shall see!" The mind must do the forming, but not everyone has equal mental faculties, as Beethoven was quoted in this book's front matter.

The American founding fathers knew this. They had a traditional Platonist philosophy, which placed the mind in control of the will and appetites. When this ideal reigned, in the eighteenth and early nineteenth centuries, the West had a beautiful and great culture. But after the '48 revolution in Europe, the masses became more assertive and the balance was destroyed. As Brahms said when he heard Mahler's first symphony: "Is this the future of music?" Reed, a Schubert biographer, said that early Romantic music is better than late Romantic music, and I would agree, with the exception of Wagner.

We see a similar disintegration in the other arts with the rise of naturalism in fiction and painting. And about 1900 Salome drinks the blood of John the Baptist on the opera stage, and it's only gone down from there. In this period, suffrage was granted to unintelligent, uneducated, and poor men, and so they got their way. This helped destroy the balance and the entirety of Western culture built on that balance. Professional wrestling and the blacks are now the cultural ideal. There was a similar collapse into particulars and subjectivism with the slide to mob rule in ancient Athens.

As we've learned, we can't legislate social psychology out of existence. Human psychology is, to a large extent, social and hierarchical. If we ignore it, it just goes out of control, or starts to follow it own course, like a river and as we saw among the Vikings. So while the Enlightenment trends of individualism may have a good motive, at least among some, it is just not tenable, if one wants to maintain some order and beauty to life. This is particularly the case with the more extreme expressions of this philosophy, like among the libertarians.

Again the issue is balance between the individual and group, or detail and form. A Columbia professor hit it on the head during the tumult of the 1960s when he said, "Individual rights versus social responsibility." This is the difficult balance to find. But find it we must if we are to see sane government that does not create a 15 trillion dollar debt, like at present in the US, and a waste land for a cultural life. In recent decades, music education has been eliminated in much of the US, so this and similar policies need to be reversed and we need to re-instill in children a love and sensitivity to beauty. Then their moral lives will start to become more beautiful, if it is accompanied by proper moral education and consciousness of the negative impulses.

Prior to the twentieth century, the term *culture* referred only to high culture. But starting about 1900 it started to refer to any fantasy that a group comes up with. This is a version of historicism and relativism. Of course this is good example of the particularism and inversion. So we need to go back to an elitist, or accurate understanding of higher human cognition and values as expressed in sound, image and language. We need to go back to the idea that we need to always present to our selves the highest moral values as expressed in image, sound and language.

This is not abstract wishful thinking, as today crime is up 1000% among whites in the US, and it is even higher in many European countries. So something needs to be done. The modernist experiment has failed in most spheres of life. "Openness" has become dogma to the point that it is stifling science and killed the arts. It has simply taken us back to the Vikings as the crime data and cultural landscape make clear.

We need to put the mind in back in control, and to have the kind of value system or hierarchy as earlier. The bad news is that society needs a mechanism to suppress the worst in human nature, and this was common knowledge before the twentieth century as we saw in Franklin's quote about social disintegration. The good news is that doing so will re-establish real justice and thus peace and harmony. During the eighteenth century, class hierarchy or elitism suppressed the worst of human nature, but today class hierarchy is dead and cannot be revived. Still, we must somehow return to rejecting our animal aspect, and individuals dominated by brute instinct, as can be seen on the street today, as funny or dismissed.

One possible approach would be to require people to take classes in the history of political philosophy, and then pass a test in political knowledge in order to vote. Tests were administered by some

American states during the 1950s. If a person cannot write a 10-page paper describing political positions, then he has no right having an influence in politics. Politics is as much a matter of knowledge as building a bridge, and Socrates makes this point several times. As one professor said, "Confused writing is confused thought." We do not want confused people electing our representatives as we do today. Such ignorant demagoguery from the media contributes to the election of charismatic but inept political leaders. Driving a car is not a right, but a privilege. Similarly, we should view voting as a privilege to be earned by the ability to not wreck the culture.

We could even pass a law requiring people who cannot vote to salute those who can. If this seems peculiar, notice that nowadays U.S. society and government demand that Whites defer to Blacks, and we have seen how destructive that is of morals. Whites are now open and receptive *to everything*. It would be a positive change to have the ignorant recognized as such and made to defer to their more educated and intelligent superiors, instead of imagined ones. Something like this would help get the lower class, and for that matter most peoples' egos, back under control, and distribute power to where natural justice and function demands. We have seen the fruits of the inversion of Platonism. It is time to return to respecting virtue. As we have professionalized political leadership, we now need to professionalize the electorate.

When I was first in college I read *Structural Anthropology* by Claude Levi-Strauss, and he said three things that seemed right and stayed with me; first, we are all ultimately after the human mind, and, second, any model for human nature, social psychology and culture has to apply with absolute consistency. He also made the good point that in the early modern period there were many different models for nature, and that this is the condition today of the social sciences. I believe that the model I have outlined in this volume helps us to achieve these goals of psychological insight and methodological unity. Notice that the inversion is evident in both high and popular culture, and in the comparison between the West and tribal societies. Simon Schama, in his *Landscape and Memory* said that the pagan Germans and the Romans existed as inversions of each other. (He also refers to the "less evolved.")

The choice is pretty simple; either mind centered or body centered. I don't think we need to become monks, but we do need to be careful about nature, or at least mostly let it in in the context of formed beauty, like the traditional decorative arts. We can't just blindly love it as Barry Manilow sings and is the common impulse today. And it is clear we need to go back to making the distinction between high and popular culture. Dancing is fine, and there are times for this, but it is not the same worth as high culture and we need to go back to this obviously correct and socially useful concept.

The traditional distinction between art and entertainment was accurate. Entertainment is more focused on the body, whereas art is more psychologically supple. This suppleness can be heard in the comparison between classical music and pop, and between high Renaissance art and middle Renaissance art. We need to create for people an aesthetic or social inducement to virtue that does not involve God. Recall here that the Greeks had the same word for both evil and ugly. There were good reasons why whites used to find the blacks to be ugly and disgusting. Of course, Whites today have become ugly and disgusting, so they feel comradery with blacks.

We need to stop romanticizing debauchery as this is bad for our health, both physical and cultural, and sets a bad example. Similarly we need to go back to romanticizing cultural greatness and its good moral effects. For instance, I recently attended a symphony concert that featured both Beethoven's Seventh Symphony and Berlioze's Symphony Fantastic.

The contrast is apt for this study. Here is how a program annotator for the Cleveland Orchestra describes the Seventh: "Many a listener has come away from a hearing of this Symphony in a state of being punch-drunk. Yet it is an intoxication without a hangover, a dope-like exhilaration without decadence." So this is good, instructive fun. It is a pleasure more of the mind, but also for the body. The Berlioz is about a literal drug induced stupor that leads to the death of the protagonist. We know who, at least so far, has won that cultural debate. Francisco Goya has an art work called *The Sleep of Reason Produces Monsters*. Of course, much of the human population does not have much of an alternative to the natural.

During the 1930s in the United States there was a large deportation of Mexicans, and Thomas Jefferson arranged for a repatriation of Africans. We need to refocus our energies. The mind is like a muscle in that it needs to be exercised by large amounts of writing before it can really think in a detailed, contextual and systematic fashion. I believe the era of base muscle flexing needs to come to an end.

With our dumbed down value system, there is no incentive for most people to really think like an evolutionary scientist. This is the only body of factual knowledge about human nature and behavior. Between my study, London and Smith's *Religion of Macho*, and the advances in evolutionary psychology during the last twenty years, there is no longer a need for estimates and guesses, at least for much of the basics of human nature.

Anne Fernald was a psychology professor who switched to animal behavior, because, as she said, "you analyze what they do, not what they say." I agree that at one level humans are more complicated because there is so much more data to organize. Using language humans communicate with great precision huge amounts of thought and emotion, while animals, at least working with what is visible, are much simpler.

But here is the rub. Because humans can communicate with more precision, scholars have the potential for greater depths of understanding because there is so much more detail. It is like the difference between understanding a rock simply by how it rolls down a hill, or what it is comprised of. The latter allows for much more control and so profitable manipulation. We live our lives surrounded by the profits from this perspective. Put another way, we can solve human social problems.

Not only is this clear in the past with the huge declines of crime and other cultural accomplishments, but, as I've just showed, it is clearly implied by the potential of greater ease of comprehension of human nature. It is only a matter of continuing to work out the correct evolutionary scientific method. So much progress has been made in the past century, that there is no doubt that this is the right path, and will take us to very near complete knowledge, as it has in all other areas of nature. A campaign among educators to actively suppress or marginalize the fear of biological determinism among themselves, students and the public will help things along. I mention all of this because, as we saw with Prof. Fernald, people are prone to pessimism about understanding human nature.

In contrast to this scenario, half of the population today simply spouts the pieties of social body generosity, love and peace, and that's the extent of knowledge, ethics and debate. This creates contemporary patterns of intolerance. We saw the effects of this wisdom on the anthropologist. Conservatives tend to want to impose virtue on the body or individual, while the left what to impose it on the social body, so they talk past each other. Though, they do draw from the same value system as we've seen, so if we can just start talking about the same things, the flawed individual and his necessary reforming commitments to the group, then maybe we can start to understand each other, reach agreements and create a sane and beautiful culture once again. The difference between left and right is not between ethical systems, but where in our personalities and social lives we direct them. The structure is the same; all that changes is where we distribute our personalities in that structure.

If we put the mind back in charge of our culture and politics, we will see the victory of mind once again. We will have achieved Thomas Jefferson's ideal of a "natural aristocracy" or the right balance between the mind and body.[295]

---

[295] For further reading on crime, race and the Christian structure of the left, see Richard Smith and Richard London, *Religion of Macho: Racial Integration, The World-Wide Crime Wave and the Left* (Bloomington IN: Author House, 2008). Roger Chartier, *The Cultural Origins of the French Revolution* (Duke University Press, 1991). Also recommended is Jennifer Homans, *Apollo's Angels: A History of Ballet* (New York: Random House, 2010). For further examples of my model in art history see Michael Marlais, John Varriano & Wendy M. Watson, *Valenciennes, Daubigny, and the Origins of French Landscape Painting.* (South Hadley, Mass: Mount Holyoke Art Museum, 2004.) And Christopher Allen, *French Painting in the Golden Age.* (London: Thames and Hudson, 2003.)

Bibliography

Aleong, A., and M. Swart (2008) "Neural Correlates of Human Body Perception." *Journal of Cognitive Neuroscience* 22 (3): 482-495.

Allen, Christopher. *French Painting in the Golden Age*. London: Thames and Hudson, 2003.

Allen, Robert C. "The Movies in Vaudeville: Historical Context of the Movies as Popular Entertainment." *The American Film Industry*. Tino Balio, Ed. Madison: University of Wisconsin Press, 1985.

Anderson, Gary A. *Sin: A History*. New Haven & London: Yale University Press, 2009.

Archer, Dane and Rosemary Gartner. *Violence and Crime in Cross-National Perspective*. New Haven & London: Yale University Press, 1984.

Arzy, S., G. Thut, et al. (2006). "Neural Basis of Embodiment: Distinct Contributions of Temporoparietal Junction and Extrastriate Body Area." *Journal of Neuroscience* 26 (31): 8074-8081.

Balandier, Georges and Jacques Maquet. *Dictionary of Black African Civilization*. New York: Leon Amiel, 1974.

Bartlett, Kenneth. *Development of European Civilization*, Audio-lecture course, (Chantilly, VA: The Teaching Company, 2011).

Bartlett, Robert. *The Natural and Supernatural in the Middle Ages* .Cambridge: Cambridge University Press, 2008.

Barzun, Jacques. *From Dawn to Decadence: 500 Year of Western Cultural Life*. New York: Harpercollins, 2001.

Bascou, Marc, Michele Bimbenet-Privat & Martin Chapman. *Royal Treasure from the Louvre: Louis XIV to Marie-Antoinette*. Munich, London & New York: Delmonico Books, 2012.

Bauerlein, Mark. *The Dumbest Generation: How the Digital Age Stupefies Young Americans and Jeopardizes our Future*. New York: Penguin, 2008.

Becker, Carl L. *The Heavenly City of the Eighteenth-Century Philosophers*, Second Edition. New Haven & London: Yale University Press, 2003.

Bailey, Colin B. "Genre Painting in Eighteenth Century France: The Huntington Collection." Shelley M. Bennett & Carolyn Sargentson, Ed. *French Art of the Eighteenth Century at the Huntington*. New Haven & London: Yale University Press, 2008.

Barber, Nigel. *The Science of Romance*. New York: Prometheus Books, 2002.

Bonfante-Warren, Alexandra. *The Pitti Palace Collections*. Westport, CT: Beaux Arts Editions, 2006.

Bureau of Justice Statistics. http://bjs.ojp.usdoj.gov/content/pub/pdf/cvus0801.pdf

Blackburn, Simon. *Oxford Dictionary of Philosophy*. New York: Oxford University Press, 2008.

Blanning, Tim. *The Romantic Revolution: A History*. New York: Modern Library, 2011.

Bolton, John. "President Obama's Foreign Policy: An Assessment". *Imprimis*, October 2009, p. 2. Volume 38, number 10. Reprinted by permission from Imprimis, a publication of Hillsdale College.

Bordes, Philippe. *Jacques-Louis David: Empire to Exile*. New Haven & London: Yale University Press, 2005.

Bretell, Richard. *Museum Masterpieces: The Metropolitan Museum of Art*. DVD lecture series. Chantilly, VA: The Teaching Company, 2007.

Brilliant, Virginia. *The John and Mable Ringling Museum of Art* .London: Scala Publishers, Ltd, 2010.

Bruce, Vicki, and Andy Young. *In the Eye of the Beholder*. Oxford, England: Oxford University Press, 1998.

Burnstein, Eugene. "Altruism and Genetic Relatedness." David Buss, ed. *The Handbook of Evolutionary Psychology*. Hoboken, N.J.: John Wiley & Sons, 2005.

Buss, David. *Evolutionary Psychology: The New Science of the Mind*. New York: Allyn & Bacon, 2012.

Byock, Jesse, trans. *The Saga of the Volsungs*. Berkeley: University of California Press, 1990.

Chan, A. W. Y., M.V. Peelen, et al. (2004). "The Effect of Viewpoint on Body Representation in the Extrastriate Body Area."*Neuroreport* 15(15): 169-188.

Chartier, Roger.*The Cultural Origins of the French Revolution*. Durham & London: Duke University Press, 1991.

Chilvers, Ian. *The Oxford Dictionary of Art*. New York: Oxford University Press, 2004.

Cohen, Selma Jeanne, Ed. *Dance as a Theater Art*. Hightstown, NJ: Princeton Book Company, 1992.

Crystal, David. *The Cambridge Biographical Encyclopedia*. New York: Cambridge University Press, 1998.

Dabhoiwala, Faramerz. *The Origins of Sex: A History of the First Sexual Revolution*. New York: Oxford University Press, 2012.

Daly, Martin, and Margo Wilson. *Homicide*. New York: Aldine De Gruyter, 1988.

Dash, Leon. *When Children Want Children*. New York: Morrow, 1989.

David, N., M.X. Cohen, et al. (2007). "The Extrastriate Cortex Distinguishes Between the Consequences of One's Own and Others' Behavior." *Neuroimage* 36(3): 1004-1014.

Degler, Carl N. *In Search of Human Nature: The Decline and Revival of Darwinism in American Social Thought*. New York: Oxford University Press, 1991.

Delumeau, Jean. *Sin and Fear: The Formation of a Western Guilt Culture*. New York: St. Martin's Press, 1990.

D'Sousa, Dinesh. *Illiberal Education: The Politics of Race and Sex on Campus*. New York: Vintage Books, 1992.

De Vecchi, Pierluigi. "Difficulty/ease and studied casualness in the work of Raphael." *Raphael: Grace and Beauty*. Nitti, Patrizia; Marc Restellini; and Claudio Strinati, Ed. Milano: Skira Editori, 2001.

De Waal, Frans. *Chimpanzee Politics: 25ᵗʰ Anniversary Edition.* Baltimore: The Johns Hopkins University Press, 2007.

Dodds, E. R. *The Greeks and the Irrational.* Berkeley: University of California Press, 1951.

Duc d'Aiguillon, M. "Motion Concerning Individual Privileges and Feudal and Seigneurial Rights." *The French Revolution: A Document Collection.* Ed. Laura Mason & Tracey Rizzo. Boston & New York: Houghton Mifflin Company, 1999.

Durgnat, Raymond & John Kobal. *Greta Garbo.* New York: E. P. Dutton and Co., 1967.

Eible-Eibesfeldt, I. *The Biology of Peace and War.* New York: Viking, 1979.

Etcoff, Nancy. *Survival of the Prettiest.* New York: Double Day, 1999.

Fagan, Brian M. *Human Prehistory and the First Civilizations.* Audio-tape lecture series. Chantilly, VA: The Great Courses, 2000.

Fears, J. Rufus. *Books That Have Made History.* Audio-tape lecture series. Chantilly, VA: The Teaching Company, 2005.

Fernald, Anne. "Human Maternal Vocalization to Infants as Biologically Relevant Signals: An Evolutionary Perspective." Jerome H. Barkow, Leda Cosmides & John Tooby, ed. *The Adapted Mind: Evolutionary Psychology and the Generation of Culture.* New York & Oxford: Oxford University Press, 1992.

Ficino, Marsilio. *Platonic Theology*: Volume I—Books I-IV. Michael J.B Allen, Trans. Cambridge, Mass: Harvard University Press, 2001.

Forsyth, Neil. *The Old Enemy: Satan and the Combat Myth.* Princeton, NJ: Princeton University Press, 1987.

Getty, J. Paul. *As I See It: The Autobiography of J. Paul Getty.* Los Angeles: Getty Publications, 2003.

Fritze, Ronald H. *New Worlds: The Great Voyages of Discovery, 1400-1600.* Westport CN: Praeger, 2002.

Gill, Meredith J. *Augustine in the Italian Renaissance: Art and Philosophy from Petrarch to Michelangelo.* New York: Cambridge University Press, 2005.

Glad, John. "Eugenics and the Public". *The Mankind Quarterly.* Fall-Winter 2009, Volume L, no. 1 & 2, p. 120.

Goff, P. A., Eberhardt, J. L., Williams, M. J., & Jackson, M. C. (2008). "Not Yet Human: Implicit knowledge, historical dehumanization, and contemporary consequences." *Journal of Personality and Social Psychology*, 94, 292-306.

Goodall, Jane. *The Chimpanzees of Gombe*. Cambridge Mass: Harvard University Press, 1986.

Gorman, Brian. "New Vision TV Sitcom Offers Extremely Diverse Characters." *The Western Star* (Canada), 53, no. 33 (February 8, 2003), p. 3.

Gottfried, Paul Edward. *Multiculturalism and the Politics of Guilt: Toward a Secular Theocracy*. Columbia & London: University of Missouri Press, 2002.

Gottschall, Jonathan. *The Storytelling Animal: How Stories Make Us Human*. Boston & New York: Houghton Mifflin Harcourt, 2012.

Greenberg, Robert. *How to Listen to and Understand Great Music, 3rd Edition*. DVD lecture series. Chantilly, VA: The Teaching Company, 2006.

Gregoire, Abbe Henri. "Opinion…on the Royal Veto." *The French Revolution: A Document Collection*. Ed. Laura Mason & Tracey Rizzo. Boston & New York: Houghton Mifflin Company, 1999.

Guelzo, Allen. "Hero, Standing." *Imprimis*, May/June, 2009. Volume 38, Number 5/6, page 4. Reprinted by permission from Imprimis, a publication of Hillsdale College.

Guerrieri, Matthew. *The First Four Notes: Beethoven's Fifth and the Human Imagination*. New York: Knopf, 2012.

Guest, Ivor. *The Paris Opera Ballet*. Alton, England: Dance Books, 2006.

Hashiloni-Dolev, Yael. *A Life (Un) Worthy of Living: Reproductive Genetics in Israel and Germany*. Dordrecht, The Netherlands: Springer, 2010.

Hayward, Steven. *The Age of Reagan*. New York: Three Rivers, 2009.

Henslin, James. *Social Problems*. Englewood Cliffs, N.J: Prentice-Hall, 1990.

Herrnstein, Richard & Charles Murray. *The Bell Curve: Intelligence and Class Structure in American Society*. New York: Free Press, 1994.

Herskovits, Melville J. *The Myth of the Negro Past*. Boston: Beacon Press, 1958.

Hight, Ainslie, trans. *Gritter the Strong*. New York: E. B. Dutton, 1913.

Hobson, Dr. J. Allen. *Dreaming: An Introduction to the Science of Sleep*. Oxford and New York: Oxford University Press, 2004.

Homans, Jennifer. *Apollo's Angels: A History of Ballet*. New York: Random House, 2010.

Hyde, Melissa & Mark Ledbury. *Rethinking Boucher*. Los Angeles: Getty Publications, 2006.

Hugo, Victor. Charles E. Wilbour, Trans. *Les Miserables*. New York: Modern Library, 1992.

Idaho Statesmen, February 15, 2010, p. C1.

Interpol. *International Crime Statistics*. Lyon, France: Interpol General Secretariat, 2002.

Jaeger, Werner. *PAIDEIA: The Ideals of Greek Culture*, vol. 1. Oxford, England: Oxford University Press, 1973.

James, Henry. *The American*. New York: Signet Classics, 1965.

Janson, H.W. *History of Art*. Second Edition. Englewood Cliffs, N.J: Prentice-Hall, 1969.

Jewell, Richard. *The Golden Age of Cinema: Hollywood 1929-1945*. Malden, Mass.: Blackwell Publishing, 2007.

Jobling, Ian. "The Crime the Media Chose to Ignore." *American Renaissance*, 16, no. 5 (May 2005), pp. 11–12.

Jones, David E. *An Instinct for Dragons*. New York & London: Routledge, 2002.

Jones, H. Stuart. *Ancient Writers on Greek Sculpture*. Chicago: Argonaut, Inc., Publishers, 1966.

Jover, Manuel. *Ingres*. Paris: Editions Terrail/Edigroup, 2005.

Kaeuper, Richard W. *Chivalry and Violence in Medieval Europe*. Oxford: Oxford University Press, 1999.

Karremans, J.C., W.F. Frankenhuis, et al. (2010). "Blind Men Prefer a Low Waist-to-Hip Ratio." *Evolution and Human Behavior* 31(3): 182-186.

Keeley, Lawrence H. *War Before Civilization*. Oxford, England: Oxford University Press, 1997.

Kerman, Joseph & Gary Tomlinson. *Listen.* Sixth Edition. Boston & New York: Bedford/St. Martin's, 2008.

Kitto, H.D.F., *The Greeks.* London: Penguin Books, 1957.

Kohler, Joachim. Steward Spencer, Trans. *Richard Wagner: The Last of the Titans.* New Haven & London: Yale University Press, 2004.

Lewin, Leif. *Planhusallningsdebatten.* Stockholm: Almquist & Wiksell, 1970.

Lewis, O. *The Children of Sanchez: Autobiography of a Mexican Family.* New York: Random House, 1961.

Linden, David J. *The Accidental Mind: How Brain Evolution has Given Us Love, Memory, Dreams, and God.* Cambridge, Mass: Harvard University Press, 2007.

Lindsey, Brink. *The Age of Abundance: How Prosperity Transformed American Politics and Culture.* New York: HarperBusiness, 2008.

Lovejoy, Arthur O. *The Great Chain of Being.* Cambridge, Mass.: Harvard University Press, 1964.

Lynn, Richard. *Race Differences in Intelligence: An Evolutionary Analysis.* Augusta, Ga: Washington Summit Publishers, 2006.

Magee, Bryan. *Wagner and Philosophy.* London: Penguin Books, 2000.

Marlais, Michael, John Varriano & Wendy M. Watson. *Valenciennes, Daubigny, and the Origins of French Landscape Painting.* South Hadley, Mass: Mount Holyoke Art Museum, 2004.

MacCulloch, Diarmaid. *The Reformation.* New York: Viking, 2003.

McGrew, W.C. Tools to get food: The subsistants of Tanzanian chimpanzees and Tasmanian aborigines compared. *Journal of Anthropological Research, 43,* 247-258.

McKenzie, Kevin. "Bringing Magic to Center Stage: The Art of American Ballet Theater." Nancy Ellison. *In Classic Style: The Splendor of American Ballet Theater.* New York: Rizzoli International Publications, Inc., 2008.

Michel, Regis. *Le beau ideal ou l'art du concept.*Paris, 1989.

Montesquieu, Charles de Secondat, baron de. 1949. *Oeuvres completes,* ed. Roger Caillos, 2 vol. Paris.

Mormando, Franco. *Bernini: His Life and His Rome.* Chicago & London: University of Chicago Press, 2011.

Morone, James. *Hellfire Nation: The Politics of Sin in American History*. New Haven & London: Yale University Press, 2004.

Mufwene, Salikoko S. ed. *Africanisms in Afro-American Language Varieties*. Athens, Ga.: University of Georgia Press, 1993.

Muller, Ulrick & Peter Wapnewski. *Wagner Handbook*. Cambridge, Mass.: Harvard University Press, 1992.

Murphy, G. Ronald. *The Saxon Savior*. New York: Oxford University, 1989.

Murray, Charles. *Real Education*. New York: Crown Forum, 2008.

"Musical Journeys: Moritzberg Festival." Staff Writer. *Gramophone* Awards Issue, 2012. Volume 90, no 1089, p. 131.

National Public Radio, "All Thing Considered," June 18, 1990.

New Century Foundation. *The Color of Crime*. Download available at: www.amren.com.

Nichols, Ashton. *Emerson, Thoreau, and the Transcendentalist Movement*. Audio-Tape lecture series. Chantilly, VA: The Teaching Company, 2006.

Nichols, Roger. "Lord of misrule: Chopin the rebel". Liner notes for CD entitled, *Chopin, pianist Simon Trpceski*. European Union: EMI Records, 2007.

Nilsson, Martin P. *Greek Folk Religion*. Philadelphia: University of Pennsylvania, 1972.

Nitti, Patrizia; Marc Restellini; and Claudio Strinati, Ed. *Raphael: Grace and Beauty*. Milano: Skira Editori, 2001.

O'Connor, David. "Architecture of Infinity-The Egyptian Temple."*Archaeology Odyssey*, September, 1999, 46–47.

Ogas, Ogi & Sai Gaddam. *A Billion Wicked Thoughts: What the Worlds Largest Experiment Reveals About Human Desire*. New York: Dutton, 2011.

Ostwald, Peter F. "Johannes Brahms, Solitary Altruist." Walter Frisch, Ed. *Brahms and His World*. Princeton: Princeton University Press, 1990.

Outlaw, Lucius T. Jr. "Reconstructions in Academic Philosophy." *Proceedings and Addresses of the American Philosophical Association*. November 2012, Volume 86, Issue 2, p. 104-124. Newark, Delaware: American Philosophical Association, 2012.

Pagden, Anthony. *Lords Of All The World: Ideologies of Empire in Spain, Britain and France, c. 1500-c. 1800*. New Haven & London: Yale University Press, 1995.

Peelen, M. V., and P. E. Downing (2007). "The Neural Basis of Visual Body Perception." *Nature Review Neuroscience* 8(8): 636-648.

Pestritto, Ronald J. *Woodrow Wilson and the Roots of Modern Liberalism*. Lanham MD: Rowman & Littlefield Publishers, Inc, 2005.

Phelps, E.A., O'Connor, K.J., Cunningham, W.A., Funayama, E.S., Gatenby, J.C., Gore, J.C., & Banaji, M.R. 2000. Performance on indirect measures of race evaluation predicts amygdale activation. *Journal of Cognitive Neuroscience, 12*, 729-38.

Pinker, Steven. *The Better Angels of Our Nature: Why Violence Has Declined*. New York: Viking, 2011.

Plato. "*Mythical Hymm of the* Phaedrus." Marsilio Ficino. Michael J.B. Allen, trans. *Commentaries on Plato: Volume I: Phaedrus and Ion*. Cambridge, Mass: Harvard University Press, 2008.

Pliny the Elder. K. Jex-Blake, Trans. *The Elder Pliny's Chapters On The History Of Art*. Kessinger Publishing. Reprint of, New York: The Macmillan Co, 1896.

Poliakoff, E. (2010). "Introduction to Special Issue on Body Representation: Feeling, Seeing, Moving, and Observing." *Experimental Brain Research* 204 (3): 289-283.

Pope John Paul II. All Popes Quoted in: http://www.mostholyfamilymonastery.com/john_paul_ii_preached_the_gospel_of_the_antichrist.php

Price, S.R.F. *Rituals and Power: The Roman Imperial Cult in Asia Minor*. Cambridge: Cambridge University Press, 1984.

Raynal, Guillaume-Thomas, abbe. 1781. *Histoire philosophique et politique des etablissemens et du commerce des Europeen dan les deux Indes,* 10 vols. Geneva.

Reed, John. *Schubert: The Final Years*. London: Faber and Faber, 1972.

Read, W. Winwood. *Savage Africa*. New York: Harper and Brothers, 1967.

Reynolds, Sir Joshua. *Discourses*. New York: Penguin, 1992.

Roslavleva, Natalia. *Era of the Russian Ballet*. London: Victor Gollancz LTD, 1966.

Ross, Janice. *San Francisco Ballet at Seventy-Five*. San Francisco: Chronicle Books LLC, 2007.

Rothstein, Bo. *Just Institutions Matter: The Moral and Political Logic of the Universal Welfare State*. Cambridge: Cambridge University Press, 1998.

Rusher, William A. "Will They Ever Learn?" *The Claremont Review of Books*, 4, no. 2 (Spring 2004), pp. 21–23.

Rushton, J. Philippe. *Race, Evolution and Behavior*. Port Huron, MI: Charles Darwin Research Institute, 2000.

Russell, Jeffrey. *Lucifer: The Devil in the Middle Ages*. Ithaca & London: Cornell University Press, 1984.

Russell, Jeffrey. *The Prince of Darkness: Radical Evil and the Power of Good in History*. Ithaca & London: Cornell University Press, 1988.

Sachs, Harvey. *The Ninth: Beethoven and the World in 1824*. New York: Random House, 2010.

Sacks, David. *A Dictionary of the Ancient Greek World*. Oxford: Oxford University, 1995.

Sargent, W. *People of the Valley*. New York: Random House, 1974.

Schama, Simon. *A History of Britain*-Vol. 1-3. London: BBC, 2000.

Schama, Simon. *Landscape and Memory*. New York: Alfred A. Knopf, 1995.

Schein, Seth L. *The Mortal Hero: An Introduction to Homer's Iliad*. Berkeley: University of California, 1984.

Schorske, Carl E. *Fin-De-Siecle Vienna: Politics and Culture*. New York: Vintage Books, 1981.

Siepman, Jeremy. *CHOPIN: The Reluctant Romantic*. Boston: Northeastern University Press, 1995.

Sölle, Dorothee. *Political Theology*, trans. John Shelly. Philadelphia: Fortress Press, 1974.

Spotts, Fredrick. *Bayreuth: A History of the Wagner Festival*. New Haven & London: Yale University Press, 1994.

Stoddard, Lothrop. *The Revolt Against Civilization*. New York: Charles Scribner's Sons, 1923.

Swanbrow, Diane (2000-03-23). "Intimate Relationships Between Races More Common Than Thought".University of Michigan. http://www.umich.edu/news/index.html?Releases/2000/Mar00/r032300a.Retrieved 2008-07-15. For a general discussion of many aspects of interracial sex see: http://en.wikipedia.org/wiki/Interracial_marriage_in_the_United_States#Interracial_marriage_versus_cohabitation

Tarnas, Richard. *The Passion of the Western Mind: Understanding the Ideas That Have Shaped our World View.* New York: Ballantine Books, 1991.

Thompson, Ian. *The Sun King's Garden: Louis XIV, Andre Le Notre and the Creation of the Garden's of Versailles.* New York: Bloomsbury, 2006.

Thomson, David. *The New Biographical Dictionary of Film.* New York: Alfred A. Knopf, 2002. And the Fifth Edition, 2010.

Tolstoy, Leo. Richard Pevear & Larissa Volokhonsky, trans. *Anna Karenina.* New York: Penguin, 2000.

Toman, Rolf. *Baroque: Architecture, Sculpture, Painting.* h.f. ullmann, 2007.

Truby, Mark. "Diversity Gives Ford a New Look." *Detroit News,* August 20, 2000, A11. Quoted in Gottfried, p. 35.

Urgasi, C., C. Berluchi, et al. (2004). "Magnetic Stimulation of Extrastriate Body Area Impairs Visual Processing of Nonfacial Body Parts." *Current Biology* 14(23): 2130-2134.

Vansina, Jan. *Paths in the Rainforests.* Madison: University of Wisconsin Press, 1990.

Valiunas, Algis. "Shall We Fight for Kind and Country?" *Claremont Review of Books,* Volume X, Number 1, Winter 2009/10.

Vasari, Giorgio. Julia Bondanella and Peter Bondanella, Trans. *Lives of the Artists.* New York: Oxford University Press, 2008.

Vieira, Mark A. *Irving Thalberg: Boy Wonder to Producer Prince.* Berkeley, CA: University of California Press, 2010.

Vyse, Stuart A. *Believing in Magic: The Psychology of Superstition.* New York: Oxford University Press, 1997.

Weaver, Robert L. "The Consolidation of the Main Elements of the Orchestra: 1470-1768." *The Orchestra*, Joan Peyser, Ed. Milwaukee, WI: Hal Leonard Corp, 2006.

West, M. L. trans., *Greek Lyric Poetry*. Oxford: Oxford University, 1993.

Whitson, James C. "Putting It Together." *Opera News*, jan. 2013, vol. 77, no 7. p. 19-20

Williams, Elizabeth Friar. *Notes of a Feminist Therapist*. New York: Praeger, 1976.

Williams, Timothy. "As Public Sector Sheds Jobs, Blacks are hit Hardest." New York Times, Nov. 28, 2011. http://www.nytimes.com/2011/11/29/us/as-public-sector-sheds-jobs-black-americans-are-hit-hard.html?_r=1

Winckelmann, Johann Joachim. Harry Francis Mallgrave, Trans. *History of the Art of Antiquity*. Los Angeles: Getty Publications, 2006.

Winn, Steve. "Angela Gheorghiu and Patricia Racette on Tosca." *San Franciso Opera Magazine*. Seattle: Encore Media Group. November, 2012. Volume 90, No. 3.

Wolfflin, Heinrich. *Classic Art: An Introduction to the Italian Renaissance.*5th edition. London: Phaidon Press, 1994

Wolfgang, Marvin E. and Franco Ferracuti. *The Subculture of Violence: Toward an Integrated Theory in Criminology*. London: Tavistock, 1967.

Wrangham, Richard and Dale Peterson, *Demonic Males*. Boston: Houghton Mifflin, 1996.

Wroe, Ann. *Orpheus: The Song of Life*. New York: The Overlook Press, 2012.

Externaliz'n sin — pp. 109-11